The art of
POETRY

CHRISTINE PERRIN, MFA

Classical Academic Press
515 S. 32nd Street
Camp Hill, PA 17011

www.ClassicalAcademicPress.com

ISBN: 978-1-60051-041-0

Cover art by
Rob Baddorf

Interior design by
Lenora Riley

Scripture quoted by permission. All Scripture taken from
THE HOLY BIBLE: NEW INTERNATIONAL VERSION®. NIV®.
Copyright © 1973, 1978, 1984 by Biblica. All rights reserved worldwide.

PGP.09.21

POEM PERMISSIONS

TABLE OF CONTENTS

INTRODUCTION

There has never been a civilization without poetry. From the beginning of time, people have sought to turn their thoughts, feelings, and stories into memorable speech to share with others. Using language, the poet preserves something precious in the world by allowing us to live next to her, to see what she sees, to enter the experience she has built for us with her words and attention to the moment. Poetry acknowledges something deep within our nature—an urge to name, say, sing, grieve, praise, out of our solitariness, to another person. It makes words into a material thing, hard and solid as a table, dense with significance. It comes from the body and the body is its instrument. It knows our body is as intelligent as our mind, and that the two intelligences are happily married.

From poets we can learn much about what it is to be truly alive. In the poem *The Rhyme of the Ancient Mariner*, Samuel Taylor Coleridge names the state which is worse than death itself, "Life in Death." The name suggests that we are capable of having a heartbeat without being fully alive to the world around us. Human forgetfulness allows fresh beginnings, but it is also an infirmity for which we need to be treated. We need a daily pin-prick of awareness to bring us back to what surrounds us. Poems are one dramatic source of this alertness. From Gerard Manley Hopkins, for instance, I've learned how to mourn and how to exalt, and how close the two lie next to each other. I talk myself out of despair for the ugliness of the industrialized world with his poem *God's Grandeur*:

> The world is charged with the grandeur of God.
> It will flame out, like shining from shook foil;
> It gathers to a greatness, like the ooze of oil
> Crushed. Why do men then now not reck his rod?
> 5 Generations have trod, have trod, have trod;
> And all is seared with trade; bleared, smeared with toil;
> And wears man's smudge and shares man's smell: the soil
> Is bare now, nor can foot feel, being shod.
>
> And for all this, nature is never spent;
> 10 There lives the dearest freshness deep down things;
> And though the last lights off the black West went
> Oh, morning, at the brown brink eastward, springs—
> Because the Holy Ghost over the bent
> World broods with warm breast and with ah! bright wings.

On my dark days, this poem reminds me I am not alone, that Father Hopkins and his precise images and sounds have gone ahead of me and meet me in my own sorrow and disgust. His bright-winged, warm-breasted, holy-ghost bird hovers over me and my imagination. The poem insists that the image of the sun rising at the brink of the darkened world to bring another day is true beyond its scientific explanation, and encourages us to believe that literal and figurative light continues to renew and tend the earth. Hope is given to us not only in the message of the words but in language that exults: the words spring up with their blending of sounds and movement to embody the movement of the sun bursting over the cusp of earth. The speaker, consoled and warmed, experiences an encircling by the "Holy Ghost," pictured as a bird who closes her wings around the world. The repetition of "b" sounds, "w" sounds, and long "o" sounds in lines thirteen and fourteen, along with the relieved and delighted interjection "ah!," creates the physical expression of solace. We experience the sensation of the movement and sound at the same time that we register the images and consider the ideas. The poet has wrought his experience of hard-won hope in such a way that we can feel, momentarily, his glad assurance. We turn from the poem back to our lives revitalized. This is only one example of the process by which the word renews the world for us. This example holds true whether or not you embrace the religious views of the poet. As a reader you can enter the sensation of transcendence over the trampled world regardless of the poem's theology.

Because they are made by other human beings at a moment of full awareness, and they are spoken from privacy to privacy into the grave of our hearts, poems enliven us. They challenge us to find meaning, they defend the importance of individual lives and allow all sorts of voices to be heard. In addition to speaking to us, poems talk to other poems, and teach us how to read conversationally. Writing is, after all, simply the highest, most intense form of reading; when you write you hone your thoughts and analysis toward precision, you attend to a text closely. All of the poets in this book have had some contact with each other and are, in some way, in dialogue with each other. In reading these poems and thinking about them you are entering a great conversation that has gone on for years and will continue.

Poetry is also a witness to human cruelty. You might think of poems as just words, but during the Russian Revolution poets and writers were killed or threatened with death. Osip Mandelstam, one of those killed, said in a poem, "And for you, I am here, to burn—a black flare, to burn." Nearly a century later, his words are still passed like a torch from reader to reader, illuminating Stalin's unspeakable acts. Throughout time poets and writers have borne witness to history.

What does this have to do with me? you ask. Well, your days are long and crammed with obligation and information and technology. You are at risk for thinking that this is knowledge. Poetic knowledge insists that beauty and truth can't be separated. It reminds us that the rational alone will not take us to full knowledge and that we should be astonished by what is true. J.R.R. Tolkien and C.S. Lewis believed that myth restores reality to its mythic proportions, that we are living a lyric truth, a story where every action has consequence, and that reading a myth or a poem makes us conscious of its enormity anew.

You will find that there are other benefits to studying poems, benefits that accrete like layers of silt in a mountain stream. Poetry fundamentally changes our relationship to language—we can no longer see words as merely serviceable vehicles. Poetry instructs us to look for the structure in any written piece. Poetry teaches us the principles of interpretation, because such questions naturally arise in the discussion of a poem. Poetry reminds us that the metaphor is the basic way of knowing the unknown and that we often describe one thing in terms of another. Poetry gives us images to cherish and to invigorate our daily experience. In April, I remember that T.S. Eliot claimed it is the cruelest month: "breeding / Lilacs out of the dead land, mixing / Memory and desire, stirring / Dull roots with spring rain." I possess Rilke's picture of *The Panther* when I am caged or when I meet someone who is. Language seems to me unimaginably deep, a record of human consciousness. And because I write poems in response to my love of what I see, I know what Adam felt like in the garden of the world naming and naming.

CLOSE READING

A soldier at attention stands erectly with heels together, arms at his side, eyes looking forward, waiting for instructions. A nurse or midwife checks the vital signs of the mother and child. A suitor notices every glance of his beloved. Close reading is learning how to pay attention to a text. This is not particularly difficult but it is hard in our times; it has to be a discipline, a habit of mind. We are busy, we are used to being active, we are addicted to being connected to other people through cell phones, the Internet, iPods, and video games. Close reading is another way to be connected, but it is different from the ways to which we are accustomed and it requires more of us. It requires time. It requires slowing down. It requires commitment. Television, magazines, and most movies don't demand your attention. They are designed to be understood easily and quickly so that you can move on—be entertained but not inconvenienced. In a botanical garden or an aquarium you take time to look at the parts of the flower or fish, you smell it or watch it swim. The same is true for a book of poems. When you read a poem, you must take time and learn to be observant. Like sea diving, there are fathoms of depth. You go to one level for a while, then deeper, then deeper. You discover there is a vast ocean to explore in any piece of art, that continues to deliver something new and unexpected with each encounter.

Being engaged to a person involves committing yourself to that person completely, making a promise to that person. Being engaged with a piece of writing is similar. There is a conversation—sometimes even an ongoing relationship—between you and the book, you and the writer. Your successful summary of a poem's structure and meaning is only a part of what you and that poem can accomplish together. The poem and its reading can't be reduced to a three-point outline or a five-paragraph essay, just as a relationship between friends can't be summarized or contained this way.

To read closely, listen to the sounds and rhythms, look at the patterns which create these, hear the language of the poem intensely, see if you can put yourself into the physical environment that the poet is creating. Start with questions that you might ask yourself about a poem. Discipline yourself to look at the images, to hear the sounds working together, to think about the subject the poet has introduced. Ask yourself if you have read anything else which would comment upon this idea. Link what is in front of you to your experience both in books and in life. Wonder at the difficult parts. Disagree. Close your eyes after you have read it a few times and see which images and words have stuck. Look up words in a dictionary, the ones you don't know but even the ones you do to see if there are nuances you might be missing. See how the rhymed words make suggestions about what the poem is saying. If you are having trouble slowing down, start with memorization and see what happens to your understanding as you commit the words and lines to memory. Try writing formally or informally on the piece in front of you.

One can't read every poem with this depth but one must learn the practice of it over time. T.S. Eliot said that "poetry may make us from time to time a little more aware of the deeper unnamed feelings which form the substratum of our being, to which we rarely penetrate; for our lives are mostly a constant evasion of ourselves." If you should accept this challenge, you will find some clarity and a language which more accurately reflects and sheds light on your experience. William Meredith in his poem *A Major Work* draws a parallel between learning to serve an art form so that we truly "read," "see," "hear" it, and learning to care for another person.

A Major Work

Poems are hard to read
Pictures are hard to see
Music is hard to hear
And people are hard to love.

5   But whether from brute need
Or divine energy
At last mind eye and ear
And the great sloth heart will move.

There are two lists of four items in this poem—can you identify them? Can you see how the two lists are linked together in a parallel structure? This is the beginning of close reading, but let's go further: why do you think the poet chose the word "move" as the final destination of the poem? Can you identify ways that you personally have experienced "brute need" or "divine energy"? What language in the poem suggests that the poet locates the actual power of poetry not in the poems themselves but in the hard work of reading them? These are the kinds of questions that you will begin to ask and answer as you are drawn more thoroughly into the skill of close reading.

In the chapters that follow, you will be guided through the elements of a poem. You will learn to look at a poem's images, metaphor, words, symbols, sound, rhythm, shape, and tone. You will combine these elements and categorical thinking in a chapter called "Putting It All Together." It wouldn't hurt to begin the book by reading the "Putting It All Together" chapter first, and then starting the elements of the poem. Later, you will examine the formal categories that poems fall under, such as genre, verse form, and shaping forms, and examine some poets who found formal strategies that were a natural part of the lives they lived. The book closes with a section on how to apply these learned skills in your home or school or with your friends. As your reading skills grow, your poetic intelligence and pleasure will grow as well. You are beginning a great work shoulder to shoulder with the writers in this book—wrestling, sifting, puzzling with the collection of words they have set down. May your great sloth heart move toward love.

HOW TO USE THIS BOOK

First Principles

Do not let this book overwhelm you. If all you do is give this book to your students as a resource that you only minimally engage, you have already made a great step. Consider having each student read around to find a poem she would like to read aloud to the class. Start your day this way. If you can't do it daily, do it weekly. Even this small step will begin to cultivate a relationship between the students and poetry that the students are free to pursue independently. Because students will fish for poems to read to the class or to family, they will likely discover other parts of this book's text as well. If some chapters seem particularly difficult given your educational background, consider using these chapters only for the anthology of poems and the activities in them. Poetry is such a natural pleasure to us, so much in harmony with our instinct and experience, we cannot help but be drawn to it, if it is introduced with pleasure. For a simplified plan on how to use this book, see Appendix C.

The Teacher's Edition

Available for purchase is a teacher's edition that "reads" or explains 37 of the book's poems, provides answers for the discussion questions, includes a supplemental poetry time line, a quiz for each chapter and a cumulative book quiz. This is in addition to the student book's "Learning to Read Closely" section, which thoroughly discusses a poem in nearly each chapter. Observing the skill we are meant to acquire is a great aid to learning it. *The Art of Poetry Teacher's Edition* is meant to help provide you, the teacher, with confidence as you lead a discussion. There are often suggestions for the discussion as well.

Three Timetables

This book is meant to fit your curriculum-scheduling needs. It is conceivable that it could be used as an intense **month-long unit,** during which your class would work on a lesson each day and limit the activities at the end of each section. An alternative would be to work on **two sections per month (or two weeks for each section) and spread it out over the school year.** If you'd like a slower pace, consider doing **several chapters a year over the course of several years**. This would be more poetic education than many receive in their high school years, especially if the student enjoys the work and is ignited to search for more poems. Considering the book according to its chapters and significant division—the elements of poetry and the formal tradition of poetry—is a helpful way to think about your use.

Academic Levels

If you are teaching younger students, cull the lessons for key points that you'd like them to receive and ignore more in-depth subject material. "The Elements of Poetry" chapters at the beginning of the book are accessible and basic to all language levels. You could save "The Formal History of Poetry" sections for later, or study those sections only for the content of their poems. You could read the poems aloud, one a day, for the remainder of the book. Have the students pick out images and metaphors or words that strike them. Have them listen for sounds that function according to the descriptions in earlier chapters. In other words, you need not teach your seventh and eighth graders the intricacies of a villanelle in order to use this book, though there is no reason why they can't learn this. You may introduce students to "The Elements of Poetry" chapters and then move on to "Growing Your Interest," where they can use and apply some of the skills they've learned. Each lesson has activities at the end of the chapter, and the later chapters demonstrate how to establish a writing group and the habits of a writer. These include keeping a poetry notebook, keeping a poetry journal, having a poetry slam, hosting a reading series, and selecting readings and resources. Older students (high school) should do very nicely with the standard approach to the text according to your curriculum needs and the time you have to spend on this activity.

Other Skills

You can also use the book to teach other skills beyond reading poetry. Poetry is a good way to learn to analyze and begin to ask questions about how to interpret. The "Learning to Read Closely" sections in the book are meant to be a guide for working out the complexities of reading. Being educated in metaphoric thinking or analogical thinking (comparing one thing to another) is essential to all thought—knowing how far a comparison can be taken and where the metaphor breaks down, or loses its parallel properties, is important. Learning to write analytically about poems strengthens writing skills. Studying the elements of a poem will reinforce your students' skills in rhetoric and in other literary reading. They will begin to think in terms of figurative language and of *how* a piece of writing means and not simply *what* it means. They will begin to write with language that is fresh and consider imaginative comparisons, even for their more analytical work. Hence, this book dovetails nicely with rhetoric and writing units as well as with literature class. Educating the imagination is an important aspect of studying poems.

Out of the Standard Classroom Use

In addition to the formal classroom, this book will work nicely for an elective class, a homeschooling cooperative group, or for at-home instruction among several students of different ages. It could also work as a poetry circle group in which students participate outside of school and with or without a teacher (perhaps a summer poetry circle). If this is your interest, start with "Growing Your Interest" to see how a workshop functions and how to keep a writer's journal and a favorite poem notebook. Plan a grand finale in which participating students have a poetry slam. Have a special recording session in which students make their own CD of cherished poems, reading them aloud. If your student is particularly musical, have her compose songs using the poems as lyrics, record the songs, and give the CDs away as gifts. There are endless creative possibilities.

Memorization

Another approach to this text is through memorization. Memorized language has long been a part of education. I had a friend whose study of sixteenth-century poetry revolutionized his own writing. When I asked him how he was able to internalize that century's work, he said he had a short attention span and so he started with memorization. (He was an English Ph.D. student.) He'd learn a poem and mull over it. What he learned about the poem was from the inside out, because he knew the lines and joints of the poem intimately. Sound and rhythm, the music of poetry, come alive when you say poems aloud from memory. One approach to this text is to start memorizing its poems and talk about the elements and formal traditions after you've committed portions of it to memory. If you have a hard time getting started, create hand motions to the words to help you remember the language visually. Observe your own best practices for memorizing (perhaps cue your memory through the poem's images, sound, line, or sentence) and observe also how you approach the poem differently when it is something you are memorizing. This is an excellent way to store up a treasure trove for moments when your mind is idle or needs distraction. I have seen young children memorize poems in minutes. It is also a wonderful word gift to recite or write to someone for a special occasion.

Christine Perrin in Your Classroom

If you are interested in having author Christine Perrin lead your school or group in a seminar regarding this book or help you get started in any of these activities, visit her consulting page at https://classicalacademicpress.com/consulting/christine-perrin/.

O1
IMAGES

{the elements of poetry}

An **image** is a **literal** or **concrete** detail that is sensory—a word or phrase that calls on the **senses** of sight, smell, taste, touch, and sound. In poems, these details are made from language and create pictures or sensations. In life we are inundated with images: the smell of bread, the blue in the sky after the sun sinks below the horizon, the feel of sand in your bathing suit, the first taste of black bottom pie. Some of these images carry great importance and emotion; some of them exist without our noticing. All images, no matter how ordinary or unusual, can be used to great effect in a poem.

Think about some of the mental pictures related to your senses that have been lodged in your brain simply because you have been alive for a decade or so. So often our memories are held in images. You can remember the flicker of afternoon light on the creek in front your house, or perhaps singing carols with your sister at the piano, the fish you ate fresh from the stream and fried in butter that time you vacationed in the Adirondacks. Images of all textures abound: figuring out your locker combination for the first time, kicking the soccer ball and smelling the cut grass, hearing the guitar riff in a favorite song. Because we live by collecting images without even trying to, they become especially important and powerful in poetry; they move us and help to bring us to the moment and the place in which the poet is speaking. Hence they become a kind of time travel machine that transports us back into our past or into the present of the speaker of the poem. A poet uses images to construct our experience of a poem because we use the received images of our daily lives to construct our own experience, identity, and culture. Poems aren't summaries or sermons or scientific equations; they are worlds that we enter and experience for a time, as if we were going to the Renaissance faire where people are dressed in costumes, speak in accents, eat drumsticks, and joust on horses.

When we use images in our writing, we bring those to whom we speak right next to us. Poet Stanley Kunitz says that "the artist in the modern world is probably the only person, with a handful of exceptions, who keeps alive that sense of the sharing of this life with others. When he watches that leaf fall, it's falling for you. Or that sparrow…." W.B. Yeats has said, "Art bids us touch and taste and hear and see the world, and shrinks from what Blake calls mathematic form, from every abstract form, from all that is of the brain only." He is making the argument that all art, poetry included, depends on the senses, on direct experience, and not just on the mind. Art moves us by appealing to our physical bodies. The art of poetry appeals to our bodies most directly when it uses images to cause us to see, touch, taste, hear, and smell the world with which the speaker of the poem would like to bring us into contact. Abstract language, such as "love," "peace," "despair," and "truth" is of deep interest to a poet, but, according to Yeats, the actual process of making or reading a poem never starts with these. Instead, poetry starts in the body, in the senses, and therefore in images.

Think about how it feels when a friend returns from a wonderful vacation and you eagerly listen for the physical details that reconstruct her experience for you. It is as close as you can come to being there and sharing the experience. At times the vividness of a retold story or event can be more intensified than the experience itself, depending both on the storyteller and the listener. This extra intensity is one quality that distinguishes poems that endure, loved by thousands of readers, from poems that are quickly forgotten.

Here's another thing to think about. Part of our experience of life is its transience—its quality of passing quickly. Philosopher Hans Gadamer says this:

> Whenever we have to hold something, it is because it is transient and threatens to escape our grasp. In fact, our fundamental experience as beings subject to time is that all things escape us, that all the events of our lives fade more and more, so that at best they glow with an almost unreal shimmer in the most distant recollection.

This writer goes on to suggest that poems and the poetic word bring time to a standstill. In particular, images in a poem mark the intersection between what is passing and what is eternal. Images bring us alive to memory—smelling the new paint of the room you worked on with your father, riding the Ferris wheel on your family vacation and feeling your stomach jump as it turned downward, or watching a face behind a rain-streaked window on the day you found out about your friend's illness. They remind us that we are alive in bodies and that time is passing.

As you study this book you will learn that many other **figures of speech**, or **figurative language**, use images. For instance, **metaphors**, or **word pictures**, make a direct and deep connection between a concrete image and an abstract idea—*my love is a rose*—or between two different concrete images—*her hair is a shining metal helmet*. **Symbols** use a person, object, image, word, or event to evoke a range of meaning beyond the thing itself: the dove of peace, the cross, the Star of David, or a host of personal symbols built over the course of a single poem. (See an example of this in the poem *The Crow*, in which the image of the crow comes to stand for a prophet who is trying to get the speaker's attention, just as prophets in all traditions come to deliver a burning message to people who do not want to hear it.) Many of the things you will notice poems doing begin with image as their basement. Images in a given poem often work together (what we might call a **family of images**) to create a larger whole. *Storm Ending* achieves this. Sometimes a single deep image is developed throughout a poem, as in *The Swing*. Jay Parini, in his introduction to the *Wadsworth Anthology*, describes the literary image this way:

> An image is a complex emotional unit, involving the whole of the reader's mind. It compels attention by its sound as well as its visual element. It conjoins thought and emotion, making a unified impression. In the very best poems, images lodge deep in the mind, where they cannot be easily removed.

As you read the following poems—closely!—may an image lodge itself deeply also in you.

LEARNING TO READ CLOSELY

Rainer Maria Rilke (1875–1926)
Translated by Edward Snow

The <u>Panther</u>*

His <u>gaze</u> has from the passing of the <u>bars</u>
grown so tired, that it holds nothing anymore.
It seems to him there are a <u>thousand bars</u>
and behind a thousand bars no world.

5   The supple pace of <u>powerful soft strides</u>,
turning in the very <u>smallest circle</u>,
is like a dance of strength around a center
in which a great will stands numbed.

Only sometimes the <u>curtain of the pupils</u>
10   <u>soundlessly slides up</u>–. Then an image enters,
glides through the <u>limbs' taut stillness</u>,
dives into the heart and dies.

*images are underlined

From the second line we understand that the speaker is investing the panther with meaning beyond the literal; in other words, we are aware that the panther means more than a panther in this poem as soon as we get to the word "tired" to describe his gaze. Then the perspective of the panther is further unspooled for us when the speaker says, "It seems to him." Though we have all looked at an animal and imagined what it might be thinking, very few of us have declared with such certainty that we know precisely what it thinks. Notice that the first **stanza** puts great emphasis on the bars by bringing them physically before us as they are, always, before the panther: three times in three **lines** they are mentioned and thus they pass inescapably before our eyes, too.

This poem uses stanzas deliberately and skillfully, demonstrating the way that stanzas function as rooms (the meaning of the Italian root of the word). Each one serves a different purpose in the poem. Notice how they end—definitively. The first stanza ends with "no world"; the second, "stands numbed"; the third, "dies." Each stanza ending ("world" at the end of the first; "numbed," the second; "dies," the third) lets the reader stay awhile in the reality of the stanza just finished. The white space between stanzas produces a longer pause than that at the end of the line.

The second stanza reveals to us the strength and agility and potential power of the panther, which is currently impotent. Unlike the first stanza, which is clipped and broken into two sentences, this stanza has a single sentence that, with each line, paces and spills onto the following line, much like the motion of the cat.

The third stanza formally demonstrates the emotional movement of the poem for us. The **caesura** (or middle of the line interruption, in this case a dash) of the second line records the possibility and hope of change represented by the entering image. The text is interrupted by an image, and the poem pauses, causing the reader to pause as the image "enters" and "glides" and "dives." Utter despair and paralysis follow when hope cannot be realized or acted upon and the image "dies." The image that "dives into the heart and dies" represents the failed possibility of a life outside the bars, of an image other than bars. The poem ends on the word of death. This poem was written originally in German, which means that in translation it is a new creation, a new poem made by poet and translator where some of the original skill and intent are lost and replaced with different sounds and shapes and words which, though changed, are often equally beautiful.

This poem is a wonderful example of how the ideas and the **shape** of a poem can work together. Poetry uses all of its lines and spaces, which prose doesn't have, to create meaning. Rilke's poem *The Panther* operates largely on the basis of **symbolism**, using images to create a picture that has meaning beyond itself. The panther is real but it is also a symbol of a state of utter despair and cagedness. There are many occasions in which an individual, a community, or even a people group experiences hopelessness and cannot imagine escaping the situation or state of mind which cages it. Rainer Maria Rilke, the poet, doesn't spell out for us whether or not this panther is meant to represent something specific, like slavery, or being trapped in a bad relationship, or an emotional or economic depression. He lets us fill in the specifics according to our own experience. He does, however, clearly express what it feels like to be in a cage and lose all hope. This cage is not simply the literal cage of the panther (though it is that); it is also the many cages that are possible in the human experience. Though many powerful poems do assign more specific meaning to their images—see the next chapter on metaphor—symbolism gives more interpretative freedom to the reader. In a poem like *The Panther*, such freedom actually helps us feel more intensely the imprisonment of the animal. We are free to assign meaning to his plight; he is not.

ANTHOLOGY

Jean Toomer (1894–1967)

Storm Ending

Thunder blossoms gorgeously above our heads,
Great, hollow, bell-like flowers,
Rumbling in the wind,
Stretching clappers to strike our ears.
5   Full-lipped flowers
Bitten by the sun
Bleeding rain
Dripping rain like golden honey–
And the sweet earth flying from the thunder.

1. Notice how Toomer's poem takes you to a distinct place, a specific experience constructed by image layered upon image. Make a list of all the verbs in the poem, then all the nouns, then all the adjectives, and adverbs.

2. We may expect images in poetry to always be nouns, *things* we can see, touch, smell, etc., but in this poem the primary image is announced by a verb—can you name it?

3. How would you describe the atmosphere created in this poem? Is the overall feeling of this poem negative or positive? Dark or light? Fearful or comforting? What specific evidence can you point to in the poem to defend your answer?

Robert Frost (1874–1963)

Dust of Snow

The way a crow
shook down on me
the dust of snow
from a hemlock tree

5   Has given my heart
a change of mood
and saved a part
of a day I rued.

1. What is the small story in this poem and what are its images?

2. What does the word "rue" mean?

3. Has anything like this ever happened to you?

4. What can you guess about the change of mood in the poet's heart? Why doesn't he name his emotions more specifically?

5. Think about the title of the poem: the image of snow dust was significant enough to the poet that in this very short poem he included its exact wording twice. Why?

Judith Kunst (1970–)

The Crow

Was it because
at last
I cleaned the window

that he threw himself
5 against the glass?
I thought, poor crow—

he doesn't know
the evergreens
and blue sky

10 are behind him.
I turned back
to my page

but *whumpp*—
the bird attacked
15 the glass again.

His long claws
scuffled at the pane
and I yelled "Crow!

go away!"
20 Again his body slapped
the glass,

again,
and then again,
and then at last

25 he caught my eye—
oh, prophet,
terrified.

1. This poem gives us another encounter between a crow and a human being. What are the specific images that place us in the scene of the poem?

2. Who is the main character? What specific evidence can you point to in the poem to support your answer?

3. How many different feelings can you find in this poem?

4. At exactly what point in the poem do we discover the crow is more than just a crow? How do you know?

5. What is a prophet? What images or feelings does that word call up for you? Why do you think the poet composed the last stanza of the poem so that it is not totally clear who is "terrified"?

6. Look again at the first sentence of the poem; what might be the significance of the speaker cleaning the window glass?

Walt Whitman (1819–1892)

Cavalry Crossing a Ford

A line in long array where they wind betwixt green islands,
They take a serpentine course, their arms flash in the sun—hark to the
 musical clank,
Behold the silvery river, in it the splashing horses loitering stop to drink,
5   Behold the brown-faced men, each group, each person a picture, the
 negligent rest on the saddles,
Some emerge on the opposite bank, others are just entering the ford—
 while,
Scarlet and blue and snowy white,
10   The guidon flags flutter gayly in the wind.

1. What are we looking at in this poem?

2. How do the images draw you into the long ago time period portrayed in the poem?

3. The poet uses two verbs that make *you* as the reader a character in this poem—what are they?

4. What, to you, is the most interesting or powerful image?

5. Have you seen anything that looks like this, or any part of this kind of scene elsewhere? How many sentences does this poem use? What is the effect of that number?

6. How does the way in which the poem is structured echo or help express the pictures?

7. What different physical senses do we get to experience through this poem?

8. Is there a mood established in the poem through the images? What is it?

Ezra Pound (1885–1972)

In a Station of the Metro

The apparition of these faces in the crowd:
Petals on a wet, black bough.

1. What are we looking at in this picture? What are the petals? What is the black bough?

2. What kind of mood does the imagery (the second line) give us?

3. Why do we need the title?

4. How is the length and shape of this poem perfectly chosen to help lodge the single image in our minds?

5. What color are the petals you imagine as you read?

6. What images or experiences in your own life are similar to those portrayed in the poem?

7. Why do you think the poet chose the word "apparition"?

Robert Louis Stevenson (1850–1894)

The Swing

How do you like to go up in a swing,
    Up in the air so blue?
Oh, I do think it the pleasantest thing
    Ever a child can do!

5   Up in the air and over the wall,
    Till I can see so wide,
River and trees and cattle and all
    Over the countryside—

Till I look down on the garden green,
10   Down on the roof so brown—
Up in the air I go flying again,
    Up in the air and down!

1. Does this poem remind you of your own experience?

2. What are some of the images that create the experience portrayed in the poem?

3. What are some of the words that create the experience?

4. What is the effect of the rhymes? Circle the rhymes. Underline the images.

5. Why do you think the poet uses the word "down" three times in the last stanza?

6. What are some feelings one might feel on a swing? Can you find one or more of these feelings in the language of this poem?

7. Is the poem about anything more than childhood swinging? How can you tell?

ACTIVITIES

1. Take five minutes and freewrite about images from one of the four seasons. (In freewriting, you write for the entire time, not planning what you say, but simply writing anything that comes to your mind, even when nothing comes to your mind. It helps to generate ideas.)

2. Describe an image that is important to you. Discuss and identify an image that's important to your class. What kind of images did you choose? Could they be called symbols? Why or why not? If they are symbols, what multiple meanings do your images represent?

3. Describe the past school year through four images.

4. Figure out which sense (of our five) is most important or strongest to you.

5. Cut out a series of images from a magazine that describes you or a relationship that's important to you. Make a collage with the images—does it matter how the pictures are arranged? Do two different arrangements convey two different feelings in you? Why?

6. Write your own version of the Ezra Pound poem. Its title should announce your location ("At…"), and the two-line body should present one glimpse, one impression of that location, using an image from nature.

7. Play an **association** game with a partner or have a single person leading the class. The leader says a word and you respond with a word that comes to your mind and then the other person (or you could go around the room with this) responds with another word. Continue for a while and see how the brain makes a necklace of these words and thoughts.

8. Write a poem like the poem titled *The Panther* but with a different animal, perhaps a snake. Describe the motion of a snake by demonstrating it. Use the lines and the stanzas to help you. If you'd prefer a different animal (say, an elephant), feel free.

9. The words "the way…" are commonly used to introduce an image that is a complete experience—not just the crow himself but *the way* he shook the snow; not just the thunder and rain but *the way* it looked and moved in the sky. Write your own version of the poem *Dust of Snow*, keeping Frost's structure but replacing his story and images with your own, either real or imagined, serious or silly.

Ezra Pound

VOCABULARY

Abstract language: words that suggest concepts, ideas, and generalizations, such as peace and justice.

Association: a leap that the mind makes when one thing or idea makes you think of another. When this is recorded it is called stream of consciousness—the stream of thought that the mind runs along at any given time.

Caesura: a pause in the middle of a line of poetry marked by punctuation.

Concrete language: words that describe particular things (bug, table, nose) as opposed to words that are abstract.

Family of images: a collection of images in a single poem that work together to form an intentional group of concrete details that create a larger picture of significance.

Figurative language: language that imposes a figure on the surface or content of what is actually there (the literal). Metaphor, simile, and symbol all do this; they suggest something beyond what they say.

Figure of speech: saying one thing and suggesting another, so that words have significance beyond the literal meaning. To compare one thing to another. Literally, to superimpose a figure upon the surface of what is truly there.

Image: a concrete detail that speaks to the senses.

Line: the place where the poet deliberately ends a line, a distinctive feature of poetry, as opposed to prose in which the lines are not broken by the writer but by the margins of the page. Also referred to as "verse" or "stich."

Literal: that which actually is there, concrete.

Metaphor: a comparison between two things that are unlike; a resemblance forged in the mind of the poet between two unlike things.

Senses or sensing: our ability to perceive with our sense organs—touch, taste, hear, see, smell.

Shape: the element that most closely involves the visible form of the poem on the page. Also referred to as "form."

Stanza: the equivalent of the paragraph in prose, a group of lines gathered as a unit in a poem.

Symbol: use of a person, object, image, word, or event to evoke a range of meaning beyond the thing itself; an important image in a poem that has multiple, unspecified meanings and suggestions in its use.

Symbolism: representing things by symbols, or investing things with a symbolic meaning or character.

Word picture: another name for a metaphor.

O2
METAPHOR

{*the elements of poetry*}

A metaphor is a figure of speech in which two unlike things are compared: the sun is a blood orange; the ocean is a grave; your smile is a butterfly. Such comparisons ask you—or force you—to see the world in a different way. Every day our mind works associatively—an image leads us to think of something like it and instantly we have associated two things that were not previously associated. Like stepping stones for the imagination, the mind follows this path of images: falling blossoms remind us of snow or the shape of a cloud suggests an animal or spaceship. Poetry takes this universal human practice and uses it to make art, layering or joining unlike images in ways that will move the reader. Good metaphors are springs that help readers make leaps in imagination.

The word "metaphor" comes from two Greek words: *meta* meaning "across," "transport," "transfer," and *pherein,* which means "to bear or carry." Together the suggestion is "to carry across." So the metaphor, which compares one thing to something it is clearly not (the sun is not an orange), carries across the meaning of one object to another (we re-imagine the sun as an orange and sometimes the other way around as well, the orange is like a little sun). If we were making a math problem out of this idea, we would write it this way: A = B. Often there is an abstract subject that is compared to a concrete object, and in this case the subject A ("hope" in the line "hope is the thing with feathers," from the anthology in this chapter) is carried by the image B ("the thing with feathers" or a bird). The writer asks us to imagine how hope could be a bird, how A could be equal to B. This act of the imagination enlarges our understanding of A, which in this case is hope.

Metaphor is the basis of poetic thinking. A poet was once asked, "Do you think in verse?" His answer was, "I don't think in rhymed iambic pentameter, but I am always drawing connections between things that were not in natural relationship to each other before my mind brought them together." Poems do this work of creating relationships between things by making unexpected comparisons. Metaphor is the natural way humans think about the unknown (the frog leg tastes like chicken), and make the familiar fresh again. For instance, when was the last time that you thought of hope as being like a bird? Emily Dickinson starts a poem with this startling insistence—"hope is the thing with feathers." At first we don't understand how an abstract concept could be compared to a living thing. But after reflection, we realize that this statement is true. Hope has properties of a bird: it flies, it survives terrible weather, it sings even when it seems there is no reason to sing. Sometimes metaphor sharpens our perception and sometimes it goes further and surprises us, which is one of the aspects most treasured about poems, for we never outgrow our love of a surprise. Poets insist that even the writer must be surprised for the poem to surprise and delight the reader. So much of what we say is tired and **clichéd** and not considered attentively; therefore, poetry is essential not only to understand the unknown but also to clarify reality—helping us to see the world in its glory and degradation and every state in between. Metaphors also help to express the emotional depth or texture or complexity of different events, situations, objects, or persons. For a good example of this, see Yeats's poem, *He Wishes for the Cloths of Heaven* in the "Learning to Read Closely" section of this chapter.

Even when we try to explain what poems are, we use metaphors. What follows are some examples of metaphors used to describe poems. This list is from Edward Hirsch's book *How to Read a Poem and Fall in Love with Poetry*.

A capsule where we wrap up our punishable secrets......... William Carlos Williams

A well-wrought urn .... Cleanth Brooks

A walk .... A.R. Ammons

A verbal icon... W.K. Wimsatt

A meteor... Wallace Stevens

A hand, a hook, a prayer, a soul in action .... Edward Hirsch

Metaphor is not only basic to poetry; it is also basic to life. Consider your own experiences. Comparisons sharpen and vivify your experience, and they are also useful. When it is snowing outside and you want to know if it will be good snow for snowballs, you ask your brother to tell you what kind of snow it is. "Like sugar," he says, and you have your answer (it will not be good for snowballs) as well as a metaphor (which is in the form of a **simile** because it uses "like"). You come home from your basketball game and your father asks you to take out the trash. "Dad," you moan, "I am a bump on a log, a sack of potatoes, a dead body, a leaden window," and your father has a more compelling description of why you are having trouble getting up from the couch. Notice that the actual nature of the comparison you make subtly changes what you are saying about your condition. If you are a leaden window, you are both fragile and heavy; if you are a sack of potatoes, you are something that can be moved, but only with difficulty.

There are many kinds of metaphor—**personification** and simile are two of the most important. Simile is a metaphor that uses "like" or "as" in the middle, and this extra word softens the comparison ("My love is like a red, red rose," or "My holes were empty like a cup"). Metaphor without the language of "like" or "as" is sometimes more bold because it makes a stronger and often stranger claim. In personification, the writer gives human qualities to an object that is not human or alive. For example, the light in spring is personified; the leaves and the wind talk to each other. Personification suggests that the world is awake in ways to which we are not attuned—as if the whole physical world were participating in our lives. Stories have often explored this idea in the figure of the dolls who wake up and talk and move at night (as in the story *Miss Happiness and Miss Flower* or the film *Toy Story*) or the museum pieces that live wild lives when the humans disappear (reference the film *A Night at the Museum*) or the trees that talk and fight in battles (reference the films *The Chronicles of Narnia* and *The Lord of the Rings*). This is a cherished intuition—that the inanimate or insensate world is more alive and active than we first thought.

Poets and thinkers have talked about the way in which objects relate to the thought lives of humans. Walt Whitman articulates this by addressing objects: "You objects that call from diffusion my meanings and give them shape." He suggests that "meanings" need objects to bring them forth, make them clear, and perhaps personify them. Yeats explained that "we are happy when for everything inside us there is a corresponding something outside us," as if the physical, inanimate world could help to draw out the subjective aspects of our own thought life and give them clearer and more physical meaning. Did it ever seem that the wind was speaking to you? Did the voice of the wind take on the emotion that you were feeling when you heard it—forlorn, perhaps, or frightened? Personifying our inner emotions in this way helps us to perceive and address them; as one child observed, personification "insides it out."

Many of our words and common phrases contain these word pictures (as metaphors are sometimes called) but the pictures have been forgotten. They have become what we call **dead metaphors**. For example, when your teacher says, "Do you grasp the idea?" is he suggesting someone has actually reached out with her hand to hold on to an idea? No, he is talking about the ability of the mind to understand an abstract thought, using the picture of a hand grasping a rope to give a clearer, sharper picture to the notion of understanding something, of having something close enough to us to be able to hold it and touch it and possess it. When we say this phrase now, we are not thinking of the physical act of grabbing on to a rope or someone's hand. Or when it is raining we might say, "It's pouring outside." This picture suggests a large amount of water being poured from a source, like a pitcher. This phrase contains a dead metaphor because our minds jump to the metaphor's meaning so quickly that we don't remember that it is a metaphor.

Part of what it means to be educated is to learn how to interpret a metaphor. One must learn what about the comparison applies to the subject of the metaphor and where the comparison ends—what the metaphor is not suggesting. For instance, consider the classic simile "My love is like a red, red rose." As readers, we must decide what aspects of love this speaker is emphasizing— its thorny quality, its sweetness, its complicated structure? Hence, there is a sifting intelligence necessary on the part of the reader to decide how the metaphor is being used. Walt Whitman said, "The reader will always have his or her part to do, just as much as I have mine." When it comes to poetry, if not all kinds of writing, the *reader's* imagination is as important as the *writer's* imagination. By listening hard and meditating on the suggestions the writer is making, particularly in his comparisons, we become a participant in the poem's sum of meaning.

Some scholars argue that buried deep in almost every word in our language is a metaphor. They say that language itself was called forth to name human situations and experiences and tools as they were needed. For instance, our word "thunder" comes from the Middle English *thoner* and the Old English *thunor*. These two words are closely related to the Norse god Thor, son of Woden, who rode through the sky in a chariot. In his hand he carried a hammer that he threw, and its head was so bright that it made lightning when it moved through the air. It returned to his hand after he threw it. When it struck the ice mountains they splintered into fragments. Thor's hammer made thunder. The Germans called this god Donar and Thunar. Notice how the story, the comparison, is literally at the root of this word (and notice, too, how the word root is also a metaphorical image). Thunder is explained by the metaphor or word picture of the god throwing his hammer through the sky. For the Norse people who worshiped Thor, his name and the word for thunder would be mixed with no little degree of awe and fear. In our time, this word still contains that story and the little charge of thunder that comes from the name of the thunder god. A more common example is the word "transgression," which to us means an error, mistake, or misdemeanor, but once meant "to cross a line." The metaphorical significance has been lost so that the current understanding is that the word is abstract. Yet once it was physical, a picture of someone crossing a line that he was forbidden to cross—like the yellow tape around a house after a fire. Poets know this…and so do good readers of poetry.

Try for one day to speak without using any metaphor—it is doubtful that you can. If you come away from this chapter understanding that metaphor is not some technical and formidable poetry tool but rather something universal and human, something poetry celebrates and makes use of, you will have succeeded in understanding its importance.

LEARNING TO READ CLOSELY

William Butler Yeats (1865–1939)

He Wishes for the Cloths of Heaven

Had I the heaven's embroidered cloths,
Enwrought with golden and silver light,
The blue and the dim and the dark cloths
Of night and light and the half-light,
5   I would spread the cloths under your feet:
But I, being poor, have only my dreams;
I have spread my dreams under your feet;
Tread softly because you tread on my dreams.

The metaphor here is buried but clear: the poet is comparing his poems to dreams spread like embroidered cloths under the feet of the listener. This has historically been an action performed for kings and important people—to spread something under their feet to walk on (the red carpet). The metaphor begins with the poet suggesting that the heavens are like beautifully decorated cloths that someone sewed pictures and perhaps ornaments onto and hung in the sky. When something is "wrought," it is elaborately embellished or ornamented, so the word "enwrought" serves to further elaborate on the kind of ornament on this "cloth," or the sky— golden and silver light, gold, the light of the sun, silver, the light of the moon. The speaker goes on to describe other familiar shades of the sky—"the blue and the dim and the dark cloths." In other words, the sky isn't simply filled with light; it also has varying shades of blue and darkness. Listen to how those shades play upon our ear both in terms of sound and **rhythm** (the way the words sound together, their flow or beat): blue, dim, dark are the words that create both the **alliteration** of the two "d's" but also the pattern of speech: "the ____, and the ____, and the ____," could be pounded out neatly on a drum. The following line works on our ear and body's movement as well with the "night, light, light" sounds repeating themselves, and the same rhythm created by the linking words: "of ____, and ____, and the ____."

The speaker (the mask or persona the poet has adopted for the poem) has an earnest, almost pleading **tone** of voice, and as a reader we sense wistfulness or soft regret at the fact that she doesn't have the heaven's embroidered cloths to spread for us. We also sense that the speaker would do anything to acquire those cloths. He wants to treat *us* like kings and queens; he wants to spread them under *our* feet, but because he is poor he must spread something else that is precious under our feet—his dreams. Here the poems are all referred to collectively as the poet's dreams. He suggests that he has collected everything that matters most to him, every strange and beautiful part of his mind (conscious and unconscious) just for us. He is casting himself upon our mercy by giving them to us, and he asks in return that we "tread softly" on his dreams.

Notice that the poem's end words rhyme, almost without trying to. The end words of lines 1 and 3 (cloths) are the same, as are the end words of lines 2 and 4. The same thing is true of the four end words of the last four lines: feet/feet, dreams/dreams. Notice as well that almost every line has nine syllables. This just barely falls short of the pentameter line (ten syllables), suggesting perhaps a fear of falling short of what one wishes, as well as of the expectations of the audience.

How are poems like dreams under our feet? When someone writes a piece of language as if he were making an alabaster statue, he puts all of his skill and hope and even parts of his deepest self into the poem. The speaker suggests that his fate, the reception of his work and even of his person, is in our hands. Who are we? We are the readers. According to Yeats, we are as powerful as kings and queens. What are poems made of, according to the poem collectively? Poems are made of delicate work, of light, of shades of color, of all the times of day, of all that matters most to human beings. This is perhaps what the critic Allan Grossman means when he says that poems keep the image of the person precious in the world—one human being speaking to another, to many others, of all that matters most deeply, and speaking with all of the skill and beauty she can muster. This would be one argument for learning to be a good reader! Sometimes life experience also prepares us to read well. For instance, because I have written poems and felt the feelings of the speaker, I understand the nature of the poem and the pleading, longing tone of voice. Your life experience will help you to read insightfully as well.

Such a small poem and yet so much contained within! Anyone making art in the world makes herself vulnerable to the opinion of others. It has been said that a work of art is not finished until it is received by others. Do you agree? This would be an excellent poem to memorize.

ANTHOLOGY

Emily Dickinson (1830–1886)

Hope is the thing with feathers

Hope is the thing with feathers
That perches in the soul,
And sings the tune—without the words,
And never stops at all,

5   And sweetest in the gale is heard;
And sore must be the storm
That could abash the little bird
That kept so many warm.

I've heard it in the chillest land,
10   And on the strangest sea;
Yet, never, in extremity,
It asked a crumb of me.

1. Hope is being compared to what? Describe Dickinson's metaphor in your own words.

2. What are some of the things a bird does that hope also does?

3. How does birdsong make us feel, according to the poet? How does hope make us feel?

4. Circle the rhymes in this poem. Does this poem have a rhythm that you can tap out on a table?

5. In what way does a wild bird that lives outside ask nothing of us? In what way does hope not ask anything of us?

6. Dickinson was a recluse who rarely stepped outside of her house—what then does she mean when she says she's heard the bird of hope "in the chillest land / And on the strangest sea"?

7. How about you—when have you felt hope or needed to feel hope?

8. According to the last two lines of the poem, can hope be something that gets hungry? Can hope be something we can feed?

William Wordsworth (1770–1850)

I Wandered Lonely as a Cloud

I wandered lonely as a cloud
That floats on high o'er vales and hills,
When all at once I saw a crowd,
A host, of golden daffodils;
5   Beside the lake, beneath the trees,
Fluttering and dancing in the breeze.

Continuous as the stars that shine
And twinkle on the milky way,
They stretched in never-ending line
10   Along the margin of a bay:
Ten thousand saw I at a glance,
Tossing their heads in sprightly dance.

The waves beside them danced; but they
Out-did the sparkling waves in glee:
15   A poet could not but be gay,
In such a jocund company:
I gazed—and gazed—but little thought
What wealth the show to me had brought:

For oft, when on my couch I lie
20   In vacant or in pensive mood,
They flash upon that inward eye
Which is the bliss of solitude;
And then my heart with pleasure fills,
And dances with the daffodils.

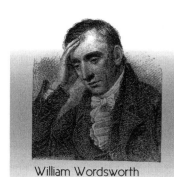

William Wordsworth

Here the speaker suggests a metaphor for himself: he is like a cloud being blown (wandering) across the hills and fields.

1. What does the speaker see? What does he do with what he sees?

2. Think about the two ways the poet represents himself: floating like a cloud and lying on a couch. How are these two images different? How are they similar—especially in relation to the crowd of daffodils?

3. What has happened between the first stanza's emotion of lonely wandering and the final stanza's emotion of blissful solitude?

4. Name two similes in this poem. Each stanza in the poem contains a pair of verbs, adverbs, or adjectives that basically mean the same thing—"vacant" and "pensive" in stanza four, for example. Find the three other pairs of words, and define any you don't know.

Emily Dickinson (1830–1886)

A Light exists in Spring

A Light exists in Spring
Not present on the Year
At any other period—
When March is scarcely here

5   A Color stands abroad
On Solitary Fields
That Science cannot overtake
But Human Nature feels.

It waits upon the Lawn,
10   It shows the furthest Tree
Upon the furthest Slope you know
It almost speaks to you.

Then as Horizons step
Or Noons report away
15   Without the Formula of sound
It passes and we stay—

A quality of loss
Affecting our Content
As Trade had suddenly encroached
20   Upon a Sacrament.

This poem describes the light in spring and personifies it. That is, it describes the light in spring as if it were a person that came to visit.

1. Where do you see the light being treated as a person in this poem?

2. Why would the speaker feel discontented loss when the light leaves? Have you ever felt this way about the light in spring, or other kinds of light—say at a carnival, in a movie theater, or in a particular spot of your own home?

3. Look up definitions for the words "trade," "sacrament," and "encroached." Explain how the last stanza is a simile describing how we feel at the loss of spring's particular light.

Anonymous

An Autumn Greeting

'Come,' said the Wind to the Leaves one day.
'Come over the meadow and we will play.
Put on your dresses of red and gold.
For summer is gone and the days grow cold.'

1. This is another example of personification—what in the poem tells you this?

2. What kind of people do you imagine the Wind and the Leaves to be?

3. Can you name the metaphor in line 3? Can you name a less obvious metaphor in line 2?

4. What is the feeling, or **tone,** of this poem, and is there more than one?

Robert Louis Stevenson (1850–1894)

At the Seaside

When I was down beside the sea
A wooden spade they gave to me
To dig the sandy shore.

My holes were empty like a cup,
5   In every hole the sea came up,
Till it could come no more.

1. Describe what is happening here as the tide rises.

2. Find and name the simile in the poem.

3. How old is the speaker in this poem? What evidence can you find in the poem to defend your answer?

4. What kind of feeling are we left with at the end of this poem? Does the sea's action leave us, or leave the speaker, with a positive feeling or a negative feeling? Can you defend both possible answers?

Langston Hughes (1902–1967)

Mother to Son

Well, son, I'll tell you:
Life for me ain't been no crystal stair.
It's had tacks in it,
And splinters,
5 And boards torn up,
And places with no carpet on the floor—
Bare.
But all the time
I'se been a–climbin' on,
10 And reachin' landin's,
And turnin' corners,
And sometimes goin' in the dark
Where there ain't been no light.
So boy, don't you turn back.
15 Don't you set down on the steps
'Cause you finds it's kinder hard.
Don't you fall now—
For I'se still goin', honey,
I'se still climbin',
20 And life for me ain't been no crystal stair.

1. Who is speaking and to whom?

2. What metaphor does the speaker use to communicate her message?

3. What does the image of the crystal stair suggest?

4. How else does the speaker's voice communicate the same message?

5. How do the line breaks contribute to the meaning?

Robert Frost (1874–1963)

Nothing Gold Can Stay

Nature's first green is gold,
Her hardest hue to hold.
Her early leafs a flower;
But only so an hour.
5   Then leaf subsides to leaf.
So Eden sank to grief,
So dawn goes down to day.
Nothing gold can stay.

1. When is the natural world full of the shade of green that the poet considers as precious as gold?

2. How is that time of year as valuable or worthwhile as gold?

3. Why is this hue, or color, hard to hold?

4. How is the losing of the green and the flowers of spring like the story of the Garden of Eden?

5. Explain the different losses charted in the poem, and then explain how the last line means more than the title, even though it is a repeated line.

George Herbert (1593–1633)

The Pulley

When God at first made Man,
  Having a glass of blessings standing by—
Let us (said He) pour on him all we can;
Let the world's riches, which dispersèd lie,
5   Contract into a span.

  So strength first made a way,
Then beauty flow'd, then wisdom, honour, pleasure:
When almost all was out, God made a stay,
Perceiving that, alone of all His treasure,
10   Rest in the bottom lay.

    For if I should (said He)
Bestow this jewel also on My creature,
He would adore My gifts instead of Me,
And rest in Nature, not the God of Nature:
15   So both should losers be.

    Yet let him keep the rest,
But keep them with repining restlessness;
Let him be rich and weary, that at least,
If goodness lead him not, yet weariness
20   May toss him to My breast.

1. In this poem we see God as a creator or mad scientist with a glass full of blessings next to him as he puts the finishing touches on humankind. What does he "pour" on Man? What does he withhold and why?

2. How does the lack of rest function in this plan to bring humankind to God? What do you think about the way man and God are portrayed?

ACTIVITIES

1. Listen to people speaking (as well as yourself) to find metaphors buried in everyday speech. Even children who are very young use metaphors. I heard one say, "Mommy, the moon is broken" once when looking up at a waning moon on a dark night for the first time. Another said, "Are we in outer space?" the first time he rode an underground subway train. Make a list of ten "found metaphors" to bring to class. Put them all in a hat and have each student draw three out and make a poem that includes at least one.

2. Make metaphors and similes by completing the following sentences. Do it thoughtfully but fairly quickly, without thinking too much about them:

The shy girl's hand in the air shook like a_____.
The old man's hands on the ancient book shook like _____.
Tree branches over my head shook their new leaves like_____.
The little boys shook with suppressed laughter like _____.
The mayor's handshake was a_____.
The mother's stern headshake was a _____.
Badly shaken, the rookie cop collapsed like a_____.
The exhausted boy just couldn't shake them; he was a_____ to their _____.

3. Choose one of the following bird activities: draw a picture of the bird of hope as you imagine it from Dickinson's poem; consider getting out bird books and sketching a bird here on this page or in your writer's notebook; study the birds in your neighborhood carefully. Will you ever see a bird now without considering the way in which its miraculous wings defy gravity and lift it into the air? This is how poetry begins to live with us each day and in the scenes we encounter.

4. Hundreds of poems have been written using birds as a metaphorical image; write a bird poem of your own. There are numerous poems about birds in this book. In preparation for writing this poem you could read through them and jot down some notes, or notice which use of them appeals to you. *Brave Sparrow, Dust of Snow, Questioning Faces* are a few of them.

5. Memorize one of the poems in this book by incorporating hand motions, and then recite it at an assembly or at dinnertime.

6. Science and metaphor: List all the metaphors you can think of that science uses to explain abstract ideas, then try to explain the metaphor and why it is a metaphor. You'll find that you are so used to these that you can hardly remember that they are metaphors. Take a science metaphor and turn it into a metaphor about nature, childhood, friendship, or fear.

7. Four of the poems in this chapter's anthology use the image or the word "field." Hold a discussion in your classroom about the many different meanings, feelings, and associations this word can evoke in us. Cast a wide net—fields of political candidates, baseball fields, etc. Also consider culture—does "field" evoke a different feeling in Arizona or Africa than in New York City? Come prepared with a little internet or library research—what are the linguistic origins of the word?

VOCABULARY

Alliteration: repetition of consonant sounds at the beginning of words next to each other (initial consonant sounds), such as roof/ruthlessness, brain/British.

Cliché: an expression that has lost ingenuity, originality, and impact and become commonplace by long overuse.

Dead metaphor: a metaphor with which we have become so familiar we are no longer aware that it is a metaphor.

Extended metaphor: a sustained comparison in which the whole poem consists of a series of related metaphors, or a single metaphor stretched throughout the whole poem. It is also called a conceit. (*Hope is the thing with feathers* does this.)

Personification: a metaphor that gives human characteristics to something that is not human.

Rhythm: the beat of the words together; the recurrence of movement and sound; the way in which sounds move; the rise and fall of words together.

Simile: a metaphor or comparison that uses "like" or "as."

Tone: the attitude of the poem, of the poet toward the subject of the poem; the emotional atmosphere of the poem.

03
SYMBOLS

{*the elements of poetry*}

A symbol is an image that stands for something more than itself. It has multiple meanings beyond the physical detail which is shown. The word comes from two Greek words: *symballein* (a verb) meaning "to put together," and *symbolon* (a noun) meaning "mark," "token," or "sign," referring to the half-coins that people would carry away as a pledge after making an agreement. Holding that broken coin in your hand was a reminder that you had promised you would do something. The thing was a sign of that promise, a recollection that something needed to be completed in order for the coin and the agreement and the relationship to be whole again. Hence, it was a half-coin that represented something beyond its monetary value.

An example of symbolism in your everyday life might be the following: some students buy clothes because they are a certain brand—Hollister, Abercrombie & Fitch, Calvin Klein. They are hoping that the clothes will not only cover their body but enhance their image, cause other people to admire them. Adults do this, too, especially with cars and other high-priced items. A new Mercedes-Benz is not just a set of wheels to get us from one place to another; it is a symbol of a lifestyle of wealth and precision. These examples are symbols that are contextualized in a given culture.

There are other kinds of symbols called **conventional** and **literary symbols**. Conventional symbols are images that many people over many areas and ages agree or understand represent certain ideas. *Spring* represents new life and growth; *rose* represents love; *moon* represents romance; *fire* represents mankind and survival; *dove* represents peace; and *winter* represents death. Furthermore, there are objects that hold history in them. In certain times and places, a plow was the most elemental tool to break up dirt and begin the process that would end with the harvest of much-needed food; hence, it appears to us as a symbol of toil. In our examination of *The Panther* in a previous chapter, you saw how the meaning of the panther was built over the course of the poem. It was not exact or simple but had a range of possible interpretations and applications. A literary symbol's meaning is built within a story or a poem and cannot be summarized in a single word.

This inexact and expansive quality distinguishes the symbol from metaphor. With metaphor, we enjoy the fact that two dissimilar things are explicitly compared, surprising us, giving us pleasure, making the original element new or understandable. With a symbol, we are aware that a meaning beyond the image exists, but it isn't single or specific; it is a suggestion, a range of additional meanings. The limits, therefore, on the possible interpretations of the symbol are more difficult to define. The equation for symbol would be A = X, in which the A of the equation is the image, and because of the way it is used in a poem or story we understand that it has great significance, even abstract significance—the X in the equation—but not a single abstract subject that we could readily pin down. (For an example of contrast see *A Noiseless Patient Spider*, in which the web-making spider is being compared to the human soul, a metaphor and specific.)

Think about your own experience and the way in which certain objects, people, or events have held meaning beyond their surface value. The flowers you received for your first drama performance that are dried and hanging from your mirror, are there not because they are beautiful any longer but because they remind you of the event and of the hard work, happiness, and personal growth that you experienced as a part of that event. The flowers are a personal symbol. You are not able to pin down their meaning to a single word but must use a string of sentences to describe it. A certain song that you remember is now symbolic of your feelings or memories of first hearing or learning it. The party that you attended, where you felt socially isolated because no one brought you into the conversation, remains a symbolic blot on the canvas of your mind. If it was a particularly bad experience, where you realized for the first time how cruel people can be and the possibility of uncomfortable exclusion, the symbol could be the house where the party was held, or even its anniversary on the calendar. The bread your mother baked and gave you after school has come to be symbolic of her love for you, along with nourishment, satisfaction of hunger, and the pleasure of the return home. Objects, persons, places, events, and actions, whether they are personal, universal, or historical, have the capability of taking on another level of meaning, to become symbols.

Literary symbols function to express remote ideas, or to put language to ideas that are so close or deep we cannot perceive them. Symbols in poetry, stories, or novels make vivid what might be faint in our emotional or cultural lives. For example, you might have had a crush on a girl in your school or church, but not until you read *The Silken Tent* (you can find it online at www. poemhunter.com) did you know how intensely you could feel about her. Or the reading of such a passionate poem may reveal to you the silliness of your crush: you couldn't compare it to the writer of that poem's feelings. Later, when you really do fall in love, or marry, you may draw upon your knowledge of this poem or image to express how you feel—or you may even learn about your own love by suddenly recognizing in yourself the passion that previously belonged only to the poet.

Ultimately, the power of symbol lies in its elusiveness—we have to go in search of the meaning of an image and build our interpretation of its suggestion. This possibility of multiple meanings in a single image is exciting; it gives us work to do and makes room for exploration. The danger of symbols in a text is that the sloppy reader may allow them to mean anything he desires and not work to pin them down to a circle of meaning. You must carefully build evidence to support your interpretation of the meaning of an image in a poem or story. Not every literal thing in a poem is a symbol; you must get used to sleuthing in order to find the images with symbolic weight. Read for literal meaning first, then look for language, description, or a tone of voice that would not normally be attached to the object or subject described. Look for **repetition** or other forms of emphasis, such as heightened sound play or the arrangement of the lines of the poem. Does the poem need a symbolic interpretation to make sense of it? Or can you read it literally without "reading into" the images? We must beware of reading into the images more than the text leads us to see, and we must use the whole context of the poem to evaluate what is symbolic.

Each poem in the anthology that follows contains an extended symbol, in which the **subject** of the poem expands to mean much more than its literal sense. When the speaker in Robert Frost's poem *Acquainted with the Night* repeatedly claims to be acquainted with the night, using a somber tone and chantlike rhythm, it begins to dawn on us that he isn't simply talking about being a night owl. The night has conventionally been associated with darkness, death, grief, and even danger. Frost draws upon these associations and constructs a literary symbol which is personal as well. Night for this speaker means all that and more: insomnia, loneliness, coldness, fear, and alienation. This is not a poem with light, and the negative aspects of the night appear to have seeped into the very soul of the speaker. The restrained speaker does not tell us the origin of this darkness—perhaps someone he loves has died, or perhaps his melancholic nature has overwhelmed him—but we experience the knowledge of this state while we read the poem. Either we, too, have had this impression and we feel companionship from its representation in the poem, or we have not and the poem serves to usher us into a new sensation which expands our awareness and experience.

When you read a poem, you work shoulder to shoulder with the writer: wrestling, sifting, puzzling with the collection of words he or she has set down. In the process, your imagination is engaged and you bring to the poem your life—memory, experience, vocabulary, and the moment in which you attend to it. So much meaning comes from this exchange, not least of which is a form of participation between you and the writer, and the poem seeps into the fiber of your experience. It becomes you.

LEARNING TO READ CLOSELY

Michael Collier (1953–)

Brave Sparrow

whose home is in the straw
and bailing twine threaded
in the slots of a roof vent

5   who guards a tiny ledge
against the starlings
that cruise the neighborhood

whose heart is smaller
than a heart should be,
whose feathers stiffen

10   like an arrow fret to quicken
the hydraulics of its wings,
stay there on the metal

ledge, widen your alarming
beak, but do not flee as others have
15   to the black walnut vaulting

overhead. Do not move outside
the world you've made
from bailing twine and straw.

The isolated starling fears
20   the crows, the crows gang up
to rout a hawk. The hawk

is cold. And cold is what
a larger heart maintains.
The owl at dusk and dawn,

25   far off, unseen, but audible,
repeats its syncopated intervals,
a song that's not a cry

but a whisper rising from concentric
rings of water spreading out across
30   the surface of a catchment pond.

It asks, "Who are you? Who
are you?" but no one knows.
Stay where you are, nervous, jittery.

Move your small head a hundred
35   ways, a hundred times, keep
paying attention to the terrifying

world. And if you see the Robins
in their dirty orange vests
patrolling the yard like thugs,

40   forget about the worm. Starve
yourself, or from the air inhale
the water you may need, digest

the dust. And what the promiscuous
cat and jaybirds do, let them
45   do it, let them dart and snipe,

let them sound like others.
They sleep when the owl sends
out its encircling question.

Stay where you are, you lit fuse,
50   you dull spark of saltpeter and sulfur.

Here, another bird poem addresses the common sparrow. In a long series of imperative sentences, the speaker gives directions in an encouraging voice to the sparrow, and we come to realize that she isn't simply talking to a bird. The title clues us in to the fact that the speaker identifies how hard it is to be a small thing in a world of large things, how much bravery it requires. Some of the bird characters that the sparrow encounters include the starlings that "cruise the neighborhood." They are like tough teenagers who articulate the rough code of behavior necessary for others to fit in. In this world of birds there is a pecking order, and brute force rules the sky. The "isolated starling" is afraid of the crows; the crows in turn band together to chase out a hawk. The details and the language of the poem work hard to paint an accurate picture both of how these birds literally behave in nature but also of how they might serve as comparisons for human behavior. We recognize in the poem words that we use to talk about human beings and the ways in which we treat each other, not birds. Hence we are sure as we pass through the **tercets** (three-lined stanzas) that the speaker is talking about how hard it is for anyone to be what he or she is, how hard it is for us to stand our ground as human beings. We are tempted to give in to the bullies, to those with power. A sparrow isn't noteworthy in the bird realm for anything except its plainness. Sparrows don't sing beautifully; they don't have pretty, bright feathers (theirs are brown). They aren't strong, they aren't special or rare—you can see bushes-full everywhere. Even the robins in the poem are stronger and more powerful, "patrolling the yard like thugs."

Despite this plainness, the speaker tells the sparrow, with increasingly resolute insistence, to "stay where you are," to do whatever necessary to hold your ground, to be what you are. The speaker acknowledges that the sparrow may need to take drastic measures to accomplish this—"Starve / yourself, or from the air inhale / the water you may need, digest / the dust." As the poem moves toward its end it gathers momentum. The admonishment becomes more intense, more earnest. The speaker calls the cat and jaybirds "promiscuous" or unfaithful. These birds steal other birds' nests as well as imitate the sounds of other bird's calls, but promiscuous is a word that belongs to the human realm of love and suggests a lack of loyalty to one to whom loyalty is owed. This voice that speaks to the figure of the sparrow understands the situation that the small, vulnerable, unimpressive bird is in—she identifies the world as "terrifying," she argues that despite the owl's question (who are you?) "no one knows." In other words: Don't let the question spook you but keep striving for what you are, keep working in your endeavors, keep making your home of "straw / and baling twine threaded / in the slots of a roof." Such a fragile place to live; yet the speaker admonishes "do not move outside / the world you've made" and later "do not flee as others have."

How do we know that this poem is not simply about sparrows? For one thing, the intensity of the tone, the sense that much is at stake in this exchange, alerts us to the fact that the sparrow has come to mean more than just a sparrow. What precisely does the sparrow represent? Of that we can only suppose the speaker is insisting that all people have a personal destiny and worth, have a self that needs to stand its ground in order to become what it was meant to be. It is possible that the speaker is also speaking to a poet-sparrow. Poets have often been compared to songbirds who sing their songs for the world to hear. Poets are often intimidated by other poets, alive and dead. The speaker may well be speaking to herself (how, after all, does she know so precisely what it is like to be a sparrow?), speaking a word of resolute encouragement to continue writing poems in her own voice, in her own way, in the "world you've made." Notice the number of surprising and intricate words the poet uses to create this particular voice.

Most people, when asked to choose a bird to represent themselves, would not choose such a humble or even worthless bird. But the speaker seems to insist that even a sparrow's song is worth singing, even a sparrow's world is worth preserving. The language surrounding the poem is also a clue to the figurative meaning that is present. We don't often think of birds as being "promiscuous" or "as snip[ing]" or even as asking a serious question such as "who are you?" The poet uses the bird world to talk about activity that goes on in the human world in many different places. Most teenagers will notice how familiar this world is to the social one in which they struggle to survive each day. Most poets struggle to establish themselves and their voices, to have a song worth listening to. This speaker wants the sparrow to continue his bravery whatever it takes, to continue singing his song and making his small life. The speaker insists that the sparrow is a "lit fuse" and a "dull spark of saltpeter (or salt) and sulfur"—dull, yes, but still burning; common as salt, and yet how could we live without salt?

Formally, the sentences and the lines are operating very differently. There isn't a line that contains a single sentence. The sentences spill (**enjamb**) over into the next line and end abruptly in the middle of lines (caesura). Several times throughout the poem the speaker refers to the fact that this life that the sparrow must live is "nervous, jittery" and that the sparrow must "move your small head a hundred / ways, a hundred times, keep / paying attention to the terrifying / world." The form of the poem, which is so unpredictable (the crazily paced and uneven sentences) and yet attempts to have a predictable shape (the three-lined stanzas), imitates the life of the sparrow. In other words, the poem conveys by its lines, its stops and starts, its sudden movements and sudden ceasing of movement, the texture of the life of this sparrow. For the space that we read the poem our body feels the pacing of this kind of life, feels the constant movement and nervousness of it. The poem becomes a space we can enter to imagine what it is to live as a brave sparrow. I am sure that you have had to live this way at some point in your life. Perhaps even now you are struggling to manage the predators and gossipy, sniping birds in your world. This poem encourages you; it demands that you stand your ground.

ANTHOLOGY

Robert Frost (1874–1963)

Acquainted with the Night

I have been one acquainted with the night.
I have walked out in rain–and back in rain.
I have outwalked the furthest city light.

I have looked down the saddest city lane.
5   I have passed by the watchman on his beat
And dropped my eyes, unwilling to explain.

I have stood still and stopped the sound of feet
When far away an interrupted cry
Came over houses from another street,

10   But not to call me back or say goodbye;
And further still at an unearthly height,
One luminary clock against the sky

Proclaimed the time was neither wrong nor right.
I have been one acquainted with the night.

The introduction to this chapter talks about night as a powerful symbol for depression or alienation in this poem; it may be helpful to read that paragraph again. This poem successfully presents night as a symbol, with a range of feelings and dark impressions, by using additional images, personification, repetition, rhyme, and rhythm.

1. Name three examples of poetic devices used in this poem, and explain how they help you, as a reader, get acquainted with the speaker's mood.

2. Name three places in the poem where the language reverses or negates a statement or action just made.

3. What is the effect of these reversals or negations on the poem as a whole?

4. Some people read this poem and absolutely love it—why do you think that is?

William Blake (1757–1827)

The Poison Tree

I was angry with my friend:
I told my wrath, my wrath did end.
I was angry with my foe:
I told it not, my wrath did grow.

5   And I watered it in fears
Night and morning with my tears,
And I sunned it with smiles
And with soft deceitful wiles.

And it grew both day and night,
10   Till it bore an apple bright,
And my foe beheld it shine,
And he knew that it was mine,–

And into my garden stole
When the night had veiled the pole;
15   In the morning, glad, I see
My foe outstretched beneath the tree.

1. Wrath is considered one of the deadly sins. What does this poem suggest about the effects of wrath?

2. How are the tree and wrath or anger related to each other?

3. How might someone "water" and "sun" their anger toward another person?

4. How might someone be literally or figuratively poisoned by another's wrath? Name one or two examples from literature, film, or your own experience that might fit this poem's scenario.

5. Look at the rhymes, arranged in couplets—two pairs of lines that each have the same end sound. Identify one or two rhyming pairs that contain opposites—the words sound the same but in some way have opposite meanings. Explain your choices.

6. Is this an adult poem or a child's poem? Cite evidence from the poem to defend your answer.

Christina Rossetti (1830–1894)

Up-Hill

Does the road wind up-hill all the way?
    Yes, to the very end.
Will the day's journey take the whole long day?
    From morn to night, my friend.

5   But is there for the night a resting-place?
    A roof for when the slow dark hours begin.
May not the darkness hide it from my face?
    You cannot miss that inn.

Shall I meet other wayfarers at night?
10   Those who have gone before.
Then must I knock, or call when 'ust in sight?
    They will not keep you standing at that door.

Shall I find comfort, travel-sore and weak?
    Of labor you shall find the sum.
15   Will there be beds for me and all who seek?
    Yea, beds for all who come.

Christina Rossetti

1. Notice that there are two speakers in this poem. Who do you think they are?

2. What is happening in this poem? What is the meaning of the road, the end, the journey, the night, the darkness, and the beds?

3. Does the language "all who seek" sound like an echo of any other text you know or have heard?

4. What is the rhyme scheme and does it have a specific effect on the meaning of this poem? What is another kind of "scheme," or ordered pattern, in the poem?

5. What is the overall feeling of this poem—and is there more than one? Cite evidence from the poem's language and construction to support your answer.

6. Why do you think the title is "Up-Hill" and not something like "The Road"?

7. What symbol or idea do you think is being constructed and explored in the poem? (Hint: it's not directly named in the text.)

William Carlos Williams (1883–1963)

To Waken an Old Lady

Old age is
a flight of small
cheeping birds
skimming
5   bare trees
above a snow glaze.
Gaining and failing
they are buffeted
by a dark wind—
10   But what?
On harsh weedstalks
the flock has rested,
the snow
is covered with broken
15   seedhusks
and the wind tempered
by a shrill
piping of plenty.

1. The speaker of the poem uses words to paint a picture of old age. Describe the picture and its symbolism. Is the picture positive, negative, or both?

2. How do the lines and their breaks and enjambment tie into the subject, to the picture which is being painted?

3. What is the effect of the sounds of the words, particularly the "ing" words?

4. What are some other words that impact the meaning of the poem and create the tone of the poem?

5. Why do you think the poem was written *To Waken an Old Lady*, as the title suggests? How might this picture wake someone up? Why might you need to waken an old lady?

Wallace Stevens (1879–1955)

The Snow Man

One must have a mind of winter
To regard the frost and the boughs
Of the pine-trees crusted with snow;

And have been cold a long time
5   To behold the junipers shagged with ice,
The spruces rough in the distant glitter

Of the January sun; and not to think
Of any misery in the sound of the wind,
In the sound of a few leaves,

10   Which is the sound of the land
Full of the same wind
That is blowing in the same bare place

For the listener, who listens in the snow,
And, nothing himself, beholds
15   Nothing that is not there and the nothing that is.

1. In this poem, winter becomes a symbol. What are some of the feelings associated with winter and why do we associate them with that season?

2. How does the poem pick up on some of these to portray "a mind of winter." Does the environmental temperature have anything to do with the emotional temperature or the feelings in the poem?

3. What is the tone or mood of the poem? What creates that tone or mood?

4. How might snow and nothingness be related to each other? How is snow empty feeling?

5. What are some of the sounds that this poem uses to demonstrate its meaning?

ACTIVITIES

1. As a class or in your notebook, brainstorm some symbols that are connected to your school, home, or country in the current political atmosphere.

2. Cut out pictures from magazines or draw one or many of the symbols you've listed.

3. Tell the story of something that happened to you at some point in your life (something significant) through symbols. Paint, sketch, or make a collage that contains this meaning visually.

4. As in the poem *Brave Sparrow*, find a symbol for something that you wish for a friend, family member, or even for your country. Discuss it as a class.

5. Choose an image and have the class freewrite on what that image means to them and associations that they make with that image. Have four people share aloud with the class what it means to them. See how different experiences attach themselves to the same image.

6. Choose an old photograph and freewrite on everything that picture contains in terms of significance or the story of your life. Then write a paragraph or poem that describes every element in an ordered way.

7. Bring an object of importance (and some mystery—not a trophy) to class and have the class guess what it might symbolize before you tell them. Then describe its symbolic value.

8. The poems in this anthology use some distinctive and simple structures that construct symbolic reflections. Frost uses the repetition of a single phrase ("I have been one acquainted with the night"); Blake uses a deceptively childlike nursery rhyme rhythm; and Rossetti uses a question-and-answer, call-and-response structure. Choose one of these three structure models and write your own poem around a single symbol or theme.

VOCABULARY

Conventional symbol: a symbol recognized by a society or culture (flag, cross).

End-stop (or end-stopped line): a line that ends with a definite halt, sometimes marked by punctuation (period, comma, question mark, semicolon, etc.), but always a thought or phrase that is complete.

Enjamb (or enjambment): in a poem, a line whose sense and rhythmic movement continues to the next line—the opposite of an end-stopped line. This technique tends to cause the reader to move on quickly at the end of a line instead of pausing. See also **end-stop**.

Literary symbol: a person, object, image, word, or event with meaning beyond itself that is defined by its context in a particular work. There are also literary symbols that are conventional, having taken on meaning because they've been repeatedly used in literature in similar ways. Winter = old age, spring = renewal, lamb = innocence.

Repetition: a duplication of words, sounds, order of words, or phrases for effect.

Subject: the basic theme the poem is exploring.

Tercet: a three-line stanza.

O4

WORDS

{the elements of poetry}

Words are the basic units of the sentence and of language. Each one has a distinctive sound, takes up a specific visual space, is a part of speech, and has singular or multiple meanings. In addition, each word has its own personal history, for usually a word has made its way through several different languages before appearing in English usage. When you read or write a poem you must learn to pay close attention to every word as well as to the ways words are combined in the whole of the poem.

Naming is the most direct purpose we expect from a word. In fairy tales, to know the name of something is to have power over it or even posses it. In the Christian story of the world's creation, land, sea, light, and trees were all called into existence by being named. Adam, the first man, was then given the task of naming all animals and plants, and this represented a kind of stewardship or husbandry of the creation God had made. Poets name the world around them and also the world within them. Poets may spend hours or days searching for the right word to capture the meaning or idea they want to convey. As readers of poems, we too must consider each word for its various meanings and suggestions, and for its connections to wider meanings as it interacts with other words in the poem.

It is possible to name many aspects of the world, and thus to speak with particularity. When we are in the presence of this attentiveness we find ourselves becoming more alert. The poet William Blake said, "to generalize is to be an idiot. To particularize is the lone distinction of merit." Centuries later another poet, Richard Wilbur, called this inventory impulse "the itch to call the roll of things." (Read his wonderful essay "Poetry and Happiness" to learn more.) Think about the pleasure you experience when you are able to name the birds, flowers, trees, or butterflies as you move through your days. This pleasure is not relegated to nature alone: any area of knowledge that you develop the terms to discuss, be it car parts or computer software or musical artists, bestows satisfaction and the sensation of skillfulness.

Words perform other functions besides naming; to understand them, we need to learn a few terms. **Denotation** refers to the literal, dictionary definition of a word (what you would find if you looked it up), its stripped-down, basic meaning. **Connotation** refers to the associations and attitudes called up by a word in addition to its basic definition. For instance, the words "aroma" and "odor" both denote scent, but each word has a different connotation. "Aroma" suggests a delightful scent; "odor" suggests something that smells bad. Likewise the words "wildflower" and "weed" have a similar denotation: a plant that grows without human cultivation. But the connotations of these words are quite different, for we desire the first but detest the second. There are many synonyms for the word "cry," yet each one suggests a different emphasis: "weep" (sorrowful, elegant, not necessarily loud); "wail" (loud, undignified); "whimper" (soft and possibly childlike or even babyish); "sob" (unrestrained); and "blubber" (emotionally and physically messy). Such distinctive, predictable reactions to these synonyms are their connotations, which are attached to each word as surely as is their common denotation.

Shades of meaning, associations, suggestions of meaning—these are part of the package with words. Consider of the definition of the word "bird." Now think of all the suggestions that go beyond the word's literal meaning—perhaps fragility, song, sky, freedom. Consider also how different birds call up different suggestions: the predators, the songbirds, doves, penguins, chickens, vultures, owls. Or take another example: think of the difference between the words "lamb" and "sheep." Even though one (lamb) is considered the immature version of the other (sheep), we have attached such different values to each that you would think that they are different species. Lambs are tender, soft, beautiful, vulnerable. Sheep are dumb, dirty, followers. Whichever of these two you choose to place in a poem will depend on the reaction you wish to provoke in your reader.

In addition to meaning, the sounds of words are important. We can fall in love with some words because of how they feel in our ears and mouths and, likewise, we can loathe certain words because their sound intimidates or irritates us or even fills us with foreboding. Poets strive to make the sound and the meaning of words work together to create a strong effect. For instance, in the phrase "vacant vast surrounding," long vowel sounds echo the literal picture of wide open spaces. Good poets hone their awareness of how specific letters create meaningful sounds. Words with a lot of sharp consonants like "p" or "k" or "t" create a harsh or fierce feeling, whereas words with sounds like "s" or "h" or "l" create a much softer or more spacious feeling. Usually you will experience the impact of a sound pattern before you are conscious of it. The sound works with the ideas in the poem to embody them; at the same time that you are thinking about meaning, you are experiencing the sensation of that meaning in your ear and mouth. Go back to the poem to perceive the pattern that created the sensation, and look to see what consonants and vowels were working together. This chapter's "Learning to Read Closely" section contains examples of this.

Up to this point we have discussed words primarily as singular units. Now we must consider two ways we talk about words used in combination in poems. Words have different emphases depending on where they are placed in the poem. The end of a line or stanza is an emphatic place for a word—you should attend to these words. In **free verse**, another technique that acknowledges the power of the line's end is called enjambment. A line whose sense and rhythmic movement continues to the next line is called an enjambed line. In the example of *The Dance* (p. 42), every line is enjambed. This method functions in *The Dance* to keep the reader in motion, to prevent us from resting at any given place in the poem, which is appropriate to its subject matter. In this poem, the power lies in the motion of the words together, not in a single word, phrase, or piece of the poem.

When the words of a poem are considered as a whole, we speak of the poem's **diction.** This is a fancy word that refers to the choice of words in a poem that combine to help create meaning. Is the speech casual (the way jeans are in dress), or is it formal (like a ball gown)? If the language is casual, is there slang (ripped jeans)? **Formal diction** tends to be elevated, dignified, exact, lofty, complex—like a tuxedo or ball gown. **Informal diction** uses plain, everyday speech, idioms, slang, contractions, and simple, common words—like a pair of jeans and a T-shirt. As you might guess, there is a range of options between these two poles. Before the eighteenth century, poetry consciously set itself apart from everyday speech. It almost always employed formal diction and rigid rhyme schemes. Since then, however, poets have increasingly sought to use a range of dictions and to speak in ways that sound natural to the ear or that reflect the way people commonly talk.

One big difference between poetry and prose is that in poetry each word possesses a great deal of importance to the ultimate meaning and pleasure of the poem. Call up the image of deep, dark, bitter espresso coffee as opposed to tall paper cups full of weak coffee, and you will have a metaphor for the value of words in poetry versus prose. One reason for this is simply that there are fewer words in poetry than in prose writing. Another reason is that words in a poem are chosen for their ability to create meaning through sound, in addition to the meaning of an idea conjured by a word. Words are therefore doing double duty, not just signifying *what* something means but *how* it means. Always we ask ourselves when studying a poem, "What does it mean?" And we follow that question with another that is equally important: "How does it make its meaning?" The tiny but powerful unit of words—their definitions, sounds, and placement on the page—is the place to begin your search for the answer to that question.

All of us have experienced an affinity for certain words. Maybe it is the name of someone we love. Maybe it is a word that sounds silly, or beautiful, or strange. I have known young children to laugh out loud when they hear a funny word-sound (such as "gum") or to say a word again and again simply for delight. Poems can introduce you to favorite words—or become the place where you, as a writer, introduce favorite words to your readers.

LEARNING TO READ CLOSELY

William Carlos Williams (1883-1963)

The Dance

In Brueghel's great picture, The Kermess,
the dancers go round, they go round and
around, the squeal and the blare and the
tweedle of bagpipes, a bugle and fiddles
5   tipping their bellies (round as the thick-
sided glasses whose wash they impound)
their hips and their bellies off balance
to turn them. Kicking and rolling
about the Fair Grounds, swinging their butts, those
10   shanks must be sound to bear up under such
rollicking measures, prance as they dance
in Brueghel's great picture, The Kermess.

The speaker of this poem is looking at a painting and telling us what he sees. The picture is called *The Kermess* by Peter Breughel. (This painting can be easily found on the Internet.) The picture involves dancing at a fair, where solid-bodied dancers are accompanied by instruments. In the space of these twelve lines, the speaker translates for us the visual scene and his sense of the experience into words. Most interesting about the poem are the words that the speaker uses to make the picture come alive and the placement of those words into lines to make it seem that we also are a part of the dance. Notice that the dancers "go round, they go round and / around." The word "round" is repeated three times, twice in a single line, and then the line itself breaks at a word that isn't often reserved for the end of the line—"and." This causes the reader to have to spill around to the next line in order to figure out what the phrase is saying. We go around the end of the line to the start of the next line in order to "chase" the word around. Thus, the poet has us doing the very thing the dancers are doing—going around.

The instruments perform a similar function in the same line that describes their sound as the "squeal and the blare and the / tweedle." Here the words the speaker chooses are especially loud and almost **onomatopoetic** (making the sound of the word's meaning); our ears hear the squeal and blare that the dancers must have heard and that the viewer of the painting imagines. Here we are also forced to spill over the end of the line, following the words "and the" and continuing in order to gain the sense of the whole to which the speaker refers. Line 4 plays with more raucous sound, with the **consonance** of "tweedle," "bugle," and "fiddles." Notice how in each of these lines the key words are strung together with linking words that are similar, the repetition contributing to the sense of going around in a circle. Soon we've moved back to the dancers' bodies, which, we are told, are round-bellied and with sound shanks—in other words, these are stout bodies with generously proportioned hips, butts, and bellies. These bodies, the speaker tells us, are "kicking and rolling" and "swinging," as well as "rollicking" and "pranc[ing]."

The repetition of the "ing" sound contributes to the sense of motion. We also know that the dancers are drinking, most likely beer, as this is a peasant celebration. How do we know it is a peasant celebration? Well, the characters aren't described elegantly and daintily or with any formality; rather, they seem to be acquainted with and cut out for hard, manual work. The viewer doesn't look down on them for this; he seems to celebrate and take pleasure in their physical presence and their actions. The festival of words that he chooses—their sounds and their movement—help confirm this: here is someone who enjoys a good dance and a glass of beer and strong, rollicking bodies. At the end of the poem, the first line returns and is repeated: "in Brueghel's great picture, The Kermess." The whole poem has come round through this repetition, just as the dancers move around and eventually come to a stop.

William Carlos Williams said that motion in a poem (the rhythm or meter) either continues or it stops. He believed this was the essential observation we needed to make about rhythm. This poem continues its motion throughout the space of its short twelve lines. There is a period in the middle of line 8 at which we briefly pause before we go round again for another period of dancing. "One more dance!" you can imagine someone imploring. Generally the intense repetition of sound and motion creates a sensation of the dance and of celebration in the body, which is clearly what this poet noticed most about the painting.

Many sound devices are operating at once in this poem. In addition to the repetition of whole words and word endings, the singular sound of "l" is strung throughout the poem, embedded within many different kinds of words: "Brueghel," "squeal," "blare," "tweedle," "bugle," "fiddles," "bellies," "glasses," and "balance." Vowel sounds on the inside of words that are near each other form another pattern called **assonance**: "squeal" and "tweedle" (long "e"), "fiddles," "tipping," "hips," "kicking," and "swinging" ("i"), "round," "pound," "grounds," and "sound" ("o"). Notice that in all of these patterns, of which there are more than is pointed out here, there are sound patterns happening at more than one level at once. For instance, the assonance of the "o" in the words mentioned in the previous sentence is matched by the consonance of the "d" sound as well. Notice as well the flavor of the words that the poet chooses—butts, prance, shanks—they are down-to-earth with a little bit of laugh in the voice of the speaker. He is having fun alongside the dancers and so are we as we read closely.

Ekphrasis is a kind of poem written in response to a piece of art. Visual art and verbal art are in the same family. Historically, many poets have responded to visual art with words and made poems this way. Consider spending a good bit of time with a work of art and then writing about what interests you in the scene or sculpture.

ANTHOLOGY

Gerard Manley Hopkins (1844–1889)

Pied Beauty

Glory be to God for dappled things—
　　For skies of couple-colour as a brinded cow;
　　　For rose-moles all in stipple upon trout that swim;
Fresh-firecoal chestnut-falls; finches' wings;
5　　Landscape plotted and pieced—fold, fallow, and plough;
　　And all trades, their gear and tackle and trim.

All things counter, original, spare, strange;
　　Whatever is fickle, freckled (who knows how?)
　　With swift, slow; sweet, sour; adazzle, dim;
10　He fathers-forth whose beauty is past change:
　　　　Praise him.

1. What kinds of things are being praised in this poem? (Look up the word "pied" before you answer.) How do the words chosen combine with the meaning to create this poem?

2. Why do you think there are only two periods in the whole poem (two sentences)?

3. Read the poem as quickly as you can out loud. What effect does reading the poem through quickly have?

4. List the things in which Hopkins finds beauty and God's glory. What kinds of things might you legitimately thank God for that the world might find surprising or not praiseworthy?

5. What things "counter, original, spare, strange" are precious and praiseworthy to you in your life?

6. Write an imitation of Hopkins's poem, or a prose paragraph, that—instead of praising God the Creator—compliments someone you know who creates things you don't totally understand but that you ultimately admire. Think perhaps of your mother, father, an older friend, or a teacher.

7. What are some of the sounds that you hear repeated throughout multiple words (list them)?

8. Give an example, from the poem, of alliteration.

9. Circle the rhymes in the poem.

10. What level of diction is being used?

11. Hopkins made this poem a kind of tongue twister. Do you think this approach adds to the overall meaning of the poem and what Hopkins is communicating about the world? Why or why not? Do you like it? Why or why not?

Hilda Doolittle (1886–1961)

Sea Violet

The white violet
is scented on its stalk,
the sea-violet
fragile as agate,
5 lies fronting all the wind
among the torn shells
on the sand-bank.

The greater blue violets
flutter on the hill,
10 but who would change for these
who would change for these
one root of the white sort?

Violet
your grasp is frail
15 on the edge of the sand-hill,
but you catch the light—
frost, a star edges with its fire.

1. What words stand out to you in this poem as interesting, distinctive, or enjoyable to say in combination with other words?

2. What interests the speaker about the sea-violets as opposed to the blue violets on the hill?

3. How does the poet describe the sea-violets? Are they big and flashy, or small and delicate? Do you think there is a relationship between the description of the sea-violet and the type of language used in the poem? Why or why not?

T.S. Eliot (1888–1965)

Preludes

I.

    The winter evening settles down
    With smell of steaks in passageways.
    Six o'clock.
    The burnt-out ends of smoky days.
5   And now a gusty shower wraps
    The grimy scraps
    Of withered leaves about your feet
    And newspapers from vacant lots;
    The showers beat
10   On broken blinds and chimneypots,
    And at the corner of the street
    A lonely cab-horse steams and stamps.
    And then the lighting of the lamps.

II.

    The morning comes to consciousness
15   Of faint stale smells of beer
    From the sawdust-trampled street
    With all its muddy feet that press
    To early coffee-stands.

    With the other masquerades
20   That time resumes,
    One thinks of all the hands
    That are raising dingy shades
    In a thousand furnished rooms.

III.

    You tossed a blanket from the bed
25   You lay upon your back, and waited;
    You dozed, and watched the night revealing
    The thousand sordid images
    Of which your soul was constituted;
    They flickered against the ceiling.
30   And when all the world came back
    And the light crept up between the shutters
    And you heard the sparrows in the gutters,
    You had such a vision of the street
    As the street hardly understands;
35   Sitting along the bed's edge, where
    You curled the papers from your hair,
    Or clasped the yellow soles of feet
    In the palms of both soiled hands.

IV.

His soul stretched tight across the skies
40   That fade behind a city block,
      Or trampled by insistent feet
      At four and five and six o'clock;
      And short square fingers stuffing pipes,
      And evening newspapers, and eyes
45   Assured of certain certainties,
      The conscience of a blackened street
      Impatient to assume the world.

      I am moved by fancies that are curled
      Around these images, and cling:
50   The notion of some infinitely gentle
      Infinitely suffering thing.

      Wipe your hand across your mouth, and laugh;
      The worlds revolve like ancient women
      Gathering fuel in vacant lots.

1. List as many of the words in this poem that contribute to its atmosphere of exhaustion and dirtiness as you can.

2. These words form images that further explain and identify this feeling of living in an ugly and uncaring place. What are some of the images?

3. The speaker tells us that he is moved by these images. Why do you think this is the case? Are you moved by them?

ACTIVITIES

1. Take the following lists of synonyms and create a chart or other visual that presents their differing connotations. You can use a web-type illustration (see www.visualthesaurus.com for great examples of this) or rank them in order from mild to extreme, negative to positive, informal to formal, or some other ordering system.

>   Fat, obese, voluptuous, plump.
>   Geek, genius, bookish.
>   Magnificent, impressive, cool.

Now come up with some of your own lists of synonyms.

2. Experiment with the way language can create a sense of motion. Make some one- or two-line "mini-poems" or fragments that give off a feeling of fast motion, slow motion, stillness—or more specific motions, such as stuttering, rolling, robotic, staccato, trudging.

3. Look at a painting and make a poem to describe it (this is called ekphrasis). As William Carlos Williams did, attempt to recreate the scene of the painting in the sound of the words you choose and the way you arrange them in lines.

4. As a class, make a picture collage of the objects in Hopkins's poem *Pied Beauty*. Cut pictures out of magazines or draw them and then place them near each other to form a pictorial version of the poem. In a way, the poem is Hopkins's personal collage method—he collected in this poem a bunch of the things he loved but that others might find off-putting, or so ordinary as to not be worth celebrating or noticing. Think of some things that you find beautiful that other people might not, and make a collage of your own. Consciously seek to communicate a love for these things through your arrangement and choice of pictures.

5. The earliest origins of poetry are an expression of the communal need for praise, grief, petition, or celebration. Write a poem that consciously reaches beyond yourself as the subject matter, that consciously seeks to say something important to a larger audience. Think about what happens to the diction of your poem as you write in this way. Does it become more formal? Discuss this as a class or with your family, and make a list of examples of communal address that use a range of dictions, from formal to informal (for example, political speech, rap song, church hymn or creed, public service announcement, etc.). Find a sample of one of these, copy out a few lines or a paragraph, and defend its choice of diction as effective or ineffective.

VOCABULARY

Assonance: repetition of vowel sounds inside words near each other, such as "tinfoil winking," "grape/shave, pine/ripe, bee/meet."

Connotation: emotional associations of a word that give words different shades of expression.

Consonance: repetition of consonant sounds at the beginnings of words next to each other (alliteration) or at the ends of words, such as book/rack, stood/rude.

Denotation: literal, dictionary definition of a word.

Diction: a writing style determined by the kinds of words you choose.

Ekphrasis: a poem written in response to, or in dialogue with, a visual piece of art.

Formal diction: elevated words, words with careful manners.

Free verse: also known as open verse, it is unmetrical verse with lines that are not measured according to syllable, stress, or length.

Informal diction: casual words, everyday language, ordinary speech.

Onomatopoeia (or onomatopoetic): a word that imitates the sound of the word's meaning, as in "splash," "sizzle," or "buzz."

05

SOUND AND MORE SOUND

{the elements of poetry}

In his *Early Prose Writings*, Dylan Thomas said, "I wanted to write poetry in the beginning because I had fallen in love with words. What I like to do is treat words as a craftsman does his wood or stone or what-have-you, to hew, carve, mold, coil, polish, and plane them into patterns, sequences, sculptures, fugues of sound expressing some lyrical impulse, some spiritual doubt or conviction, some dimly realized truth I must try to reach and realize." Your body is as intelligent as your mind, and poetry reminds us of this. Your ear and sense of motion will come alive when you hear poetry read aloud (even if you're reading to yourself). This is one of the reasons that poetry exists. Long ago, before there were books, tribes or even just families would gather in front of a fire and tell tales, remember important information, and practice religious rituals through this very method of speaking rhythmically to each other. This is how the **epic** began, how all story took root. We call it the oral tradition. Not having a written language was no barrier for story and song—on the contrary, it stimulated a level of communal sharing and linguistic complexity that we have trouble achieving today. (Imagine being able to recite an epic poem more than 600 pages in length, as the ancient bards did!) For this lesson, be sure to read the poems aloud, numerous times, and in different voices.

In addition to rhythm in a poem, sound creates the music of poetry. Poets choose words for their sound as well as for their meaning. Words that mean the same thing but have different sounds produce different effects. For instance, consider the words "rock" and "stone." One has a harsh sound while the other has a smooth sound, so smooth that the silence closes around it when you finish saying it. Poems must be read aloud in order for you to be attuned to these nuances. Their energy and beauty comes forth only when the instrument of the body plays them for the air and the ear. When you speak a poem, you feel it in your mouth, on your tongue, with your breath. In this way, poetry has always had a relationship to music. **Lyric poetry** came from songs and was first sung to the accompaniment of a harp or lyre, hence the word lyric. **Narrative poems** were part of an oral folk tradition that included **ballads**, in which a story was told to music. Today we are most likely to hear the ordered sounds of poetic language in songs—the most popular of which, rap and country, make conscious and extensive use of repetition and rhyme.

Rhyme is a large part of the sound experience in poetry. We recognize rhyme most readily when words at the end of the lines of a stanza repeat the same sound. They do this in a pattern and create what is called a **rhyme scheme**, in which an expectation is created for the end words of each stanza to sound the same. Below is an example from Robert Frost:

> The people along the sand
> All turn and look one way.
> They turn their back on the land.
> They look at the sea all day.

If we assign a letter to each end rhyme, the scheme of this stanza would be *abab,* and we would expect succeeding stanzas of the poem to continue alternating rhyme sounds. The pattern would continue with either more words that rhyme with "-and" and "-ay" sounds or with new rhymes that would be labeled *cdcd* and so on.

Useful terms have been developed to describe different kinds of rhymes. When two or more words or phrases repeat the same sounds they are called **full** or **perfect rhymes** (such as "ripe" and "tripe," "enough" and "snuff"). When words look alike but don't rhyme they are called **eye rhymes** (such as "comb" and "womb"). Rhymes that are not exact, such as "again" and "rain" are called **slant**, **half**, **near**, **off,** or **imperfect rhymes** (other examples include "filled" and "still," "is" and "has"). Sometimes a poet will repeat a word exactly to create a rhyme.

Rhymes have been part of the pleasure of poetry for hundreds of years. Rhymes create expectation and shape in a poem, and establish a sense of pleasure and of challenge—can the poet pull it off? Rhymes that contribute to the meaning and the music of a poem are a sign of skill. They tell us that the poem is going to have a pattern; they help the poet to measure off lengths of verse and create resting points. Echoing sounds also contribute to the rhythm, especially when they occur at the end of a line. The end rhyme is like a bell that tells us that the line is finished and shows our ear where the next one begins. Rhymes also help us to remember words; say a poem aloud and afterward you will likely remember the words that were rhymed. There are times, however, when rhymes are used to disguise badly written verse. Therefore, we mustn't judge whether or not a poem is successful by whether or not it has rhymes.

Rhyme is not the only sound-making tool in poetry, however. There are some other animals in the menagerie of sound that you will be happy to meet. Here, as elsewhere, you have already experienced the pleasure of feeling various sounds in your mouth and ear, but you may not know the name for them. You may not know from where the delight comes, or what combination of sound-tools created the particular linguistic moment that struck you. Here are some descriptions that will help you trace the music to its source.

One of the most common sound makers is onomatopoeia, which comes from the Greek and means "making a name." This long funny word is the term for any word that imitates the sound of what the word means, such as "buzz," "moo," "chirp," "rumble," "splat," "sizzle," "puff," "slosh." In all of poetry we want the sound of the poem to echo its sense. In other words, we want the meaning to be understood in the sounds. Onomatopoeia is one of the easiest and most immediate ways to experience the physical pleasure of words within poetry. We all have found words we couldn't stop saying or words that made us laugh or buzz with pleasure. When words in a poem are more generally pleasing and harmonious we call them **euphonic**. When they are noisy, jangling, rough, or harsh we call them **cacophonic**. These three terms refer to the particular pleasure words give us.

Much like playing in the sand or at the water table in preschool or in the city fountain, **alliteration** is another sound maker with which you have played. Alliteration is the repetition of consonant sounds that are at the beginning of words (initial consonant sounds), such as in Frost's line "the woods are lovely, dark and deep," or W. H. Auden's "the shingle scrambles after the suck / ing surf," or Hopkins's "It will flame out, like shining from shook foil." This pattern can go on throughout a poem, and there can be multiple sounds carried within the poem (see anthology examples). Tongue twisters exaggerate this device to the point of absurdity, as in "Peter Piper picked a peck of pickled peppers." Unlike rhyme, alliteration does not predictably appear at a certain place in the line. (Rhyme happens so frequently at the end of a line that we may mistakenly think it can *only* appear at the end.) If we use the metaphor of visual art, alliteration is used more as a subtle shading tool whereas rhyme is often used as the sturdy line drawing that undergirds the whole picture.

Other subtle sound tools include: Consonance, which is the repetition in two or more nearby words of similar consonant sounds that come after different vowels, such as book/lack, knock/ pluck. There are times when the repetition happens within a single word, such as little and goldenrod. If it happens at the end of lines it can substitute for end rhyme. Assonance is the repetition of vowel sounds within words (two or more) in a line or lines of verse: "the chalk walk falls" (W. H. Auden, *Look Stranger*).

Silence is the last important element of sound that you will learn to recognize as you read and recite poems. Not only is it important to pay attention to what a poet chooses *not* to state explicitly (in terms of message), it is important also to notice when a poem falls silent or pauses. Punctuation marks delineate a poem's silence. A period or exclamation mark is akin to a whole rest in music—a full stop—and a comma is a fraction of this—a half stop. When reading a poem out loud, continue its flow smoothly across lines and stanzas, unless the punctuation tells you to slow or stop.

All of these sound-tools work together to produce the effect that the emotion and message of a given poem needs. They play over our ears and merge harmoniously, often without our being aware of it. Jazz great Duke Ellington once described his life in music as "Roaming through the jungle of 'oohs' and 'ahs,' searching for a more agreeable noise, I live a life of primitivity with the mind of a child and an unquenchable thirst for sharps and flats." You are becoming tuned to the music of human language when you pay attention to sound in poems, speech, and songs. Poetry, in particular, uses specific sound devices to communicate what it is saying before it is entirely understood.

LEARNING TO READ CLOSELY

Gerard Manley Hopkins (1844–1889)

Peace

When will you ever, Peace, wild wooddove, shy wings shut,
Your round me roaming end, and under be my boughs?
When, when, Peace, will you, Peace? I'll not play hypocrite
To own my heart: I yield you do come sometimes; but
5   That piecemeal peace is poor peace. What pure peace allows
Alarms of wars, the daunting wars, the death of it?

O surely, reaving Peace, my Lord should leave in lieu
Some good! And so he does leave Patience exquisite,
That plumes to Peace thereafter. And when Peace here does house
10   He comes with work to do, he does not come to coo,
He comes to brood and sit.

Aren't we all in some way struggling to find peace? Peace is being free from anxiety, distraction, annoyance, and fear; it is a state of tranquility or serenity. As you talk about this poem together, ask yourselves when you feel peaceful, and what words of your own or in this poem best describe peace. Hopkins, a Jesuit priest who lived in England and Wales in the nineteenth century, lived a life full of struggle. If you read his journals and letters, you'll see that he believed he could not write poetry and also be a good priest. His chief desire was to serve God as a good and obedient priest, yet he found the compulsion to write poems irresistible. We are glad he did write poetry, especially his poems about that very struggle, for they help us define and work through our own difficulties.

Hopkins's poem *Peace* creates a space in which the sounds and movement of the language tell us as much about the words as the dictionary definitions do. Hopkins is best known for his outrageous use of sound, the devices of which he uses all the time. He combines them with images and rhythms, and their pull on us is magnetic. Often you will understand what a Hopkins poem means by its sounds before you have broken down the meaning of the words. His poems are generally short, which helps us to tackle their dense sound activity, and they also generally have simple, straightforward titles.

In the poem *Peace*, the speaker personifies Peace, addressing it directly as if it were a being that could understand speech and reason. Quickly, for the sake of our metaphoric imaginations, the speaker compares the figure of Peace to a wooddove, or wild dove. The speaker calls out with yearning and frustration to the non-domesticated bird who won't stay put, won't come to rest and live under his boughs or in his house. The language is densely imitative of the statement—it is complicated, the flow of the sentence (what we call syntax) is complicated and fractured, with interruptions throughout the middle of the line. The word order is sometimes switched—"your round me roaming end," instead of "when will you stop roaming around me?" The reader's tongue must work hard to handle all the alliteration: wild/wooddove, shy/shut, round/roaming, when/will/wild/wooddove/wings. Other sound repetition happens simultanously in the middle of words and at the end of words, with consonance (similar sounds at the end of words), such as round/end, and assonance (similar sounds in the middle of words), such as round/bough.

What is all this saying? The first two-and-a-half lines simply ask a question of Peace: When will you come and be with me? But the language poses the question in a way that makes us know that peace is moving, won't stay put, won't come to roost, won't let itself be held, and won't even seek shelter under your roof. If you've ever owned a bird, you understand what the speaker is saying. If even a caged bird, let alone a wild bird, gets loose, it is difficult to catch. It flaps from spot to spot, usually leaving a trail of dung! The movement of the words in relationship to each other in these lines embodies this anxious, flapping motion of seeking peace. The third line of the poem repeats the question in shorthand—"When, when, Peace, will you, Peace?"—using the second "Peace" almost as a verb, with choppy, insistent, pleading phrases separated by commas.

Notice the rhyme scheme at the end of the lines: in the first stanza *abcabc*, in the second *debde*. The rhymes are widely separated from each other, so our ears have to wait for the same sound again. This, too, enacts the sensation of chasing something not easily caught, of waiting for something that one desperately wants but can't possess or control.

In the last half of the first stanza, the speaker explains that his relationship with Peace is complicated—sometimes the bird, Peace, *does* come, but its presence is "piecemeal" (or pieced together like a quilt, not sustained like a single piece of fabric) and "poor." (The peace the speaker occasionally experiences doesn't seem to do much to stop war or death in the world.) Notice how the speaker continues to repeat the word "Peace"—in five lines we hear the word six times. This both calls attention to the subject and the pursuit, but it also seems to focus on the failure to rest, to catch the bird, to hold it and be with it in a way that will last, or in a way that will affect more than just the speaker alone.

After a stanza break where the questions linger in the quiet (white space between stanzas creates a longer pause than at the end of lines), the speaker introduces a new figure in the poem: "my Lord," or God, the author of both peace and the speaker himself. It's as if the speaker knows that chasing after the bird of peace won't work; he must try a different approach, perhaps appeal to a higher authority. Even though this poem isn't a sonnet, we experience the sonnet form in the question-answer, call-response structure of the poem. Having questioned Peace and received no response except greater awareness of the need for peace in the world and in himself, the speaker questions God. He is asking the question: Foregoing, or "reaving," peace, what small good can you give me instead? And the answer comes: He gives "Patience," or a willingness to wait, trust, and hope. Patience, the speaker says, can "plume," or rise up, and change into peace over time. "Plume" is an interesting word choice because it refers to feathers, which are the things that allow birds to fly—patience "plumes to Peace." And when peace does come to take up residence, according to this speaker, he will do so with work to do—as if peace has something to accomplish—though this work may, in fact, be accomplished only by the seemingly passive acts of brooding and sitting.

What a tangle of sound, thought, and movement! You must read poetry aloud to understand it, for just seeing this poem on the page doesn't clarify it. The act of reaching for something (in this case peace) comes through in each phrase, in the punctuation, and in the rhythm that this movement creates. Look at the odd places where the lines are punctuated and feel the jerky movement that this conveys. The chase of a bird, or of a feeling, comes through at every level. Do you know that feeling of longing for peace—or something else—and not being able to catch it? The speaker in this poem suggests that waiting for it is part of finding it in the end, and that should you find or catch peace, it will enlist you into a mission. Filled with newfound, hard-won peace, you will have work to do.

ANTHOLOGY

Gerard Manley Hopkins (1844–1889)

God's Grandeur

The world is charged with the grandeur of God.
  It will flame out, like shining from shook foil;
  It gathers to a greatness, like the ooze of oil
Crushed. Why do men then now not reck his rod?
5 Generations have trod, have trod, have trod;
  And all is seared with trade; bleared, smeared with toil;
  And wears man's smudge and shares man's smell: the soil
Is bare now, nor can foot feel, being shod.
And for all this, nature is never spent;
10   There lives the dearest freshness deep down things;
And though the last lights off the black West went
  Oh, morning, at the brown brink eastward, springs—
Because the Holy Ghost over the bent
  World broods with warm breast and with ah! bright wings.

1. Start unpacking this dense poem by underlining all alliteration, then underline assonance, then consonance. It may take you a while. Circle the rhymes. Write out the rhyme scheme. Is there onomatopoeia? What are the emotions that this poem's sounds and words communicate to you?

2. The poem starts by telling us that the world is "charged with the grandeur of God." What does this mean? Look up the word "charged" and "charge" in a good dictionary. Is the poet saying more than one thing about the world in relation to God's grandeur?

3. Can you name the three or four basic "characters" or "actors" in this poem? (Hint: They aren't necessarily people.)

4. Break this poem down into three or four parts. Give each part a title or a phrase that describes its general thrust—as if you were writing an outline of the poem. If you were organizing this poem, would you end it positively or negatively? Why?

Gerard Manley Hopkins (1844–1889)

I wake and feel the fell of dark, not day

I wake and feel the fell of dark, not day.
What hours, O what black hoürs we have spent
This night! what sights you, heart, saw; ways you went!
And more must, in yet longer light's delay.
5   With witness I speak this. But where I say
Hours I mean years, mean life. And my lament
Is cries countless, cries like dead letters sent
To dearest him that lives alas! away.

   I am gall, I am heartburn. God's most deep decree
10 Bitter would have me taste: my taste was me;
Bones built in me, flesh filled, blood brimmed the curse.
   Selfyeast of spirit a dull dough sours. I see
The lost are like this, and their scourge to be
As I am mine, their sweating selves; but worse.

1. This is a poem of depression, in which the speaker addresses his own heart in the night and describes how hard it is to be in a place of emotional and spiritual darkness. What metaphors does he use to describe this inner darkness? What sound-making devices does he use?

2. Alliteration is very noticeable in this poem. Make note of all the places where alliteration is used and talk about its effect in the poem.

3. Note the rhymes at ends of lines, and look at rhymes that occur in the middle of lines.

4. Beyond the poet's depression, what is the conflict in this poem? Who is the poet accusing or criticizing?

5. Do you see any hope in this poem?

6. Explain why you like or dislike this poem.

William Blake (1757–1827)

The Tiger

Tiger, tiger, burning bright
In the forests of the night,
What immortal hand or eye
Could frame thy fearful symmetry?

5   In what distant deeps or skies
Burnt the fire of thine eyes?
On what wings dare he aspire?
What the hand dare seize the fire?

And what shoulder and what art
10   Could twist the sinews of thy heart?
And when thy heart began to beat,
What dread hand and what dread feet?

What the hammer? what the chain?
In what furnace was thy brain?
15   What the anvil? What dread grasp
Dare its deadly terrors clasp?

When the stars threw down their spears,
And water'd heaven with their tears,
Did He smile His work to see?
20   Did He who made the lamb make thee?

Tiger, tiger, burning bright
In the forests of the night,
What immortal hand or eye
Dare frame thy fearful symmetry?

1. In Blake's time, the tiger was considered "the most rapacious and destructive of all carnivorous animals," meaning it was incredibly fierce, dangerous, cruel, and bloodthirsty. How does knowing this contribute to your understanding of the larger meanings of the poem?

2. In your own words, what is the basic question the speaker is asking? Why do you think the poet chose to address the poem directly to the tiger? Are there others directly or indirectly involved in this dialogue?

3. Circle the rhymes in this poem. What pattern do the rhymes follow? What is the effect of the rhyming words at the end of lines being close together (for example, "bright" and "night")? Is the *aabb* pattern found in the first stanza carried throughout the poem? What is the rhythm or pattern of stresses? What kind of rhymes does the poem use (slant or full)? Underline the rhymes that are slant or partial rhymes.

4. What do you think are the symbolic meanings of the lamb and of the tiger? Why is a lamb introduced? What do you think of the basic question "Did He who made the lamb make thee?"

5. In contrast to the speaker's long and detailed description of the tiger, we are given only the single word "lamb." Why are there no corresponding details about the characteristics of a lamb? Are they needed? Why or why not?

William Blake (1757–1827)

The Lamb

Little Lamb, who made thee?
Dost thou know who made thee?
Gave thee life, and bid thee feed,
By the stream and o'er the mead;
5   Gave thee clothing of delight,
Softest clothing, woolly, bright;
Gave thee such a tender voice,
Making all the vales rejoice?
Little Lamb, who made thee?
10   Dost thou know who made thee?

Little Lamb, I'll tell thee,
Little Lamb, I'll tell thee:
He is callèd by thy name,
For He calls Himself a Lamb.
15   He is meek, and He is mild;
He became a little child.
I a child, and thou a lamb,
We are callèd by His name.
Little Lamb, God bless thee!
20   Little Lamb, God bless thee!

1. What do you notice about the rhymes in this poem? Circle them all. Underline the slant rhymes.

2. What is being discussed through the image of the lamb? What is the lamb a symbol of—first generally, then historically or theologically?

3. The voice of this poem is a child's voice. What do a child and a lamb have in common and why does it make sense to have the child speaking to the lamb? What does Christ, the Lamb, say abut children and the kingdom of God?

4. Why was Christ called the Lamb, according to Christian theology?

5. Now compare this poem by Willam Blake to his poem *The Tiger* and see if your understanding of each is increased. Find the one adjective Blake uses in both poems to describe these two different animals.

6. Consider the poems *The Lamb* and *The Tiger*. Which of these poems does it make sense to call a poem of innocence and which would be called a poem of experience? Why? Sometimes reading several poems by the same writer helps your interpretation of each poem.

Sir Walter Ralegh (1552–1618)

To His Son

Three things there be that prosper up apace
And flourish, whilst they grow asunder far;
But on a day, they meet all in one place,
And when they meet they one another mar:

5   And they be these: the wood, the weed, the wag.
The wood is that which makes the gallow tree;
The weed is that which strings the hangman's bag;
The wag, my pretty knave, betokeneth thee.

Mark well, dear boy, whilst these assemble not,
10   Green springs the tree, hemp grows, the wag is wild,
But when they meet, it makes the timber rot;
It frets the halter, and it chokes the child.

Then bless thee, and beware, and let us pray
We part not with thee at this meeting day.

1. Begin by defining any words in this poem you don't know.

2. In this poem, a father is speaking to his son. Summarize, in your own words, what he's saying. It may be helpful to list the three things the father references. What happens when these three things "meet all in one place"?

3. Notice the rhymes and how neatly they fit together; does this work well with the theme?

4. The father sums up his message in the final stanza with two pairs of alliterated words: "bless" and "beware;" "pray" and "part not." What paradoxes or ironies of love or parenting lie hidden in these yoked words? Can you think of an instance in your own life when you wanted to bless someone with a warning? Did it work?

Robert Burns (1759–1796)

To a Mouse

On turning her up in her nest with the plough, November 1785
Written in Scottish dialect

Wee, sleeket,* cowran, tim'rous beastie,	sleek
O, what panic's in thy breastie!	
Thou need na start awa sae hasty,	
Wi' bickering brattle*!	noisy, scurrying
5 I wad be laith to rin an' chase thee,	
Wi' murd'ring pattle*!	plowstaff

I'm truly sorry Man's dominion
Has broken Nature's social union,
An' justifies that ill opinion,
10   Which makes thee startle,
At me, thy poor, earth-born companion,
    An' fellow-mortal!

I doubt na, whyles, but thou may thieve;	
What then? poor beastie, thou maun* live!	must
15 A daimen*-icker* in a thrave	chance / corn-ear
'S a sma' request:	
I'll get a blessin wi' the lave,*	remainder
An' never miss't!	

Thy wee-bit housie, too, in ruin!	
20 It's silly* wa's the win's are strewin!	fragile
An' naething, now, to big* a new ane,	build
O' foggage* green!	mosses
An' bleak December's winds ensuin,	
Baith snell* an' keen!	sour

25 Thou saw the fields laid bare an' wast,	
An' weary Winter comin fast,	
An' cozie here, beneath the blast,	
Thou thought to dwell,	
Till crash! the cruel coulter* past	plow
30 Out thro' thy cell.	

That wee-bit heap o' leaves an' stibble,
Has cost thee monie a weary nibble!
Now thou's turn'd out, for a' thy trouble,
    But* house or hald.*   with no / hold
35   To thole* the Winter's sleety dribble,   bear
    An' cranreuch* cauld!   hoarfrost

But Mousie, thou are no thy-lane,*   not alone
In proving foresight may be vain:
The best laid schemes o' Mice an' Men,
40   Gang* aft agley,*   go / awry
An' lea'e us nought but grief an' pain,
    For promis'd joy!

Still, thou art blest, compar'd wi' me!
The present only toucheth thee:
45   But Och! I backward cast my e'e,
    On prospects drear!
An' forward, tho' I canna see,
    I guess an' fear!

1. It's crucial that this poem be read out loud before beginning to unpack it. Does your tongue grow more comfortable with the strange dialect as you read? Does the fixed rhythm and basic rhyme structure help you both pronounce and understand the poem?

2. Number each stanza, then describe the main point the speaker makes in each.

3. There's a line in this poem that has become extremely famous—a commonplace. Can you find it?

4. By the end of the poem, what has changed in the speaker?

e.e. cummings (1894–1962)

in Just—

in Just—
spring   when the world is mud—
luscious the little
lame balloonman

5   whistles   far   and wee

and eddieandbill come
running from marbles and
piracies and it's
spring

10   when the world is puddle-wonderful

the queer
old balloonman whistles
far   and   wee
and bettyandisbel come dancing

15   from hop-scotch and jump-rope and

it's
spring
and
              the

20   goat-footed

balloonman   whistles
far
and
wee

1. Read this poem aloud several times. Start by looking for all the alliteration you can find.

2. Then look for other patterns of sound such as assonance and consonance.

3. How do the line breaks combine with the festival of sound to create a movement that brings you inside the dizzying world of spring?

Robert Frost (1874–1963)

Mowing

There was never a sound beside the wood but one,
And that was my long scythe whispering to the ground.
What was it it whispered? I knew not well myself;
Perhaps it was something about the heat of the sun,
5   Something, perhaps about the lack of sound—
And that was why it whispered and did not speak.
It was no dream of the gift of idle hours,
Or easy gold at the hand of fay or elf:
Anything more than the truth would have seemed too weak
10   To the earnest love that laid the swale in rows,
Not without feeble-pointed spikes of flowers
(Pale orchises), and scared a bright green snake.
The fact is the sweetest dream that labor knows.
My long scythe whispered and left the hay to make.

A scythe is an implement with a long, curving blade fastened to a handle. Before farm machinery, the scythe was used to cut field grasses for hay.

1. How does the writer describe the sound of his blade?

2. What is the effect of this sound and what thoughts does it suggest to the dreamy speaker?

3. How does the speaker feel about the labor of mowing?

4. How does he express his feelings about his work in the sounds of the words both at the ends of lines and among other words as well?

ACTIVITIES

1. Play a rhyming game with the class in which someone says a word and the class spontaneously tries to find as many rhyming words as possible.

2. Choose five pairs of rhymes, such as eye and goodbye, song and long, sight and might, speak and weak, know and low, and write a poem from them.

3. Use a rhyming dictionary to look up new rhyming combinations.

4. Read a poem aloud at the beginning of every class. Let each student choose or simply read straight through a book of poems. Read the poems in this anthology or try another anthology, such as the excellent *A Child's Anthology of Poetry* edited by Elizabeth Hauge Sword. Make a point of listening to the sounds of the language; jot down the rhyming or alliterative words as you hear them.

5. Write a nonsense poem in which you play with sound (reference Lewis Caroll's poem *Jabberwocky* on p. 72).

6. Go to a noisy place, such as the lunch room, a construction site, or a public swimming pool, and listen quietly. Then describe both the sounds and the feeling that you have as you sit in the midst of them. Try to use words that are onomatopoetic—that create, either singly or in combination with each other, what you've been hearing and feeling in response to the scene.

7. Go to a quiet place and do the same; explain the silence, using words and combinations that are quiet and harmonious. If you are truly interested in the subject of silence, read Max Picard's book *World of Silence*. Spend some time each day for a week listening to the silence and trying to describe it and your thoughts in it.

8. Take a fast from language. Spend a whole day, or a mealtime, without speaking. See what happens to your relationship to language. What do the words feel like when they return to your mouth? How do you feel about them? How much more closely are you following them?

9. Do a mini-study on Gerard Manley Hopkins's life. Keep a Hopkins-like journal, making a record of the natural world or of some other aspect of the world with which you have contact, writing down detailed descriptions on a regular basis. The following is an excerpt from Hopkins's journal. Notice the care of his investigation. Try to write a journal entry that matches it.

> There are round one of the heights of the Jungfrau two ends or falls of a glacier. If you took the skin of a white tiger or the deep fell of some other animal and swung it tossing high in the air and then cast it out before you it would fall and so clasp and lap round anything in this way just as this glacier does and the fleece would part in the same rifts: you must suppose a lazuli under-flix to appear. The spraying out of one end I tried to catch but it would have taken hours: it is this which first made me think of a tiger-skin, and it ends in tongues and points like the tail and claws: indeed the ends of the glaciers are knotted or knuckled like talons.

VOCABULARY

Alliteration: repetition of consonant sounds at the beginning of words next to each other (initial consonant sounds): roof/ruthlessness, brain/British.

Ballad: a narrative poem originally meant to be sung with a regular rhyming stanza.

Cacophony: harsh, rough sounds, such as "screech."

Epic: a long, narrative poem that tells the stories central to the myths and beliefs of a people group.

Euphony: smooth, pleasing, harmonious sounds, such as the word "lilting."

Eye rhyme: words that look like they rhyme to the eye but don't to the ear, as in love/move.

Lyric poetry: short musical poems spoken in the voice of an individual; one of the three main categories of poetry.

Narrative poetry: poetry that tells a story; another of the main categories of poetry.

Perfect or full rhyme: when sounds fully resemble each other; sound alike, as in brake/shake.

Rhyme: when words repeat or echo the same sound.

Rhyme scheme: the pattern of rhymes used in a poem; indicates which words rhyme with each other.

Slant, half, near, off, imperfect rhyme: words that nearly rhyme but not exactly, such as brake/spoke.

06
RHYTHM

{the elements of poetry}

Our lives are full of natural rhythms: our heartbeat, our breathing, our walking with two feet. We rise when the sun rises and sleep when it sets; we eat at three different watches of the day. In an earlier age, work in the fields and around the home took on rhythms in time and space. Women cleaned on one day, baked on another, and did laundry on another. When they scrubbed the laundry on the washboard they most likely did it rhythmically. When they kneaded the bread, they felt the rhythm of their hands pushing and pulling it. Farmers milked cows, hoed the earth, scythed the grasses and wheat. Though many of us don't do these things now, we still orient our lives around set routines. The way you brush your teeth, practice your free throws, or tap your fingers while you read a book all take on predictable rhythmic shapes.

Anytime we use language, whether speaking or singing, we find rhythms. Churches, mosques, and synagogues all incorporate clear patterns of repetition in worship, whether formal or informal, through liturgy, chanting psalms, saying prayers, and even preaching. (For an example of this, listen to one of Martin Luther King, Jr.'s speeches or sermons online on YouTube.) One of your primary tasks as a reader of poetry is to realize that language has the capacity to create rhythm. Children listen to nursery rhymes and chants, then easily recite them from memory because of their obvious rhythms. Television and radio commercials use rhythm in an equally obvious but more sophisticated way—the words slow down or rhyme when companies want you to remember their product; they speed up and use technical vocabulary when they want you to overlook its dangers or inadequacies.

Rhythm comes from a Greek word that means "time or flow." Rhythm is the recurrence of movement and sound, the way sounds move, the rise and fall of words together. One of the physical conditions of speech is that the voice rises and falls with words in **stressed** or **unstressed syllables**. In poetry, rhythm is achieved through the deliberate arrangement of stressed and unstressed **syllables** combined with the silence of periods, commas, and breaks in lines and stanzas.

How do we read rhythm in a poem? We start by revisiting something we learned as much younger students: the smaller units of syllables. If you look at a page in the dictionary, you will see that any word longer than one syllable is divided into its separate syllables, sometimes with a small mark over the emphasized syllable. In this book, we will illustrate emphasis with capital letters, like this: exPLORE and exPLORer. The mark or capital letters are there to help us pronounce the word out loud; to tell us which syllable we must stress with our voices in order for the word to roll smoothly from our mouths. Every word has a stressed syllable, and every word that is two syllables or longer is a combination of stressed and unstressed sounds. Say the word "exploration" out loud—which two of its four syllables did you stress? EXploRAtion. Note that the stress falls differently in this word than in the two-syllable word exPLORE. Try saying these words again, but switch the stress to different syllables—they sound unnatural and awkward, don't they? Stressed syllables aren't something the dictionary invented; they happen naturally in speech. In everyday speech our voices rise and fall in a rhythm that is ordered simply by the desire to communicate clearly. In poetry, the rhythm of language is ordered and patterned to achieve specific meanings and effects. The most deliberately ordered, rigidly structured rhythm is called **meter**.

Do you remember this favorite nursery rhyme?
> Hickory, dickory, dock,
> The mouse ran up the clock.
> The clock struck one,
> And down he run,
> Hickory, dickory, dock.

This simple poem has a pleasant rhythm that we come to expect as the lines go on. Poetry deliberately creates these kinds of rhythms for emphasis and for pleasure. When you read a poem, try to tap out the beat. Where the syllables are emphasized, hit the table (for instance, the syllables HICK, DICK, and DOCK). Notice how your voice emphasizes certain syllables and not others (for instance, the light syllables in the first line: ory, ory).

Rhythms are different in every language, for our voices rise and fall very differently if we are speaking a smooth, flowing language like French or Spanish, than if we are speaking a more guttural, clipped language like German or Russian. In a language such as Chinese, the meaning of a word can change based on the tone in which it is spoken.

In English poetry, the natural rhythm, the one that is easiest for the voice to create, is called **iambic pentameter.** This is a fancy term that is easy to understand when you break it down and define it. "Iambic" refers to a pattern of alternating stressed and unstressed syllables as in "the MOUSE ran UP the CLOCK." (A non-iambic pattern might look like this: "ROdents ran UPward to REACH their reWARD.") An **iamb** is word or phrase that has two syllables with the first one unstressed and the second one stressed. Some examples of words that create an iambic rhythm just by saying them are the following: Detroit (deTROIT), away (aWAY), against (a GAINST). An iamb doesn't have to be a word; it can also be a phrase. Here are some examples of phrases that form an iamb: what kept (what KEPT), his eyes (his EYES), the gaze (the GAZE). An easy way to make iambs when you're writing a poem is to use articles (a, an, the). These tiny words tend to be unstressed, so if you put them next to a word that begins with a stress, you've got the beginnings of an iambic pattern: an APple, the CAR, his COATsleeves.

Iambic pentameter describes a string of five iambs put together in a line. You will learn more about the different kinds of emphasis that create meter, but for now knowing this basic yardstick (used up until about the 1800s for most of the decisions about where to end a line in poetry) gives you a great start: five iambs to a line, or ten syllables in which five stresses alternate with five unstresses. William Shakespeare wrote hundreds of lines in iambic pentameter. Here are some examples that indicate stressed syllables and unstressed syllables:

shall I comPARE thee TO a SUMmer's DAY
(Shall I compare thee to a summer's day?)

bright STAR! Would I were STEADfast AS thou ART
(Bright star! Would I were steadfast as thou art.)

the SHATtered water MADE a MISTy DIN
(The shattered water made a misty din.)

One reason iambic pentameter is considered the most natural English poetic line is because it is the longest one you can easily say without taking a breath. However, many poems are written in an iambic pattern but with shorter lines, or fewer iambic **feet**. A line of four iambs is called **iambic tetrameter**, a line of three iambs is called **iambic trimeter**, and a line with seven iambs is called **iambic hexameter**. You will notice that many hymns, nursery rhymes, and popular songs are arranged in tetrameter or trimeter lines because the shorter lines are more easily understood and more quickly memorized.

Rhythm is one of the reasons that poems must be spoken aloud. They are meant to affect us with their music, and rhythm is a huge part of this music. Simply reading poems with our eyes does not do justice to the way in which our body feels the movement in the words.

Understanding syllabic stresses in language is like studying how the organs and vessels of the body work. We know we sneeze and digest food, but to understand more about these experiences, we have to go inside the systems of the body. We have to learn the technical terms used to describe what these systems are doing naturally and easily, all the time, whether we study them or not. Rhythm and meter are a significant part of the insides of poems. When you evaluate them in the way that this chapter has discussed, you are **scanning** the poem. Understanding rhythm helps you to understand what matters in the poem, why you respond to it the way you do, what the writer is emphasizing, and what your mouth, eyes, head, and heart are registering as you read.

LEARNING TO READ CLOSELY

Walt Whitman (1819-1892)

When I Heard the Learn'd Astronomer

When I heard the learn'd astronomer,
When the proofs, the figures, were ranged in columns before me,
When I was shown the charts and diagrams, to add, divide, and measure them,
When I sitting heard the astronomer where he lectured with much applause in the
      lecture-room,
5   How soon unaccountable I became tired and sick,
Till rising and gliding out I wander'd off by myself,
In the mystical moist night-air, and from time to time,
Look'd up in perfect silence at the stars.

The rhythm of this poem is particularly useful. Notice how closely it matches the sense or thoughts that the speaker is articulating. The poem is spoken in the voice of someone who goes into a lecture hall to learn about the heavens and the stars from a learned astronomer. It opens with a long list of the elements taught in the classroom—figures, proofs, charts, diagrams, and how "to add, divide, and measure." This list gives us a direct taste of the speaker's experience. We are told it is laborious, that the speaker becomes "tired and sick," and likely bored. The list of words is not particularly melodious or lyrical but difficult both in length and in the nature of the individual words that are heaped upon each other. Notice how the **anaphora**, or the repetition of the opening word in several successive lines, "When" gives us that sense of heavy repetition. The lines of the poem get longer with each addition to the list. Line 4 is the longest and spills past the margin. This lengthening of the rhythm by lengthening the line is especially effective when combined with the repetition and the long list—it creates the actual sensation of being tired and sick, or of being overwhelmed. Haven't we all felt flooded in a lecture-type experience, overloaded and unable to receive any more information and instruction?

Another aspect of this speaker's particular circumstance is the contrast between direct experience and book learning. Notice how the rhythm and the type of diction changes as soon as he leaves the lecture hall and goes outside. The lines become shorter and more melodic. The words change from hard sounds ("chart," "diagram") to "ing" sounds such as "rising" and "gliding." The sound devices also intensify—the words "mystical moist" are alliterative, as are "time to time." The last line, almost written in iambic pentameter, is particularly musical. Its rhythm brings us to a place of rest and harmony, just as the speaker's circumstances change from tedious to comfortable. The speaker has been released from the droning voice of the astronomer and enters joyfully into the "mystical" night air, which suggests that he is spiritually enlivened as well. The mysteries of the universe are present outside under the stars, while in the classroom (at least this particular one) access to those large wonders is blocked.

The poem might be arguing for the value of direct experience of things, rather than indirect classroom learning and book learning—or it may simply be an incident in which the classroom couldn't do justice to the overwhelming beauty and strangeness of the night sky. Either way, it is a wonderful example of how rhythm works with words, the length of lines, and the beat of words to combine with the meaning and make itself known to us. This is a wonderful example of what Hans Gadamer describes as "a saying where its own presence is in play," meaning that the poem means with all it does, not simply with its arguments, but also with its lines, words, images, and sounds. All of these combine to create a presence that fully releases the meaning to us.

ANTHOLOGY

A.E. Housman (1859–1936)

When I was one-and-twenty

When I was one-and-twenty
  I heard a wise man say,
"Give crowns and pounds and guineas
  But not your heart away;
5 Give pearls away and rubies
  But keep your fancy free."
But I was one-and-twenty
  No use to talk to me.

When I was one-and-twenty
10 I heard him say again,
"The heart out of the bosom
  Was never given in vain;
'Tis paid with sighs a plenty
  And sold for endless rue."
15 And I am two-and-twenty
  And oh, 'tis true, 'tis true.

1. What do the words "rue" and "vain" mean?

2. What are guineas?

3. This poem is about giving the heart away. Can you summarize what the message is on this subject?

4. What does the speaker seem to be saying about being young? According to the speaker, what happens as we get older and look back on the things that people tried to tell us when we were younger?

5. The wise man says, "keep your fancy free." How do you know that the speaker failed to follow this advice? What do you think might have happened?

6. What is the tone of this poem? Does the speaker feel glad, regretful, or uncaring about what happened to him in the recent past? What evidence can you point to in the language of the poem to support your answer?

7. See if you can tap out the rhythm of this poem, emphasizing the syllables that are stressed. (If you are unsure, look up a few of the words in the dictionary to see their stress marks.) Do you get used to the rise and fall of the words and the lines? Does there seem to be an organized pattern to this poem?

8. Are there iambs in the lines? Can you mark the lines to show where the iambs are and how many there are? How many iambs are you counting in each line? (Hint: It alternates every other line.) Do you like the repetition of the rhythm that creates an expectation and then fulfills it?

9. Why did the poet write "two-and-twenty" instead of "twenty-two"?

10. Why did he repeat the phrase "'tis true" at the end of the poem?

Lewis Carroll (1832–1898)

Jabberwocky

'Twas brillig, and the slithy toves
Did gyre and gimble in the wabe;
All mimsy were the borogoves,
And the mome raths outgrabe.

5   'Beware the Jabberwock, my son!
The jaws that bite, the claws that catch!
Beware the Jubjub bird, and shun
The frumious Bandersnatch!'

He took his vorpal sword in hand:
10   Long time the manxome foe he sought—
So rested he by the Tumtum tree,
And stood awhile in thought.

And, as in uffish thought he stood,
The Jabberwock, with eyes of flame,
15   Came whiffling through the tulgey wood,
And burbled as it came!

One two! One two! And through and through
The vorpal blade went snicker-snack!
He left it dead, and with its head
20   He went galumphing back.

'And hast thou slain the Jabberwock?
Come to my arms, my beamish boy!
O frabjous day! Callooh! Callay!'
He chortled in his joy.

25   'Twas brillig, and the slithy toves
Did gyre and gimble in the wabe;
All mimsy were the borogoves,
And the mome raths outgrabe.

1. Perhaps because this poem doesn't make complete sense we are able to see the rhythm more clearly. Pound out the beat of this poem. How many syllables are there in each line? How many stresses?

2. What is the pattern of emphasis? Put marks on two or three lines to show the emphasis (what was stressed, what was unstressed).

3. The last lines of stanzas 3–6 are visually shorter than those in other stanzas. Does this have any special effect on you as a reader?

William Butler Yeats (1865–1939)

An Irish Airman Foresees his Death

I know that I shall meet my fate
Somewhere among the clouds above;
Those that I fight I do not hate
Those that I guard I do not love;
5   My country is Kiltartan Cross,
My countrymen Kiltartan's poor,
No likely end could bring them loss
Or leave them happier than before.
Nor law, nor duty bade me fight,
10   Nor public man, nor cheering crowds,
A lonely impulse of delight
Drove to this tumult in the clouds;
I balanced all, brought all to mind,
The years to come seemed waste of breath,
15   A waste of breath the years behind
In balance with this life, this death.

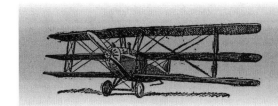

1. The speaker in this poem knows that he is going to die; what clues suggest that he knows this; and in what kind of mortal situation does he find himself?

2. Is there any aspect of this poem that seems to emphasize balance to you? Does the speaker want to avoid death or embrace death, and why?

3. To what extent do you think this tension characterizes the way a soldier *must* think?

4. Draw a line to divide the poem into two logical parts—why did you choose that dividing place? How would you describe how the two parts are different?

5. Looking at the rhythm in the lines (pounding it out as you go along), is there any difference in the rhythm of the two parts? Is a difference needed? Why or why not?

6. Notice the words that rhyme. What are some of the other words that aren't at the end of the lines that share similar sounds (such as "impulse" and "tumult" in lines 11 and 12)? What is the effect of these rhymes or repeated words that take place inside the lines?

7. What is the meter or rhythmic pattern of this poem?

Emily Dickinson (1830–1886)

A bird came down the walk

A bird came down the walk:
He did not know I saw;
He bit an angle-worm in halves
And ate the fellow, raw.

5   And then he drank a dew
From a convenient grass,
And then hopped sidewise to the wall
To let a beetle pass.

He glanced with rapid eyes
10   That hurried all abroad,–
They looked like frightened beads, I thought;
He stirred his velvet head

Like one in danger; cautious,
I offered him a crumb,
15   And he unrolled his feathers
And rowed him softer home

Than oars divide the ocean,
Too silver for a seam,
Or butterflies, off banks of noon,
20   Leap, plashless, as they swim.

1. Look first at the way this poem uses rhythm. Go through a whole stanza and mark where the words and phrases are stressed and where they are unstressed. How many iambs are in each line?

2. What happens in the third line of each stanza? What is the effect of that change?

3. Do you like to be able to predict that the change is coming? Do you like it when the poem does the same thing in each stanza?

4. How do you feel at the end of a poem when you have been carried along through it by a regular rhythm? How does it feel when the rhythm changes?

5. How do the choices Dickinson made about rhythm in the poem match the way the bird acts?

6. In this poem, the speaker personifies the bird, attributing to it human qualities. What are some of the clues that the poet believes that this bird is thoughtful and aware? What does the speaker do to befriend the bird?

7. What is the metaphor that the poet creates to describe the bird's leaving after the speaker offers it the crumb? Have you ever felt like you would befriend a wild animal if you could? Have you had any such experiences as this?

8. Write a list of all the end-words in this poem. Which of them rhyme or slant-rhyme? Is there a pattern of rhymes that you can describe?

Robert Frost (1874–1963)

Fire and Ice

Some say the world will end in fire,
Some say in ice.
From what I've tasted of desire
I hold with those who favor fire.
5   But if it had to perish twice,
I think I know enough of hate
To say that for destruction ice
Is also great
And would suffice.

1. This poem's meter changes in different places in the poem. There is a steady iambic beat but sometimes there is a sudden shortening of the lines. Map out the places that are iambic tetrameter and then the places where the lines are shorter.

2. Is there a reason related to the meaning of the poem that would cause the writer to vary the length of the line? How would you describe that reason?

3. What argument or question is being debated in this poem?

4. What positions does the author take in the argument? On what authority does he base his opinions?

5. Which of the following adjectives accurately describes the *tone* of this poem: peaceful, angry, matter-of-fact, childlike, mature/wise, fearful, or courageous? Give evidence from the poem to support your choices.

6. Which do you think is more destructive, fire or ice? Why?

ACTIVITIES

1. Turn on the radio or play a music CD and tap out the drum beat. Do this with several different songs. Then read several poems aloud and do the same thing.

2. Get out the dictionary and look up some words to see the way in which the dictionary marks syllables.

3. Figure out the syllabic emphasis for each of your classmate's names. Write yours down. Try to say it with the emphasis on the unstressed syllable(s).

4. Stand up and form a line, then read a poem out loud and have each student take a step forward for each stressed syllable and a step backward for each unstressed syllable. Do this slowly at first and then try to get faster and smoother as a group.

5. Have students compile a list of words with everyone in the class contributing any two- or three-syllable word that comes to mind. Make a list on the board and form teams, then see which team is first to figure out the stress pattern for each word (award one point for each correct answer). Then take words from the board and string them into iambic pentameter lines. The content doesn't have to make sense, but the rhythmic pattern does. The team with the most correctly patterned lines wins.

6. Make a list of rhythms from life, such as seasonal rhythms, classroom rhythms, cooking rhythms, etc., and try to imagine what would happen without these rhythms, and tell a group story or write your own essay to describe what a day would be like without rhythm.

7. Take a poem that you've written in open verse and convert it to one of the meters described in this chapter. You will likely need to rearrange words and change phrases. See what happens when you put a restriction on words and word combinations. You might stumble onto an arrangement you like even better than your original wording. If you're stumped for an original poem, take a paragraph from a favorite novel or story and do the exercise with that.

8. Go to a poetry reading at a local college or community event. Check out recordings of poets reading their own work at the library or online.

9. Memorize poems to see what happens to the rhythm when you aren't reading it from the page.

10. Form small groups of three. Have each group choose a poem from this book to recite to the class or for the teacher. Have each member read the poem aloud in your group, and then discuss where the stress in the reader's voice should naturally fall. Also, decide how long a pause should be held at commas, periods, line and stanza breaks, and other punctuation. Talk about the pace of the poem—should it be read slowly, swiftly, or change pace as the poem progresses? Where should it be read softly and where should it be read loudly? Choose one person from your group to formally recite the poem to the class.

VOCABULARY

Anaphora: several lines, phrases, clauses, or sentences that begin with the same word or phrase.

Foot: a unit of measure in a metrical line.

Iamb: word or phrase that has two syllables, with the first one unstressed and the second one stressed.

Iambic hexameter: seven iambs together.

Iambic pentameter: five iambs together.

Iambic tetrameter: four iambs together.

Iambic trimeter: three iambs together.

Meter: the rhythmic measure of a line of verse.

Scan: to identify and determine the pattern of stressed and unstressed syllables of a poem.

Stressed syllable: a syllable in which the emphasis of the voice (or intonation) falls. For example, the first syllable in the word "BARking" is stressed.

Syllable: a basic unit of speech consisting of a single cluster of sound, which can be as simple as "I" or as long as "breathe."

Unstressed syllable: a syllable in a word or phrase in which the emphasis does not naturally fall. In the word "basic," the emphasis is on the first syllable not on the second, so we say that the second syllable, "ic," is unstressed.

07
SHAPE: STANZA AND LINE

{the elements of poetry}

Everything that exists has **shape**. As we have discussed with rhythm, **imagery**, and other poetic elements, shape, also called "form," is a part of life. You've known for years the three different forms water can take: liquid, solid, gas. The same substance, different forms, each exhibiting very different qualities and effects. Think, too, about the fact that on Saturdays and Sundays you have to figure out what the shape of your day will be because you do not have school. Think about learning the grammar of visual art—you start with shapes and see how every thing you want to paint can be broken down to basic geometrical forms.

Art cannot exist without form. Ideas in a piece of art are always working together with the skill of its shape, and this is true for any art form—music, visual art, poetry, dance. Shape is the element that most closely involves the visible form of the poem on the page. Like the other elements of poetry you have learned about in this book, shape emerges naturally from the history of human experience. Just as words were created because they were necessary (someone needed to talk to someone else about the thing they took out on the lake to fish and so the word "boat" came about), shape in poetry came about as communally accepted forms to hold certain thoughts and experiences. Shapes came from culture-specific experiences in harvest fields and in kings' courts, and they came from universal human experiences, like the need for breaks or breaths in oral storytelling or singing. Hundreds of years later, more shapes came from artists' reaction against set poetic shapes and traditions—poets made poems that went on and on without breaking at all. One poet, Jack Kerouac, even made a poem written out entirely on a roll of calculator paper. Still other poets, rather than reacting against traditional shapes or forms, took them and filled them with nontraditional ideas or images.

In poetry the two fundamental elements of form are the line and the stanza. A line is the basic compositional part of a poem. Other names for line are "verse" and "stich." As mentioned earlier, the line is essential to what distinguishes poetry from prose (or verse and prose). A line of poetry ends before the edge of the page; it is a deliberate break, a decision on the part of the writer to turn to the next line. A line can also be longer than the prose equivalent, extending past the natural breaking point of the width of the page, as do most of Walt Whitman's poems (see chapter 14). When this happens, the second line is indented to show the continuation. The poet determines the length of a line one of several ways:

- By using meter (see chapter 6), such as iambic pentameter, iambic tetrameter, or **hymn meter** (as with Emily Dickinson), in which there are a set number of syllables: and stresses (five or four) in the space of the line.

- By ending the line with a rhyme, using however many words as necessary to reach the rhyming word, or confining the rhymed line to a set meter or length. Sometimes the set length and rhymes are part of an established scheme or pattern to which individual lines must conform in order to make the shape or form of the whole poem.

- By using another less clear or measured rhythm: a line length that feels "right" and in some way supports or expresses the content of the language. Some poets settle into a comfort level with very short lines (Robert Creeley, Kay Ryan); others find they are most at home with very long lines (C.K. Williams, Walt Whitman).

- By stopping the line to make a pause in what is being said—either a natural pause because of the grammar (a phrase stays together) or because it is the approximate length of a breath, or an unexpected, unnatural pause because suspense is being created or a certain word is being emphasized.

Like any element of artistic expression, the length of a poetic line is infinitely flexible in the hands of its maker. Often in the midst of writing, a poet will recast the poem into very short lines, very long lines, or lines that are stepped in gradual indentations. This kind of drafting and revising is freeing, but a poet will usually find that committing herself to a fixed form or shape is freeing as well. The focus can then be turned to filling the fixed shape with sound, rhythm, and imagery.

The other significant element in the shape of a poem is the stanza. The word "stanza" comes from the Italian word meaning "room." Each group of lines in a poem is like a little, self-contained room. Think about rooms in your house—different things happen in different rooms, though they are all part of the same house. In your bedroom you sleep and spend time alone, while in the kitchen, food is prepared. This represents the purpose of stanzas: they give the poem space and time to develop, provide opportunities for different things to happen at different times, and give a sequence to the events of the poem. There is white space before and after stanzas. Those spaces of rest, silence, and nothingness are important to the poem, just as the landing on the stairwell in your house where you watch and wait for a friend to pick you up is important.

Stanzas, paragraphs, chapters, acts, scenes—these ordering units can all be traced to the history of oral culture (oral tradition), for as you tell a story or sing a song it is necessary to pause, to catch your breath, and to emphasize what you're saying with brief silence. It is also necessary for speakers and listeners to bring some order or organization to the flow of ideas and scenes. Over time, especially at the end of the Middle Ages, poets became interested in making more complex stanzas, beautiful in their ornamentation and demanding in their poetic skill.

In our era, poets make use of the full range of stanza lengths. Here is a list (see anthology for some examples):

Number of lines	Term for stanza
1	**monostich**
2	**couplet**
3	**tercet**
4	**quatrain**
5	**cinquain**
6	**sixain** or **sestet**
7	**septet**
8	**octave**

Many different poems have been written using each of these lengths of stanza, but the most basic and common in history is the quatrain, which has four lines to the stanza. The couplet has also been a very popular stanza form. In the sixteenth, seventeenth, and eighteenth centuries it was used widely for satirical, witty, wisecracking poetry (called the heroic couplet— read Moliere's plays for a great example). In our era, the couplet form is often used for more meditative poetry, which allows for frequent spaces between thoughts. As you read, pay attention to the ways in which the groupings of stanzas affect the poem's music and meaning. Different shapes make different statements possible.

Some people have looked at the historical shapes of poetry as a lock or a rule—inherited forms obeyed and imitated blindly with a lack of creative freedom. Yet the great poet Robert Frost calls form not a lock or a rule but a "harness," suggesting that a poem, like a horse, needs direction, and that direction isn't always a burden, but a guide. The long tradition of fixed line and stanza length, of complicated rhyme schemes, and even of experimental departure from these forms shows us something important about our nature as human beings. It shows us that the human spirit is hungry to find order for the expression of its heart, mind, and soul—and it is just as eager to break or revise that order. Thus we can be assured that while there are certainly new poetic shapes to be discovered, such discovery is always aided by an understanding of what has been shaped and reshaped in the past.

LEARNING TO READ CLOSELY

Robert Hayden (1913–1980)

Those Winter Sundays

Sundays too my father got up early
and put his clothes on in the blueblack cold,
then with cracked hands that ached
from labor in the weekday weather made
5   banked fires blaze. No one ever thanked him.

I'd wake and hear the cold splintering, breaking.
When the rooms were warm, he'd call,
and slowly I would rise and dress,
fearing the chronic angers of that house,

10   speaking indifferently to him,
who had driven out the cold
and polished my good shoes as well.
What did I know, what did I know
of love's austere and lonely offices?

Sunday is a day that we all expect to be different from other days. We usually don't go to work outside the home and often even our housework is put aside. Some go to church as, we can surmise from the poem, this family did. If we read only the title of this poem and nothing more, we might get a feeling of rest and fond nostalgia. Yet it takes only the first two lines to quickly see that the feeling of this poem is not what you might expect. The speaker's father is getting up early and getting dressed in "the blueblack cold." With the tiny word "too" in the first line we know this is something he does every day, and by the third and fourth lines we know that what the father does after he rises and dresses is manual labor that makes his hands "cracked" and aching. Years or perhaps decades later, it has struck the son that no one, including himself, thanked his father for starting those fires, for getting up early, for working a difficult job to help keep the family and household functioning.

This poem is made of three stanzas of uneven length and unmetered lines. In the first stanza, the poet has chosen to list each item of service on its own line. This adds to the sensation of it being labor and to our sense that it was a long list of acts. Line 5 ends the list abruptly with a caesura that pulls the speaker out of his meditation with the bitter realization that his father was not thanked for this gift. Ending the stanza on that note leaves the reader, along with the speaker, pondering this sad thought. The white space between stanzas (or rooms) reinforces the discomfort of this awareness.

The first stanza, as with the others, does not rhyme, but still engages a multitude of sound patterns. Many long vowel sounds wind their way throughout these five lines: clothes, cold (long "o"), ached, labor, weekday, made, banked, blaze, thanked (long "a"). In addition to vowel sounds (called assonance) there are prominent consonant sounds: "c/k" (clothes, blueblack, cold, cracked, ached, week, banked, thanked), "b" (blueblack, banked, blaze). Some consonant sounds are repeated at the beginning of words in a short succession (alliteration) "clothes/ cold," "weekday/weather," "banked/blaze." The effect of rhyme is different, more ordered, less haphazard, but these other sound-types can reinforce the mood or feeling that is developing in the poem. They can order the poem in a way that is different from consistent, expected, echoed sound at the end of a line. The long vowel sounds tend to reinforce a sense of longing, and the hard "k" sounds harsh. This first stanza draws the portrait of the father in the context of the home. Closing the first stanza with the bald statement "No one ever thanked him" leaves us in the moment of unhappy recognition. It communicates the sense that it is too late for thanks or to make amends, either because the father is gone (perhaps he has died) or because the moment of thanks has passed.

The second stanza, another room, shifts its attention to the speaker as an adolescent who explains that by the time he woke, the heat created by his father's hands had already begun to warm the house. The speaker brings us into the experience by creating the often repeated morning scene—the cold "splintering, breaking," the father calling up the stairs to get the children out of bed, the reluctant riser "slowly ris[ing] and dress[ing]." We are surprised at the end of the second stanza when the speaker describes his fear of the "chronic angers of that house." He does not elaborate on what those angers were or how intensely they characterized the family. We know that they are important, for again he has chosen the last line of the stanza to place this piece of information, which leaves the reader in the presence of its knowledge and creates emphasis. This line is enjambed to the next—it crosses from one stanza into the next— which suggests the overflow of anger, both in terms of its role in the family as well as the impact of its presence. The second stanza uses temperature symbolically—the physical warmth and cold of the house is a reflection of the emotional temperature of its relationships. There is coldness (indeed, later the speaker refers to his own "indifference" toward his father, which is a type of coldness), but there is also warmth of several varieties. After all, the poem is being written to commemorate the love that was shared and not entirely acknowledged. Yet there was also the warmth of anger—too much emotional heat that, like the warming fire, can singe and burn.

Perhaps the greatest beauty of this poem is its accurate portrayal of how love and hurt lie close to each other. The family life wasn't perfect, it would not be suited for greeting card sentiment, but it is honest. It also seems to acknowledge that despite our imperfect love for each other, the abiding reality of the exchange is the love. The sound reinforces the angers as well as the warmth. When an old house warms up it creaks and shivers, the wood itself pops and breaks. But anger also splinters and breaks, so the sounds work on both a literal and a figurative level (or symbolic level, suggesting something beyond the concrete meaning). This second stanza is full of "s" sounds and "k" sounds that seem to mimic the warmth as well as the harshness.

In the third stanza, the adult speaker finishes by admitting his part in the hurt of the family, explaining his childish blindness that wasn't able to see what his father had done for the family, despite whatever he hadn't done. In a climax of emotion the speaker calls out with a voice mingled with thanks and grief, "What did I know, what did I know?" He understands now, perhaps because he himself is a father, perhaps because of the insight that time gives, perhaps because his father is gone and the speaker can now examine more closely his father's legacy, love's offices (or the jobs of love) are "austere and lonely." "Austere" means "stern, forbidding, grave, unadorned," all qualities that we sense were true of the father.

Then suddenly we understand, as the speaker does, that these may also be qualities of love. Love's job can be stern and unfancy. The act of loving, the speaker seems to say, is not chiefly a sentiment, a warm tingling feeling, but rather it is a grave, hardworking, self-sacrificing, thankless task. It is a lonely task; sometimes you do it without being understood. The repetition of that final phrase, and the poet's choice to make it a question, gives the reader the sense of the son's anguish and regret. Once again, the stanza ends with a lingering regret, a lingering sense that this knowledge has come too late and is something the son will have to bear. The long vowel sounds have returned to this final stanza, in particular the long "o" (cold, know, lonely), which contributes to the quality of moaning.

This is powerful and moving and speaks beyond the lives of the specific individuals in the poem. Don't we all have regrets about the way we've treated those closest to us? The poem is a beautiful example of how free or open verse makes a shape and uses the line and stanza for structure, even when there isn't meter and rhyme. The decisions of where to break the lines seem governed by the dawning awareness of the speaker—he is piling up the facts of the situation, the story. Each piece of information has its own line; each piece is a kind of evidence in the court of the law of the heart. The lines aren't precisely uniform, but we can see that the first stanza establishes an average line length that basically holds for the rest of the poem.

Each stanza draws a different perspective: the father, the speaker as an adolescent, the speaker as an adult. Each stanza ends at a place that is difficult and resonant. The last anguished question seems to be asked of the darkness.

There is something austere about this speaker's tone of voice. He presents the facts, unadorned—there aren't many adjectives beyond what will communicate the necessary message. The speaker is determined to give us an accurate picture; he isn't trying to make himself or his father look better than they were, as often happens in funeral speeches, for example. From the beginning of the short poem (fourteen lines) we hear regret in this voice, and there is the sense that the speaker's failure cannot be easily set right. That failure is communicated in every element of this poem, including and perhaps especially in its inelegant shape: the unpatterned, unrhymed lines and stanzas. The skillful use of silence in this poem also communicates the speaker's sense of failure, while at the same time creating space for reverence, remembrance, and perhaps in some way, forgiveness.

One of the reasons we write poetry is to bear witness to something, to correct something that can't be made right in life. There is relief and even honor in naming an experience for what it is, for all its mingled pain and love. What makes this a superior piece of art is that it is broad and skillful enough for all of us to find it true to our own experience, and at the same time it is particular, publicly stating what should have been said privately years ago. In this way again the poem is less like a formal funeral speech and more like a humble gravestone, carved painstakingly with the few words that truly matter. Looking at such a tribute, our own hearts contract and expand.

ANTHOLOGY

Henry Wadsworth Longfellow (1807–1882)

The Day is Done

The day is done, and the darkness
 Falls from the wings of Night,
As a feather is wafted downward
 From an eagle in his flight.

5 I see the lights of the village
 Gleam through the rain and the mist,
And a feeling of sadness comes o'er me
 That my soul cannot resist:

A feeling of sadness and longing,
10 That is not akin to pain,
And resembles sorrow only
 As the mist resembles the rain.

Come, read to me some poem,
 Some simple and heartfelt lay,
15 That shall soothe this restless feeling,
 And banish the thoughts of day.

Not from the grand old masters,
 Not from the bards sublime,
Whose distant footsteps echo
20 Through the corridors of Time.

For, like strains of martial music,
 Their mighty thoughts suggest
Life's endless toil and endeavor;
 And to-night I long for rest.

25 Read from some humbler poet,
 Whose songs gushed from his heart,
As showers from the clouds of summer,
 Or tears from the eyelids start;

Who, through long days of labor,
30 And nights devoid of ease,
Still heard in his soul the music
 Of wonderful melodies.

Such songs have power to quiet
 The restless pulse of care,
35 And come like the benediction
 That follows after prayer.

Then read from the treasured volume
 The poem of thy choice,
And lend to the rhyme of the poet
40 The beauty of thy voice.

And the night shall be filled with music,
 And the cares, that infest the day,
Shall fold their tents, like the Arabs,
 And as silently steal away.

Henry Wadsworth Longfellow

1. Look at the lines and stanzas of this poem; notice that they are almost entirely uniform. Describe this sameness, how the lines are decided and how the stanzas are working.

2. How many beats (stressed syllables) does each line have? How many unstressed syllables? Can you make a case for why this rhythm, called **anapestic** rather than iambic, might best suit a lullaby such as this? (Think about the word "lullaby" itself and how well its sounds match its meaning.)

3. Does each stanza have its own subject? There will, of course, be themes running through the whole thing.

4. How does the writer use rhyme to reinforce both the line and the stanza?

5. For what does the speaker wish? What is the speaker's mood?

6. What are some of the striking comparisons in the poem?

7. Why does the speaker want a "humbler poet" as opposed to a "grand old master" or "bard sublime"? Does the language of the poem reflect this wish at all? Does the poem end in "quiet" or "benediction" as the poet wishes?

8. Is there any precedent or anything familiar about the idea of having a poet sing the cares of the day away?

9. Does the poem soothe you in any way? Remember the books from when you were younger in which the story ended in a child being put to bed? Your parents probably read them right before your own bedtime because they hoped the books would relax you and make you realize how sleepy you felt. Does this poem function similarly for you? Try reading it at the end of a long, tiring day.

Edna St. Vincent Millay (1892–1950)

Afternoon on a Hill

I will be the gladdest thing
    Under the sun!
I will touch a hundred flowers
    And not pick one

5   I will look at cliffs and clouds
        With quiet eyes,
Watch the wind bow down the grass,
    And the grass rise.

And when lights begin to show
10   Up from the town,
I will mark which must be mine,
    And then start down!

Edna St. Vincent Millay

1. Examine the way this poem takes shape—notice the lines and the uniform pattern that every other line has. What is that pattern (first and third lines, second and fourth lines)?

2. Which lines rhyme? How would you label the rhyme scheme?

3. Do you think there is any reason, according to the meaning of the poem, that the second and fourth lines of each stanza are half as long as the first and third? Does it correspond to anything the speaker is talking about or emphasize anything related to the subject of the poem?

4. What is the mood or tone of the speaker's voice?

5. Have you ever purposed in your heart at the start of a day how that day will be, imagining it in its entirety?

6. Why do you think the speaker plans to touch "a hundred flowers" but not pick any?

7. How does the quiet of the eyes get reproduced in the poem, and what in the language of the second stanza suggests quietness? Have you ever been quiet this way, and do you do it regularly?

8. How much time will the speaker have spent frolicking happily alone by the time the poem ends? Have you done this? If not, why not? What would your own poem about the ideal day look like?

9. Consider the approach of night and the final two lines of the poem. Is the speaker's tone assured, happy, safe? Is there anything in the language that might suggest a different kind of tone? If your answer is "yes," explain it.

William Butler Yeats (1865–1939)

The Lake Isle of Innisfree

I will arise and go now, and go to Innisfree,
And a small cabin build there, of clay and wattles made;
Nine bean rows will I have there, a hive for the honey bee,
    And live alone in the bee–loud glade.

5   And I shall have some peace there, for peace comes dropping slow,
Dropping from the veils of the morning to where the cricket sings;
There midnight's all a glimmer, and noon a purple glow,
    And evening full of the linnet's wings.

I will arise and go now, for always night and day
10   I hear lake water lapping with low sounds by the shore;
While I stand on the roadway, or on the pavements gray,
    I hear it in the deep heart's core.

1. Notice how the stanzas function in this poem. All three contain beautiful descriptive details of Innisfree, so what makes each stanza different? Are they self-contained (do they stop at the end of the stanza in terms of the sentence), and do they each have a distinct idea?

2. How does the rhyme scheme contribute to the shape of the poem?

3. What determines the line length?

4. In your own words, describe the speaker's feeling about Innisfree. How do the sounds and rhythms contribute to communicating his emotion?

5. Do you feel this way about a particular place of your own? Describe it, and try to pin down why it evokes such feelings in you.

6. Is there a conflict in this poem? How would you describe it?

7. Do you think it is necessary for the speaker to actually physically "arise and go" to this place of peace, or is to "hear it in the deep heart's core" sufficient? Do you think the speaker would agree with your answer? Why or why not?

Marianne Moore (1887–1972)

The Fish

wade
through black jade.
   Of the crow-blue mussel-shells, one keeps
   adjusting the ash-heaps;
5   opening and shutting itself like

an
injured fan.
   The barnacles which encrust the side
   of the wave, cannot hide
10   there for the submerged shafts of the

sun,
split like spun
   glass, move themselves with spotlight swiftness
   into the crevices—
15   in and out, illuminating

the
turquoise sea
   of bodies. The water drives a wedge
   of iron through the iron edge
20   of the cliff; whereupon the stars,

pink
rice-grains, ink-
   bespattered jelly fish, crabs like green
   lilies, and submarine
25   toadstools, slide each on the other.

All
external
   marks of abuse are present on this
   defiant edifice—
30   all the physical features of

ac-
cident–lack
   of cornice, dynamite grooves, burns, and
   hatchet strokes, these things stand
35   out on it; the chasm-side is

dead.
Repeated
   evidence has proved that it can live
   on what can not revive
40   its youth. The sea grows old in it.

1. Notice the regular irregularity of these lines as they are indented strangely in a predictable pattern. What is the pattern?

2. How is the pattern both regular and irregular at the same time?

3. What is the effect of the pattern? Do you feel yourself taking on the fish's-eye view as it weaves through the ocean depths?

4. How does breaking the lines and stanzas at strange places shape the way in which you perceive the fish and its movement?

William Carlos Williams (1883–1963)

The Red Wheelbarrow

so much depends
upon

a red wheel
barrow

5   glazed with rain
water

beside the white
chickens

1. This is another poem that breaks its lines in unusual places. How does the shape of the lines and stanzas relate to the physical object being described?

2. How does the lack of punctuation and capitalization affect the poem and the way you read it?

3. What is the effect of beginning the poem with a line that suggests symbolic importance and then paints a clear but simple picture?

4. What are two different ways that you might interpret the meaning of this poem?

ACTIVITIES

1. Cut poems up into lines and try to put them back together as you think they should be. Then try to arrange them in a different way and see how the poem changes. Do this activity with a poem someone else cuts up for you that you've never seen in its whole form.

2. Do what Emily Dickinson did and collect lines of poetry written (or typed) on scraps of paper. You could type up a bunch of lines and then cut them apart. Take the lines from different poems and then fashion a poem from them.

3. Do the same thing as above but with stanzas. See how the sequence of the stanzas is important to the poem, and try to discover if this helps you to understand how a stanza is a room that leads us somewhere (especially if a story is being told).

4. Find a poem in this book that you like and set it to music—which is to say, layer or juxtapose its form on top of a different art form. You can do this by writing a melody and literally singing the poem— it can be your own original notes or a melody you already know. Or you can do this by finding a more complex piece of music to play in the background while the poem is recited. Think of this as a "sound collage." Hymn writers and classical composers have been doing this for ages—try listening to Aaron Copeland's music for Emily Dickinson's poems, or to Ralph Vaughn Williams's music for William Wordsworth or Robert Frost's poems. Pop musicians do this also—a recent term for it is "sampling"—try listening to songs by Moby and by many rap artists.

5. Try writing a poem, made up of a few important images, in which you experience a realization by the last stanza. See how the stanzas divide the images into separate moments and how this builds to a final moment. Pick a few images that are common to you, perhaps things that sound musical as you say them, and let them lead to a specific emotion: wonder, terror, joy, ordinary happiness.

6. Take a poem and change where the lines end and begin, and then talk about how this changes the meaning of the poem. William Carlos Williams's poem *To Waken an Old Lady* works well for this exercise.

7. Write your own poem and play with the lines, ending them in different places. What difference does it make?

8. Write a poem that uses stanzas to progress clearly from one point to another—either backward or forward in time, or from one emotional state to another. Experiment with different ways of ordering the rooms in your poetic house.

9. Make a list of things that are a certain color. Use the list to write a poem in stanzas.

10. Use the library, this book, and internet poetry sites to find examples of poems with each type of stanza: monostich, couplet, tercet, etc. Share them with your class, or put them together into a packet for reference as you write your own poems.

VOCABULARY

Anapestic: a foot of three syllables, two short followed by one long, or two unstressed followed by one stressed.

Hymn meter: a pattern of sound that lends itself to songs that a lot of people can easily sing, like nursery rhymes and church hymns. It is a closed poetic quatrain—a four-lined stanza whose end rhymes are *abab*, in which iambic tetrameter alternates with iambic trimeter. Also known as common meter.

Imagery: a concrete piece of information gathered with the senses.

Stanza types:

Monostich: a one-line stanza.

Couplet: a two-line stanza.

Tercet: a three-line stanza.

Quatrain: a four-line stanza; the most common stanza in English.

Cinquain: a five-line stanza.

Sestet (or sixain): a six-line stanza.

Septet: a seven-line stanza.

Octave: an eight-line stanza.

08
TONE:
PUTTING IT ALL TOGETHER

{*the elements of poetry*}

Poems are the expression of a single human voice; they are intimate, personal, and specific. When they are successful, poems speak to many people and their subject becomes universal—relevant to many people beyond the speaker—and yet they also remain individual. Figuring out who is speaking in a poem is primary: we want to know what the voice has experienced, what perspective on the world he or she has, what language he or she uses, and sometimes even what the speaker might be hiding or not saying.

When we speak aloud to each other, we hear tone of voice—that is, the way in which what we say sounds. In conversation, the quality of voice is more obvious than it is in a poem, and we can usually determine the speaker's tone very quickly. If your older brother told you he is getting married, his tone would tell volumes about how he feels about the impending change: happy, sad, overwhelmed, disbelieving, private, bitter. If you were evaluating your older brother's pronouncement, you'd also look at his body language and listen for the timbre of his voice. Writing can express many emotions, as can our voices. Tone is the attitude of the poem toward its theme or ideas. Think of the different parts of the poem (images, title, subject, sounds, diction, repetitions) as body language that gives you clues to its emotional core. Sleuthing the tone of a poem involves listening to *how* a poem is saying, versus *what* a poem is saying.

The theme of a poem is the subject, but the tone of a poem projects the speaker's feelings on that subject. Even when two poems are about the same subject, they can be very different in their ultimate meaning, in their stance toward that subject, in their tone. This is part of poetry's distinctiveness, for no two poems have the same impact on us or the same texture or feeling.

Learning to interpret the tone of a poem is essential to becoming a strong reader of poetry, and it will also help you to be a better reader in general, for interpretation is a skill that we use every time we open a magazine or textbook, click on a website, or watch a movie. In poetry you must learn to evaluate all of the elements of the poem and tally their sum. When you eat a fine meal with friends or family, it has many separate parts that must be combined for the complete experience. There is bread and oil or cheese, salad, a main dish, and perhaps a special drink or a dessert. There is laughter, conversation, and moments of quiet savoring of the taste and smell and happiness you feel. Similarly, a poem, to be complete, is made of parts that must combine to make a piece of art. As a reader, you must learn to understand the role of the different parts and to savor them. This process takes time and practice, alone and with other people.

Preceding this chapter have been discussions of each of the formal elements of poetry— the various poetic devices available to the poet. Now it is time to put these various elements together to understand how they interrelate and how to approach a poem as a meaningful whole. Different poems care about different elements—not all of them treat the same parts equally. Part of your job as a reader is to understand which elements in a poem matter most. Some poems need more probing than others to be understood. How much probing a poem needs does not determine its worth or merit. Such analysis increases our pleasure and ability to fully absorb the poem; however, don't allow the analytic work to take away from your initial delight and physical response to the poem. T.S. Eliot reminds us that "genuine poetry can communicate before it is understood." Seek first, therefore, to experience the poem at a gut level and then go in search of the particulars that made that experience happen.

Always begin by experiencing the poem with your body: as sound in your ear, shape in your mouth, breath in and out of your lungs. You are the poem's instrument, and your reading of it makes possible the life it was meant to have. Delight is the first order of importance, and the work of separating out a poem's parts is meant to add to that initial catch of your breath. Read a poem aloud slowly several times and, if possible, with several different voices.

Reading literature of high caliber in this attentive way sustains our inner lives. We live in a time when the language we use and the massive amount of information with which we come into contact does not adequately reflect the inner complexities (or even the simplicities) of our experience. When we read closely and imaginatively we learn about ourselves and are able to enter the mind of another who may not be like us, thus expanding our self-knowledge and our ability to imagine someone different from ourselves. Reading this way does justice to the ambiguities of our experience and enlarges our understanding. Learning to interpret a text is a natural part of the reading process and deepens our pleasure and understanding. Once you finish high school and possibly college and get a job, what habits of mind and heart will you bring to your work, family, and friends? How will you define the purpose and meaning of life? These are the questions that learning to read poetry prepares us to answer.

Robert Frost, who wrote the poem that follows, describes the process of tonal interpretation as searching for "the speaking tone of voice somehow entangled in the words and fastened to the page for the ear of the imagination." How we interpret the emotional edge of the content of a poem largely determines its vital meaning. To understand Frost's poem *Stopping by Woods on a Snowy Evening*, a range of interpretive skills is required, for its tone is essential to its interpretation and complexity.

LEARNING TO READ CLOSELY

Robert Frost (1874–1963)

Stopping by Woods on a Snowy Evening

Whose woods these are I think I know.
His house is in the village, though;
He will not see me stopping here
To watch his woods fill up with snow.

5   My little horse must think it's queer
To stop without a farmhouse near
Between the woods and frozen lake
The darkest evening of the year.

He gives his harness bells a shake
10   To ask if there's some mistake.
The only other sound's the sweep
Of easy wind and downy flake.

The woods are lovely, dark, and deep,
But I have promises to keep,
15   And miles to go before I sleep,
And miles to go before I sleep.

The speaker is on a trip through a deep wood on his way toward home. (The speaker could be a woman, for there isn't anything to suggest gender.) He wonders whose woods he's crossing and seems to be glad he is alone, away from the owner of the property, away from anyone's watching eyes. The speaker stops in these woods, which are filling up with snow and longingly wishes to stay there. It is the darkest evening of the year and everything is frozen. The only sounds are the speaker's horse and the wind and snow. Despite the starkness, the woods are lovely. After a time of contemplation he shakes himself out of the reverie and urges himself forward, to finish the miles that lay ahead. This represents a simple moment, as in a pause in one's work or journey, something we have all experienced in some form.

We feel the pull of the rhythm and sound of the first line of that last stanza, "The woods are lovely, dark, and deep," and in that pull we sense the speaker's own desire for something the woods hold. Perhaps the speaker longs for freedom from the "promises to keep" that await him at the end of his journey. Don't we all sometimes long for release from our commitments when they grow heavy? Haven't we all experienced the draw of stillness and solitude, away from the intensity and demand of life?

But the atmosphere is dark—"the darkest evening of the year"—and it is also cold, "frozen," "fill[ed] up with snow." Still, this darkness is somehow connected to the loveliness. This is not necessarily a scene that everyone would consider lovely, though many of us have probably encountered the depth of a snowy wood or some other equally stark landscape with awe and a sense of its intense, forbidding beauty. This kind of loveliness is both inviting and distancing, compelling in its very foreignness to our everyday lives.

The poem creates the stillness of the woods with its sounds and rests. Observe that each stanza ends with a period; it is contained within itself and does not run on to the next stanza, and is, in fact, its own complete sentence. This has the effect in two distinct places of coming to rest, coming to stillness. The sound and motion stop for a time. The meaning of the scene harmonizes with the sounds, especially the last stanza, which creates a kind of echo chamber of similarity. The fact that the last two lines end in repetition furthers the sense that something has come to rest, some ultimate layer of silence has been added where language slips away.

This poem is written in rhymed quatrains. The rhyme scheme is interesting for the very limited set of sounds used in its end rhymes: *aaba bbcb ccdc dddd*. The outcast sound in one stanza becomes the primary sound for the next stanza (the single *b* rhyme of the first stanza becomes the triply rhymed sound of the second stanza, etc.) and this pattern links the subjects as well as the sounds. Nothing is wasted; the sound themes keep getting picked up and applied. This creates a strong music that draws us in, but it also suggests a gesture of continuing return, a going back to something, an inability to leave something behind. In the final stanza there is an eerie similarity to the sounds of all the end words, almost as if the sound has gone to sleep. In both the case of the returning thought as well as the end sounds coming to rest, the rhyme mirrors the ideas of the poem.

This is supreme craft, because while we feel the harmony of sounds we don't feel that the poet is forcing the ideas or language to make the rhyme. Thus the shape of the poem also contributes to its tone. The rhyme scheme of this poem makes a contribution to the speaker's inner tug-of-war. The fact that one of the previous stanza's sounds gets picked as a rhyme in the following stanza (the *b* sound of stanza 1 becomes the dominant sound of stanza 2) demonstrates both the desire to linger and to drive oneself onward. The rhyme of the last stanza comes to an absolute rest without variation in a kind of lyric sleep, a standstill at the very moment when the speaker is insisting he or she will go on. These are the kinds of cues that we factor together as we attempt to determine the writer's attitude toward the subject, the intention of the poem's emotional direction.

What is the speaker feeling? What does he truly want? Whether the voice (tone) is weary, irritated, depressed, or longing matters greatly to our interpretation of the poem. The fact that the speaker chooses the word "promises" in the last stanza to describe what causes him to leave the lovely silent woods gives us one clue. A word like "appointments" might suggest an irritated tone of voice when he regretfully decides not to stop and linger on the way home. "Promises" suggest something that is of ultimate concern in the way in which we lead our lives, commitments that go deeper than our desires in the moment, however strong they may be.

Does the speaker joyfully turn away from the woods and head toward his tasks and promises, invigorated by his moment of contemplation? Or is he more keenly aware of his weariness, of the weight of his responsibilities? Some have argued that this speaker longs not just for rest but for the ultimate sleep of death. A few of the poem's details support this interpretation: The speaker is standing in a dark snowy wood and doesn't want to leave. He refers to sleep, which is sometimes considered a small death because we are not active in the world when we sleep.

We sometimes actually refer to death as "falling asleep." Frost actually borrowed lines from the Thomas Beddoes poem *The Phantom Wooer*, in which the line "our bed is lovely, dark, and sweet" refers to death. With such an interpretation, the longing in the tone of the poem would be intense, perhaps haunted. On the other hand, rather than death, the poem may symbolize the speaker's wish to leave the social world of obligation and falseness for the bare beauty and starkness of the natural world. In either case, it is clear we aren't simply getting information here—a mileage tally—but a deep sigh against what is before the speaker and what must be undertaken. All of these elements create a mood that helps us to determine the tone of voice.

Whatever the interpretation, most can agree that there is awe and longing in the voice of the speaker, either for the ultimate stillness of death or a less weighty one, such as peace or release from something pressing. The imagery is simple and complete: a winter scene. Metaphor as a poetic device is almost nonexistent in this poem—a "downy flake" suggesting that snowflakes are like feathers is the only one. The whole poem is certainly symbolic, though we likely won't agree on what precisely is being symbolized. This is the nature of a literary symbol—it resists exact interpretation and gives us some room to apply our own imagination. The word choices suggest the gravity of the speaker's concerns. The sound and formal aspects of the poem support its meaning (or sense). The meter is iambic tetrameter and is quite regular, which adds to the mesmerizing, lovely stillness.

This poem is beloved for obvious reasons. We have all felt similar moments of this mysterious mix of serenity and longing. Why take so many words and such trouble to say simply, "I would like to stay in this place but can't?" One five-year-old student who was asked this question about Frost's poem answered forcefully, "He says it like he means it!" Yes—this is precisely the purpose of poems. For the length of the poem, we enter the speaker's experience and understand ourselves and others with momentary clarity and pleasure.

A Checklist of Sorts

The following questions and suggestions are offered to help you synthesize a poem's elements and prepare for a close reading of it. As you read them over, try to consider relationships and how the different elements combine. Here is a list of elements to refresh your memory: image, metaphor, words, symbol, sounds and sound patterns, rhythm, shape, tone.

1. What does the title make you expect? Does the body of the poem fulfill your expectation or surprise you into a different space or perspective?

2. Use a dictionary, a literary reference book like *Benét's Reader's Encyclopedia*, and online research to define and explain anything in the poem you don't understand.

3. Who is speaking and to whom (who and what are the characters or actors in the poem)? What is the speaker's point of view? What kind of person is he? What does she think of the subject or theme, and does this opinion (tone) stay constant throughout the poem? Are any of the characters changed by the end of the poem?

4. What is the situation, occasion, or trigger for the poem? What is the physical setting? How does this context shape the poem? What is its relationship to specific images, metaphors, or symbols in the poem?

5. What is the poem's imagery? Find the images and ask if they make a pattern or relate to each other in any way. Does tracing the images give you a sense of the poem's concerns or movement—is there a logic to the images and their unfolding? How do they impact you? Have you experienced these images in everyday life? How is their presentation different from your experience?

6. What is happening at the level of sound and rhythm? Do the sounds suggest meaning? Do they create an atmosphere (harsh, soft, longing)? Are there numerous sounds of one type (like long vowels)? What type of words (diction) does the poem use—high, low, casual, formal? How does the rhyme scheme create structure? How does it contribute to meaning? What is some other meaningful repetition in the poem and what does it contribute?

7. Paraphrase/summarize the poem—what is its theme or central idea and how do the other elements develop it? How does the figurative language—symbols, metaphor, etc.—contribute to the poem's meaning? Do you feel these metaphors were necessary to this poem—do they contain conviction? How do they combine with other elements to create an event—something that you participate in as a reader, rather than something you are simply hearing about secondhand?

8. How do this poem's concerns, emotions, ideas, and images relate to your experience as a person? Do you agree with these ideas? Are you moved by them? Are they worthy content for a poem? How light or weighty are they? What is your reaction to the poem—do you like it? Do you think it is well made? Does it move you even if you don't agree with it?

9. What do you know about the time period and cultural context in which this poem was written? What do you know about the author of this poem? How does this poem fit with the rest of this poet's work? What formal traditions does this poem follow and what expectations do they create? How is the poem fulfilling or departing from these traditions and expectations? How does this knowledge contribute to your reading of the poem?

10. Assume there is a reason for everything and try to account for it in terms of meaning, skill, pleasure, or some other desired effect.

11. Seek opportunities to argue about and discuss your interpretations with others, to see how they understand this poem.

ANTHOLOGY

Gerard Manley Hopkins (1844–1889)

Spring and Fall

to a young child

> Margaret, are you grieving
> Over Goldengrove unleaving?
> Leaves, like the things of man, you
> With your fresh thoughts care for, can you?
> 5   Ah! as the heart grows older
> It will come to such sights colder
> By and by, nor spare a sigh
> Though worlds of wanwood leafmeal lie;
> And yet you *will* weep and know why.
> 10   Now no matter, child, the name:
> Sorrow's springs are the same.
> Nor mouth had, no nor mind, expressed
> What héart héard of, ghóst guéssed:
> It is the blight man was born for,
> 15   It is Margaret you mourn for.

1. In what manner or tone does the speaker speak to the young child Margaret?

2. What do you guess is the speaker's age?

3. What is the relevance of the poem's title? What layers of meaning are in the words "Spring" and "Fall"?

4. The speaker's tone suggests that he understands Margaret's weeping and has experienced it himself. Do you believe him and, if so, what in the poem makes you believe him?

5. How does the speaker's sympathetic tone combine with his message and the statement that he is making about the plight of mankind? How do the tone and theme of the poem work together?

6. How do the first and last lines of the poem work together with the title?

Robert Louis Stevenson (1850–1894)

Evensong

The embers of the day are red
Beyond the murky hill.
The kitchen smokes: the bed
In the darkling house is spread:
5   The great sky darkens overhead,
And the great woods are shrill.
So far have I been led,
Lord, by Thy will:
So far I have followed, Lord, and wondered still.

10   The breeze from the enbalmed land
Blows sudden toward the shore,
And claps my cottage door.
I hear the signal, Lord—I understand.
The night at Thy command
15   Comes. I will eat and sleep and will not question more.

1. What is the tone of voice of this poem and how does it contribute to the poem's meaning?

2. What in the language or shape of the poem helps you to decide its tone?

Robert Frost (1874–1963)

The Road Not Taken

Two roads diverged in a yellow wood,
And sorry I could not travel both
And be one traveler, long I stood
And looked down one as far as I could
5   To where it bent in the undergrowth;

Then took the other, as just as fair,
And having perhaps the better claim,
Because it was grassy and wanted wear;
Though as for that the passing there
10   Had worn them really about the same,

And both that morning equally lay
In leaves no step had trodden black.
Oh, I kept the first for another day!
Yet knowing how way leads on to way,
15   I doubted if I should ever come back.

I shall be telling this with a sigh
Somewhere ages and ages hence:
Two roads diverged in a wood, and I—
I took the one less traveled by,
20   And that has made all the difference.

1. What are the cues that help you to understand the importance of the road the speaker has chosen?

2. What do you make of the fact that the speaker tells us he will be "telling this with a sigh / Somewhere ages and ages hence"? Does it suggest that there is no sigh in that voice now?

3. What is the current tone of voice in the poem? What poetic devices or elements help create that sense or atmosphere?

William Blake (1757–1827)

Jerusalem

(from *Milton*)

And did those feet in ancient time
Walk upon England's mountains green?
And was the holy Lamb of God
On England's pleasant pastures seen?

5   And did the Countenance Divine
Shine forth upon our clouded hills?
And was Jerusalem builded here
Among these dark Satanic Mills?

Bring me my bow of burning gold!
10   Bring me my arrows of desire!
Bring me my spear! O clouds, unfold!
Bring me my chariot of fire!

I will not cease from mental fight,
Nor shall my sword sleep in my hand,
15   Till we have built Jerusalem
In England's green and pleasant land.

William Blake

1. When a situation fills our minds with questions, it is often the first inkling that something is amiss or not quite right in that situation. In this poem, the speaker begins with questions—two stanzas' worth. What is he asking? Is there a larger question underneath the literal questions? (You may need to research what Blake means by "Satanic Mills" to answer this.)

2. In the second half of the poem, the speaker changes from asking questions to making exclamations. What fuels the strong emotions he is expressing and what is the relationship between the questions in the first half of the poem and the exclamations in the second half?

3. There is more than one tone in this poem. What are they and do they combine to form a dominant impression?

4. Symbol, repetition, and rhyme are crucial poetic tools employed in this poem. Identify one example of each and explain how it contributes to the poem's meaning or to its tone.

Annie Kantar (1976–)

World

After Stephen Dunn's "A Bowl of Fruit"

My twins, I've spent days arranging
This dark paradise, all for you,
Knowing how much you love water
And I've been careful to make sure
5   Each pool is body temperature,
That the waves rise with the waves,
And for your pleasure I've included
Five small meals a day,
Which may signify to you my intention.
10   No doubt you've begun to question
Why waves rush over me too
When I talk to you, and (knowing you)
Whether this paradise
Is a paradise at all. And perhaps it's true
15   That I've covered the way out,
Painted over it perfectly,
Though this would be a mystery
That can only be solved
By bursting me open,
20   Diving with your heads,
Then your shoulders, and your hands.
It would be the kind of bold probing
I'd love for you to love, the new
Mess of our still life breaking open
25   Into life, the discovery that the secret opening,
If real, will not permit you any distance.
But surely by now you've come to realize
There is no way out, only this world
You swim in.

1. This poem is spoken in the voice of a mother to her unborn children who are growing inside her. Try to trace the different tones expressed in her conversation with them. Is there humor? Is there love? What is the nature or texture and quality of that love? What particular sound, rhythm, shape, image choices did the poet make to communicate that love?

2. What do you think she means by the final assertion—"surely by now you've come to realize / There is no way out, only this world / You swim in"?

ACTIVITIES

1. To practice tone of voice, say some short phrases aloud, varying their meaning by changing the tone. For instance, try saying, "I'm getting married," with dread, then surprise, then delight. Have a different person say each variation and make the class guess who is expressing what emotion. Try it with, "Oh, it's you," or "Nice job!" Make up some other phrases that illustrate this concept of tone.

2. Pick a couple of poems whose tone can be argued, and argue. Have students write privately about the matter for five to ten minutes, making a case for a certain tone of voice in the poem and then make a debate panel with judges to decide which argument wins.

3. Read a single poem aloud with different tones of voice and have the class vote on which one seems most appropriate to the material.

4. As a class, listen to music (with or without words) that has a certain mood. Assign a topic that can mean different things to different people (for instance, the changing of the seasons) and have students write out how the music affects the tone of the topic. You could also write a poem together as a class with everyone offering a line, the tone of which is to be decided ahead of time by the teacher or students.

5. Go to www.feelingfacescards.com to find examples of facial expressions that correspond with certain emotions. Then read several poems out loud and have the students express the tone of the poems using different facial expressions.

6. Write a poem two times using two completely different tones of voice.

7. Have students privately read several poems aloud and study them. Then have the entire class talk about the poems, encouraging them to note how the collaborative aspect of the conversation helps them understand each poem more fully. Students will observe that each person is drawn to different elements within the poem. One may be more attuned to sound, another to emotion, another to visual aspects of a poem. (It is helpful if the conversation is guided by someone with a bit more experience in the reading of poems.)

ACTIVITIES (CONTINUED)

8. Set a timer for ten minutes and begin freewriting in response to a poem read out loud that is also printed on a handout or in a book in front of you. Write without stopping about whatever comes to mind in answer to the question, "What is this poem saying?" Then set the timer again and write for ten minutes without stopping on the question, "How is it saying it?" You can also do this as a spoken exercise with a partner, in which one person speaks uninterrupted on the first question and the partner speaks uninterrupted on the second, then the partners switch.

9. Assign different students to each introduce a poem to the class. These people are responsible for using the checklist on p. 97 and coming up with a close reading of the poem outside of class and then leading the discussion of the poem in class. These students should be sure to come with questions for the class to explore some of the wonderings of the poem.

10. To get conversation going on beyond the boundaries of class time, create a class blog (web log) for any of the above activities that are to be done outside of the class. Have the students read the blog before or during class as part of the classroom activity.

11. Have a group or an individual teach a poem to the class.

09

HISTORY OF FORM, MOVEMENTS, GENRES

{the formal history of poetry}

An Introduction to the History of Form

All cultures at all times have had poetry. For hundreds of years poetry was not written, but was passed down from mouth to mouth, memory to memory, through the generations. Through oral poetry, different cultures preserved important information about the many elements of society: farming, religion and worship, the history of conflicts and their resolutions, the celebrations of births and marriages, and burial ceremonies. As you might guess, the seer or poet (there were no scribes or authors) had a significant role in premodern cultures. In earliest times, the vocation of poetry involved the spiritual life (it often still does) and the seer had shamanic or priestly responsibilities. One generation of seers taught, or apprenticed, the next in the rhythms of language and the art of storytelling. They had to learn to condense or expand a story depending on the event and time frame of the telling. They had to learn the rhythms that best suited different stories. Along the way, of course, they also learned to innovate, adding their own unique elements to the forms and the stories.

The first type of poetry to be written down was epic poetry—long, narrative poems that tell the stories central to the myths and beliefs of a people group. Ezra Pound called the epic a "poem containing history." Some examples of this type of poetry are *The Odyssey* and *The Iliad*, *Epic of Gilgamesh*, and *Mahabharata*. In Greek, the word "epic" means both song and narrative, and considering the astonishing length of epic poems, you can see why the musical rhythms of poetry were a natural device used to preserve these important narratives in the memories and hearts of a given people.

Song stories have always existed to rhythmically tell the story of ourselves with word pictures and other figures. This is the way we think, learn, and record the meaning that we experience in our lives. From the beginning of time it has been this way and it continues to be this way. By studying this book you are learning how to be a seer, a bard, and as such how to carry on the tradition in your times. This is not simply an academic exercise or busywork. Try to learn the craft and find poems that move you, that make you want to respond by writing your own, that urge you to memorize them and pull them out of your brain and heart when you need them most. You are entering the stream of story-making history when you perform these activities.

Historic Poetic Movements
Major movements in English-language poetry

The evolution of poetry and its various forms took place in specific locales. A chronology (literally "time study") of poetic development helps to understand the large movements that emerged in history and how they shaped the poems we read and write today. What follows is a short history of poetic movements.

History and literature do not fit in boxes, lists, or tidy categories, and yet the human mind needs to organize thoughts categorically and understand poems in relation to time and place. No one has ever sat down to intentionally write a poem that fit in one of these categories, because historic movements are identified many years after they happen. When we are in the midst of a time period, we have difficulty seeing what values and structures define it. "Hindsight is 20/20," some say, meaning that when we look back after something is finished, we are able to see, understand, and make a discerning judgment about what happened. Similarly, we can look backward at these impulses in poetic form and subject and recognize patterns. Patterns help us organize. As you think about these categories, however, remember how limited and ineffectual they are to communicate fully what happened in literature in a time or place, or to characterize a time period as uniform in its intentions. Writers are shaped by their time and the times that came before them, but they are also distinctive, rare, imaginative human beings creating out of their individual temperaments, their attachments, their instincts. Poems are not just interesting for the time in which they were born. Trying to categorize movements in poetry is similar to trying to label different kinds of people. There are some obvious general groupings, but people resist being defined in simple ways. You are as distinctive as your fingerprints, but at the same time you are as categorical as a homo sapien. Don't let the historical categories that follow, organized and limited by time, distract you from the direct experience of the poem itself—the language, the ideas, the shape, the physical expression. (To teachers and students alike: if this information is overwhelming to you, skip it and move on; come back to it after you have absorbed more of the poems themselves.)

Gerard Manley Hopkins, whose poetry appears in this book, exemplifies the complexity of this categorization process. He lived during the Victorian period and there are certainly some marks of this in his work. Largely, though, his writing was concerned with the pure music of language and with his own personal interests. He was deeply involved with the natural world, with religious thought and the life of a priest. His sense of form and the music of the poetry was so distinctive that many people would say that though he lived in Victorian times he wrote like a modernist. Even to say he wrote like a modernist is to simplify the matter, because he was uniquely himself, without much thought or exposure to his times. The only other poet with whom he was in contact was his friend Robert Bridges. He had no contact with literary circles after his schooling. Nonetheless, he lived during this period and held certain views that reflected his time, and it is useful for us to look at him in that light and to put him next to his contemporaries (as well as those writing before and after). Interestingly, his study of classical literature was vast and he knew and taught Latin and Greek. Keep this example in mind as you look at the useful but incomplete categories established by scholars to help us organize our thinking about poetry in relationship to time and place. This list is not meant to suggest that what was happening in other parts of the world is not valuable, but simply to limit the scope of the project to a manageable size.

Classical poets wrote in Greece and Rome during ancient times (approximately 1200 BC–AD 455). There were many different schools of poetry or trends of poetry within the classical period. They range from the lyric poem (brief, spoken by the individual, musical) to the epic poem (the story of a culture's happenings, heroes, and rites over many years). Some examples of form that emerged from this period are **pastoral** verse, **eclogue**, **ode**, and **elegy**. Some influential classical poets were Homer, Horace, and Virgil. Classical poets saw poetry as imitating life, both in the natural world and in the human world. The golden age of Greece, the founding of the Roman Republic, the Roman imperial age, and the patristic period are all subsets of the classical period of literature.*

Medieval is a general term given to poetry written during the Middle Ages (roughly from the fifth century through the fifteenth). During this period, the Catholic church exercised wide influence on all creative work. Many writers and visual artists came from monasteries and were therefore anonymous because they were working as a body for the good of the church, sharing all things in common. Much of the content of medieval poetry is based on the lives of the saints or on scriptural stories and themes. Drama was an active poetic form, as were romance or adventure tales. In the latter category, knights, kings, and distressed ladies were leading characters. The Arthurian legend springs from this time, set down by Thomas Malory. The so-called Dark Ages occured during the earliest part of this period. Chaucer, Dante, and Petrarch, though very different poets, all wrote during the medieval period.

Chaucer

Renaissance, which means "rebirth," defines work written in the fifteenth through eighteenth centuries in England. During the earlier part of this period, classical influences were strong, but during the later Elizabethan period some of the great authors that we know well today— Spenser, Sidney, and Shakespeare—wrote with great innovation and somewhat in reaction to the classical period. Meditative and highly structured, dense poetry flourished during this period by writers including John Donne, George Herbert, Richard Crashaw, Henry Vaughan, Robert Southwell, and Thomas Traherne. The Protestant Reformation took place during this time.

The **Neoclassical** movement peaked during the eighteenth century (approximately 1660–1790) in England and once again took its inspiration from classical forms and preferences. Are you beginning to see the pattern of action and reaction in movements—a seesaw? Literary

*The classical period was not English-language but was the root of the English language; to expand your study beyond this, try this excellent resource: *World Poetry*, edited by Clifton Fadiman.

movements are very much like families in which there are some children who do things the way their parents did them, and some who rebel against family traditions to do things their own, new way. The heroic couplet was popular during this time. This was the age of the Enlightenment, which emphasized the power of the human being to solve all problems and mysteries through logic. Dryden, Pope, Swift, and Burns wrote during this period, and the American Revolution occurred in this era as well.

Romanticism is another period in English literature that ranged from the late eighteenth century to the late nineteenth century (approximately 1790–1830). In this period, self-expression and intense feeling were dominant values in poetry. The poem was considered something that grows naturally like a plant, taking a natural shape. The imagination was supremely valued and the poet was considered an innate genius rather than a trained craftsman. After the Industrial Revolution, poetry was considered a good vehicle for the critique of culture. Instead of looking outward in an attempt to describe the world outside the self, the romantic poet tended to define her inner world, or to define the outer world through the veil or vision of the inner self. Wordsworth, Coleridge, Shelley, Keats, and Byron were writing poetry at this time. **Blank verse**, the **sonnet**, and the Spenserian stanza were widely used, along with many experimental **verse forms**. A down-to-earth, natural speaking voice was preferred rather than fancy, elevated language.

The **Victorian** period was named for Queen Victoria's reign (1832–1901) and tended to idealize the moral purity or innocence of the medieval world. In England, Hopkins, Tennyson, Robert and Elizabeth Browning, Arnold, and Christina and Dante Rossetti were writing. Later, in America, Whitman and Dickinson were also composing poetry, and free or open verse began to be shaped to fit the twentieth century.

Modernism began at the turn of the twentieth century and lasted until about mid-century as an extension of Romanticism. It valued many of the same principles of Romanticism with its own distinctive new emphases. Many writers that you've read are included in this category: T.S. Eliot, Ezra Pound, Wallace Stevens, William Butler Yeats, W.H. Auden, Ranier Maria Rilke, Dylan Thomas, Robert Frost, and Marianne Moore. Many movements have been gathered under the umbrella of modernism but are more narrowly defined: imagism, Harlem Renaissance, Black Arts movement, Beat movement, formalism, Fugitive movement, confessional school, New York School, language poets, Black Mountain school, and new formalism. World Wars I and II are included in this period. They had an enormous influence on culture and thought and led to disillusionment and experimentation in poetry and the sense that old forms had trouble containing new ideas and experiences.

Postmodernism is a much debated, complex category that has been used to describe the time we are living in now. It is difficult to have an objective perspective on your own times, and for that reason most era-naming solidifies after the era has passed. Many have argued that postmodernism is simply an extension of modernism and that it is too soon to explain its distinctiveness from that movement. It is safe to say that both movements are opposed to easy realism and have an intellectual bent. Jay Parini says that "Modernism is a house that adds a wing called postmodernism. The wing eventually becomes the main house." It is also safe to call the work of your own time "contemporary poetry."

Historic Genres of Poetry: Lyric, Narrative, Dramatic

Poems exist in categories of time, as we've just discussed, and they also exist in categories of shape and kind. Just as words came about because people needed them, so too genres of poetry came about because people needed poetry for different things in different generations. For instance, you can see how the epic was useful to Greek culture: it collected their stories as individuals and as a large community, it reminded them of what was important to their culture, it created a myth to pass on to their children and shape their understanding as a people group. Later, when epics were no longer being written (they arrive on the scene at the very beginning of written language), these divisions naturally evolved into new forms. Each culture has gravitated toward different genres and forms according to what it values. All aspects of a group of people affect this unconscious choice. All three of the following genres have been written in the last century.

The development of genre is not an unchanging situation. Even now there are conversations about the narrative-lyric, a hybrid category that draws from each of these classic genres. Dividing poetry this way helps you to understand some of its uses over the centuries of English language. In reality, poets don't usually sit down to write a certain kind of poem, except to exercise their writing muscles or develop skills in an area of weakness. Ideas, images, and music are cultivated in their thoughts and in their reading and slowly poets work it out in language on the page. We categorize as we look backward and try to create structure for what has naturally occurred, and in this way the art of poetry gains some helpful definition.

Lyric poetry: A lyric is the expression of an individual who thinks out loud with an emotion. Poems like these are musical and usually compressed, with meaning packed into a small space. In Greece, where lyric poetry traces its roots, these poems were sung, chanted, or recited to the accompaniment of the lyre—the poet's harp instrument. Lyric poems tend to be meditative and brief. The challenge of the lyric is to have this personal meditation matter to others, to strike on a subject that begins in the self but has resonance and significance to more than just the speaker. Typically there is a dominant emotion that characterizes the whole poem but becomes clearer as it goes on. Most of the poems in this anthology are lyric poems, because it is the predominant form used by contemporary poets.

Dramatic poetry: Dramatic poetry is written for a play. In Greece, there were two kinds used: tragedies and comedies. Tragedies show a man of nobility with a tragic flaw related to pride (or hubris) that results in his fall, which causes the audience to feel fear and pity and to work out their own concerns by watching the dramatic presentation. Comedies show a community with a flaw of some kind, often related to stubbornness, self-pity, or pride, and use satire, witty wordplay, and the arrival of a stranger or outsider to create so much chaos that the flaw is revealed and resolved. Everything in the community is restored and ends "happily ever after." In Shakespeare's comedies many characters get married at the end. Sophocles, Aristophanes, Euripides, and Dionysus are all playwrights of note from Greek literary history. This book will not venture into the realm of dramatic poetry (though there are two examples from Shakespearean plays in the section on blank verse from *The Tempest* and from *Julius Caesar*) but consider reading a Shakespearean play aloud each year, not only in the classroom but for an evening of fun.

Here are some recommended selections of dramatic poetry from Shakespeare:

- From *Two Gentlemen of Verona*, act 4, scene 2 (Host) beginning, "Who is Silvia?" and ending, "To her let us garlands bring."
- From *Love's Labour's Lost*, act 3, scene 1 (Biron) beginning, "And I, forsooth, in love!" and ending, "Some men must love my lady and some Joan."
- From *Twelfth Night*, act 1, scene 1 (Duke Orsino) beginning, "If music be the food of love, play on," and ending, "That it alone is high fantastical."

Dramatic poetry is less often written in the twentieth and twenty-first centuries, though Yeats, Eliot, and Lorca all wrote plays in verse. Musical comedies include verse and song but not much dramatic poetry.

Narrative poetry: Narrative poetry tells a story that contains characters and a plot (rising action, conflict, movement toward climax, resolution), starts at a different place than it ends, and involves sequence (first one thing, then another), suspense (what will happen?), and

Homer

consequence. The elements of poetry complement the story. The ballad is a form of narrative poetry that continues today, though interestingly these are usually sung, so there is a strong lyric component. The epic poem (Homer's *The Illiad* and *The Odyssey*, for instance) is considered an early narrative form, though it too was sung or chanted and so included elements of every possible use of language, even including aspects from *Farmer's Almanac* (weather predictions and home medical remedies). The epic stories came out of a time when there was no written language, so the storyteller fulfilled significant and varied roles. He passed on information, history, spiritual practices, and myths in order to entertain and instruct. Stories have been a part of every culture—in them we describe ourselves, define ourselves, and allow ourselves to live our lives through the prism of another set of characters and circumstances.

In our own contemporary context, the categories of narrative and lyric poetry are sometimes not as distinct as their definitions suggest. There is a narrative-lyric blend that emerges where the elements of both genres are loosely present. *Stopping by Woods on a Snowy Evening* is a good example of this blend. Many poems have a storytelling element to them, so questions that we often ask about narrative are, who is speaking and what is the situation of the speaker? It can also be helpful to separate narrative-lyric poems into sections that we examine almost like scenes of a movie or play in order to better trace the rise and fall of an experience.

VOCABULARY

Blank verse: unrhymed iambic pentameter (used widely by Shakespeare and Milton).

Eclogue: a pastoral poem, often in dialogue form.

Elegy: a lament or mourning for someone who had died. It seeks consolation and describes the circumstances and nature of the loss.

Ode: a song or lyric that is solemn, heroic, and elevated, often for an occasion. This form began by celebrating people but developed into a commemoration or study of various objects or occasions.

Sonnet: a poem of fourteen lines in iambic pentameter with varying rhyme schemes: Petrarchan (or Italian), which is divided into eight rhymed lines and six rhymed lines; and Shakespearean (or English), which is divided into three quatrains and a final couplet.

Verse forms: all traditional or received forms with structural rules or keys that guide the poet in decisions about line length, rhyme scheme, stanza length, and other patterns.

10
VERSE FORMS

{the formal history of poetry}

All traditional or received verse forms have structured rules or keys that guide the poet in decisions about line length, rhyme scheme, stanza length, and other patterns. Verse forms, like shaping forms and narrative forms, evolved within specific cultural contexts, and it helps to understand the history of how each form came to be as you learn its specific structure. Why do writers and readers of poetry continue to enjoy and use these old, often foreign forms—and how do they keep them alive in totally new cultural contexts? It is one of the mysteries of poetry and of art and perhaps even of life that adopting the seeming "straitjackets" of particular forms and traditions inspires creativity and new life rather than restricting it. This is why your parents pondered carefully what to name you when you were born. Your full name represents a received form within which you will create your own unique personhood. Your name and your life are at once fully rooted in history, yet fully original. Such are the poems you will read in this chapter: examples of poems from every era and every attitude of life that closely adhere to verse forms that emerged in a specific setting but have heartily stood the test of time. Don't forget the poetic devices of image, metaphor, symbol, tone, sound, and words as you begin looking at these structures that have housed meaning in specific ways over the years. Don't let formal study or imitation of these classic forms take precedence over the other elements of poetry. Enjoy them whole!

Villanelle

This form's natural beginning was as an Italian rustic song of the harvest. *Villano* is an Italian word for "peasant," and *villa* is Latin for "country or farm house." People sang songs in rounds as they harvested crops in the fields. Imagine the repetitive motion of the scythe and the way in which the repetitive lines of the villanelle might accompany that gesture. By the time it was written down, the villanelle had taken shape as a French pastoral poem. It became very popular in France and eventually moved to England in the 1900s when England was borrowing heavily from French poetry. The twentieth century has used it well as a form that provides a structure for powerful emotions such as love, loss, and obsession.

This form has nineteen lines and includes five tercets (three-lined stanzas) and one quatrain (four-lined stanza). There are two repeated, alternating refrains. The first line is a refrain and is repeated in lines 6, 12, and 18; the third line is also a refrain and is repeated in lines 9, 15, and 19. The end words of these lines rhyme throughout the poem, simply by virtue of their (more or less) exact repetition. The middle lines of each stanza must rhyme with each other as well, giving the villanelle two basic rhyming sounds. This means there is a lot of repetition—whole lines and sounds—which is why it's such a useful form to express obsession or intense emotion. Contemporary poets create a more natural sounding "song" in the villanelle form by enjambing (causing lines to run on into the next line as opposed to ending the sense and rhythm of the line when the line ends). The whole is usually written in iambic meter, and the classic form uses a five-foot or pentameter line.

LEARNING TO READ CLOSELY

Elizabeth Bishop (1911–1979)

One Art

The art of losing isn't hard to master;
so many things seem filled with the intent
to be lost that their loss is no disaster.

Lose something every day. Accept the fluster
5 of lost door keys, the hour badly spent.
The art of losing isn't hard to master.

Then practice losing farther, losing faster:
places, and names, and where it was you meant
to travel. None of these will bring disaster.

10 I lost my mother's watch. And look! my last, or
next-to-last, of three loved houses went.
The art of losing isn't hard to master.

I lost two cities, lovely ones. And, vaster,
some realms I owned, two rivers, a continent.
15 I miss them, but it wasn't a disaster.

—Even losing you (the joking voice, a gesture
I love) I shan't have lied. It's evident
the art of losing's not too hard to master
though it may look like (*Write it!*) like disaster

Contemporary versions of the villanelle often present feelings that aren't entirely clear or explicable. The speaker in *One Art* uses the repetitive villanelle form to revisit a subject that isn't resolved or entirely clear and explores it through repeated contact and from approaching the material from different angles. The speaker in this poem insists for many lines that "The art of losing isn't hard to master." Yet the second repeating refrain acknowledges that the experience of loss can seem difficult indeed, "like disaster." This second refrain changes throughout the poem but always ends with the word "disaster." The speaker's tone of voice seems overly insistent, cheerful, and bright from the opening of the poem: it isn't hard to lose things; loss is surmountable, you can become an expert at it. Breezily the speaker insists that things themselves seem intent on becoming lost and then rattles off a list of the kinds of small losses we all incur: "door keys," an hour, the name of an acquaintance.

As the poem unfolds stanza-by-stanza, the types of losses incurred become weightier. There is a cascade of loss down the page that builds in mass and significance. We start with "door keys" and move on to "places, and names, and where it was you meant / to travel," which suggests forgetfulness, or possibly hopes that die naturally in the course of living. By the fourth stanza we are up to family heirlooms and houses—places that were home but to which we will not return. The speaker is also admitting that she will "miss them." This admission takes the breezy confidence down a peg, but still the speaker will not admit to the disaster that we sense lurking around the poem. By stanza five, enormous losses in the physical world—"realms I owned, two rivers, a continent"—have gathered on the list.

Yet despite, or because of, this careful buildup of losses, we are totally unprepared for the disaster waiting for us in the last stanza. The speaker turns from addressing some abstract audience (the reader perhaps) and addresses a specific individual. The emotional unraveling of the insistent voice, which tells us over and over again that this art form (loss) is manageable, becomes dramatically visible in the last stanza. It begins with a dash as if to suggest that something is being interrupted or extended. We are suddenly painfully aware here that a beloved has been lost—we see this in the keen memories placed in parentheses. The little parentheses seem to function as the speaker's attempt to control the entrance of memory, but it pushes through nonetheless just as the phrases "the joking voice, a gesture / I love," thrust their way into the poem.

The speaker insists that it is not lying to say that this, too, is no disaster, not hard to master. Yet as readers we are aware that the very use of the word "lied" suggests the possible presence of untruth that we've been perceiving in the voice from stanza 1. The voice contains too much insistence, confidence, self-mastery. It is the caesura, or pause, that occurs with the period after the word "lied" that gives us time as readers to ask the question "Why do you need to assure us you aren't lying?" The shifty, legal-sounding phrase that abruptly breaks at line 17—"It's evident..."—further arouses our suspicion of this speaker's claims of emotional indifference to loss. In the next line the speaker admits this art is in fact "too" hard to master, admitting difficulty but still attempting to qualify the extent of the difficulty, still insisting on mastery. In the last line the speaker confesses that it does look like disaster and has to speak commandingly to herself to write the word that all along she has attempted to avoid: "disaster." It is as if the speaker believes that as long as she can keep that word at bay, contained through the formal restraints of the villanelle, the disaster won't be real and she can command her emotional life.

The art form of the villanelle has long been and continues to be a medium for managing a deep and unutterable pain. By the poem's end that pain—made real for us by the poet's craft— has broken through the strictly controlled structure of the villanelle. While the villanelle has been perfectly executed, it was not able to control the emotional matter. This is a truly masterful marriage of form and content.

ANTHOLOGY

Edwin Arlington Robinson (1869-1935)

The House on the Hill

They are all gone away,
The House is shut and still,
There is nothing more to say.

Through broken walls and gray
5   The winds blow bleak and shrill;
They are all gone away.

Nor is there one to-day
To speak them good or ill:
There is nothing more to say.

10   Why is it then we stray
Around that sunken sill?
They are all gone away,

And our poor fancy-play
For them is wasted skill:
15   There is nothing more to say.

There is ruin and decay
In the House on the Hill:
They are all gone away,
There is nothing more to say.

1. This villanelle is simpler than some others you'll encounter. The repeated lines state directly "They are all gone away, / There is nothing more to say." Well, one might respond, if there is nothing more to say, why are you writing a poem about it? But the speaker seems to be asking the same question: Why are we still drawn to this place despite its air of abandonment? What makes this theme of an inexplicable curiosity or of being drawn to a place compatible with the villanelle form?

2. What do you notice about the words that are rhymed? Do they help to solve the mystery at all?

3. Have you ever been inexplicably drawn to a place, or to a place/experience filled with "ruin and decay"?

4. What might be the positive value in meditating on or writing about such a negative compulsion?

Sestina

This form was developed in France by medieval troubadours. The inventor of the form (invention isn't owned solely by the world of science) was Arnaut Daniel. He belonged to a group of twelfth-century poets who entertained people with their verse. The word *trobar* means "to invent or compose verse." Troubadour poets were the rock stars of their eras—they served as court poets for noblemen and competed with each other to make funny and complicated verse structures.

The sestina is a favorite form among modern poets. Ezra Pound once called the form "a thin sheet of flame folding and infolding upon itself." The form can be fun to work with and is good for playful spirits as well as more serious emotions.

The sestina has thirty-nine lines, divided into six stanzas with six lines in each and an envoi of three lines at the end. The same six end words are used and repeated in a prescribed, varied order throughout the poem. Like a cross-country drill in which the runner from the back runs to the front of the line to lead for a little while, the order of the repeated words is strictly dictated. In the first stanza, the end word of the last line is the end word of the first line of the second stanza. Are you confused yet? After the first stanza establishes the six set end words, each of the succeeding stanzas rearrange the prior stanza's end words this way: 6, 1, 5, 2, 4, 3. The final envoi must use the six words again, two in each line, in any order desired. It's easiest to grasp this form by looking at an example and marking it up yourself with numbers to see the pattern. The repeating words don't usually rhyme, though feel free to try. Sometimes contemporary poets alter the end words with suffixes, homophones, or slant rhymes to keep surprise in the poem. The challenge, of course, is to sustain a fresh and real meaning in your chosen theme through such a long, rigidly prescribed form.

ANTHOLOGY

Sir Philip Sidney (1554–1586)

Old Arcadia

Book 4, page 2; Agelastus speaking

Since wailing is a bud of causeful sorrow,
Since sorrow is the follower of ill fortune,
Since no ill fortune equals public damage,
Now prince's loss hath made our damage public,
5   Sorrow pay we unto the rights of Nature,
And inward grief seal up with outward wailing.

Why should we spare our voice from endless wailing,
Who justly make our hearts the seats of sorrow,
In such a case where it appears that Nature
10 Doth add her force unto the sting of fortune,
Choosing alas, this our theatre public,
Where they would leave trophies of cruel damage?

Then since such pow'rs conspire unto our damage
(Which may be known, but never helped with wailing)
15   Yet let us leave a monument in public,
Of willing tears, torn hair, and cries of sorrow.
For lost, lost is by blow of cruel fortune
Arcadia's gem, the noblest child of Nature.

O Nature doting old, O blinded Nature,
20   How has thou torn thyself, sought thine own damage,
In granting such a scope to filthy fortune,
By thy imp's loss to fill the world with wailing!
Cast thy stepmother eyes upon our sorrow,
Public our loss: so, see, thy shame is public.

25   O that we had, to make our woes more public,
Seas in our eyes, and brazen tongues by nature,
A yelling voice, and hearts composed of sorrow,
Breath made of flames, wits knowing naught but damage,
Our sports murd'ring ourselves, our musics wailing,
30   Our studies fixed upon the falls of fortune.

No, no, our mischief grows in this vile fortune,
That private pangs cannot breathe out in public
The furious inward griefs with hellish wailing;
But forced are to burden feeble Nature
35   With secret sense of our eternal damage,
And sorrow feed, feeding our souls with sorrow.

Since sorrow then concludeth all our fortune,
With all our deaths show we this damage public.
His nature fears to die who lives still wailing.

Sir Philip Sidney

1. See if you can piece together the meaning of this complex poem by starting with the end words. What do they suggest the poem is about? What are the six words that keep repeating? Do they contain a summary of the "story" of the poem?

2. Do you remember, as you are reading the poem, that these words are being repeated at the ends of lines, or does the subject of the poem distract you from them?

3. Describe in your own words what the poem's last stanza—in particular the last line—is saying.

Dante Alighieri (1265–1321)
translated by Dante Gabriel Rossetti (1828–1882)

Of The Lady Pietra Degli Scrovigni

O the dim light and the large circle of shade
I have clomb, and to the whitening of the hills,
There where we see no color in the grass.
Natheless my longing loses not its green,
5 It has so taken root in the hard stone
Which talks and hears as though it were a lady.

Utterly frozen is this youthful lady,
Even as the snow that lies within the shade;
For she is no more moved than is the stone
10 By the sweet season which makes warm the hills
And alters from afresh from white to green
Covering their sides again with flowers and grass.

When on her hair she sets a crown of grass
The thought has no more room for other lady,
15 Because she weaves the yellow with the green
So well that Love sits down there in the shade,—
Love who has shut me in among low hills
Faster than between walls of granite-stone.

She is more bright than is a precious stone;
20 The wound she gives may not be healed with grass:
I therefore have fled far o'er plains and hills
For refuge from so dangerous a lady;
But from her sunshine nothing can give shade,—
Not any hill, nor wall, nor summer-green.

25 A while ago, I saw her dressed in green,—
So fair, she might have wakened in a stone
This love which I do feel even for her shade;
And therefore, as one woos a graceful lady,
I wooed her in a field that was all grass
30 Girdled about with very lofty hills.

Yet shall the streams turn back and climb the hills
Before Love's flame in this damp wood and green
Burn, as it burns within a youthful lady,
For my sake, who would sleep away in stone
35 My life, or feed like beasts upon the grass,
Only to see her garments cast a shade.

How dark so'er the hills throw out their shade,
Under her summer-green the beautiful lady
Covers it, like a stone cover'd in grass.

1. This sestina is also an elegy for a dead beloved. How does the speaker feel about his dead lady?

2. How does the repetitive form of the sestina serve to communicate his, almost illogical, attachment to her?

3. How does the writer use the six base words to get a range of meanings, so that though the words are repetitive, the meaning is expanded?

4. Look up some contemporary sestinas online to see how the old form has been updated. Look for: *Sestina* by Elizabeth Bishop, *After the Trial* by Weldon Kees, and *Sestina: Here in Katmandu* by Donald Justice.

Sonnet

The word "sonnet" comes from the Italian *sahn-et* meaning "little song," or from the medieval Latin *sonitus*, which means "murmur, soft sound or noise." The sonnet is a poem with fourteen rhymed iambic pentameter lines. It originated in Italy in the thirteenth century and didn't migrate to England until 200 years later. In the Sicilian court of Frederick II (AD 1220), officials (including the emperor) passed these poems back and forth (a bit like notes in class). It is believed that Jacopo da Lentini invented the sonnet.

The most important aspect of the sonnet in terms of ideas and structure is the construction of its parts. There is an initial body of lines that present an argument, meditation, scene, portrait, list, or small story, and then there is a turn (or *volta*, which means "turning, or turning point") where the argument, narrative, or question of the first part is answered or resolved.

In English poetry, two distinct versions of the sonnet emerged and have survived as active verse forms—the Petrarchan (or Italian) and the Shakespearean (or English). The differences between them concern the location of the turn or *volta* and a variation in the rhyme scheme. In the Petrarchan sonnet (named for the Italian Renaissance poet Petrarch, 1304–1374), the turn comes in the eighth of fourteen lines; in the Shakespearean sonnet, the turn comes toward the end, in the twelfth line. The Petrarchan sonnet tends to have a reasoned tone with an argument and response (call and response) motion, leaving time after the turn to give another point of view some room to develop. The Petrarchan sonnet has the following as its basic rhyme scheme: *abbaabba cdcdcd*. Poets have experimented with various endings that alter this basic scheme, including the following combinations for the last six lines: *cdece ccdccd cddcdd cdecde cddcee*. As you can see, there is a lot of room for variation in the rhyme schemes. An interesting note on Petrarch is that he created many sonnets for a lady, "Laura," who never existed!

In the Shakespearean form, there are three quatrains (four-line stanzas) and one couplet, with the *volta* usually taking place at the couplet. You can tell, without having read many sonnets, that this means the Shakespearean will have more emphasis on the problem, scene, or argument, with a very quick and sometimes unexpected change at the end. Often the resolution is a general one and less developed than that of the Italian sonnet. To adjust for this, the end couplet is often the most declarative, powerful part of the sonnet. The Shakespearean rhyme scheme is *abab cdcd efef gg*.

The sonnet has been successfully used by many poets writing in English, some of whom have adapted the form slightly. These include Sir Thomas Wyatt, John Keats, Robert Frost, William Wordsworth, Percy Bysshe Shelley, Alfred Tennyson, Elizabeth Barrett Browning, Robert Lowell, John Berryman, and Gwendolyn Brooks, to name a few. Poets writing today are still using and changing this tight music box of a poem.

LEARNING TO READ CLOSELY

John Milton (1608–1674)

On His Blindness

When I consider how my light is spent
   E're half my days, in this dark world and wide,
   And that one Talent which is death to hide,
   Lodg'd with me useless, though my Soul more bent
5 To serve therewith my Maker, and present
   My true account, least he returning chide,
   Doth God exact day-labour, light deny'd,
   I fondly ask: But patience to prevent
That murmur, soon replies, God doth not need
10 Either man's work or his own gifts, who best
   Bear his milde yoak, they serve him best, his State
Is Kingly. Thousands at his bidding speed
   And post o're Land and Ocean without rest:
   They also serve who only stand and waite.

John Milton

In this poem, Milton uses the Petrarchan sonnet form to explore an argument that he has been having with himself and perhaps with his God. The two-part form—eight lines in the first and six lines in the second—works handily with the poet's theme of wrestling with the burden of his blindness. The biographical information is that Milton himself did go blind. Imagine what it is like to be a great reader and writer and then to lose your sight. This is what the speaker is grappling with as he examines his dilemma in a dialogue with himself, speaking it aloud, and ultimately hearing an encouraging, reassuring response.

The sonnet opens with the metaphor of light being spent, almost like money or any resource that we have and then use up. We know from the poem's title that the spent light is in fact spent sight. We know from the words, "When I consider" that the speaker is evaluating how he has used his light, his time. He alludes to the "Talent which is death to hide," which references both his gifts as a writer and the gospel parable of the talents—in which the master left money with his servants and then the master returned to see how the servants had invested the money. The speaker feels that his talent (reading and writing) is "Lodged with [him] useless," though he wishes to serve his maker, God, with his gift and skill.

The speaker worries that the "Maker" will return and chide him for not using his talent (this happens to one servant in the parable of the talents). He cries out asking if God expects him to labor without his light—does God expect him to read and write without sight? It is at this anguished question that the first part of the sonnet concludes, and the punctuation of line 8 signals the turn, for the semicolon marks the only heavy pause in the whole poem.

The one who answers the question is Patience, personified; Patience insists that God doesn't need our work, for he is kingly and has thousands to do his bidding. Rather, says Patience, the way in which we serve God best is to "bear his milde yoak," another reference to a New Testament passage, in which Milton was well versed along with all of Greek mythology and history. This suggests that accepting the burdens we are given is part of our good service to our Creator. The poem ends (still spoken in the voice of Patience) with the encouraging assurance that both action ("Thousands at his bidding speed / and post o'er Land and Ocean without rest") and inaction ("They...who only stand and waite") are forms of service that God values, needs, and in which He delights.

The sonnet form demonstrates the inner argument that this speaker (presumably Milton) is having with himself. In the first lines he states his case and has his day in court, much like Job, the long-suffering Old Testament figure who requests a confrontation with God. In the second part of the poem the answer comes back to the speaker in the call and response pattern of the sonnet. The end rhymes encapsulate his struggle: "spent," "wide," "hide," "bent," "present," "chide," "deny'd," and "prevent" (before the turn) and "need," "best," "State," "speed," "rest," and "waite" (after the turn). In these compressed lists we can see the speaker's concern about his work and his need to perform for a king (his Maker); the sorrow and fear he experiences as he contemplates his lack of performance; and the answering encouragement to trust the King—"rest," "waite"—in other words, to accept his state.

One of the things that makes this poem great is its tone. The speaker's question is a terrible one—how can I make something good out of my life if the tools I need have been taken from me? Yet he asks it "fondly" and refers to it as a "murmur." The speaker puzzles through the maze of his thoughts and fears; he wrestles, but the opponent with whom he wrestles—God—is someone he loves, someone with whom he has had a long relationship. The tone of the poem gives the feeling of an argument you might hear between a husband and wife in a healthy marriage. The problem is real and there are two sides, but great love and affection are present as well. In fact, John Milton ultimately wrote his greatest work, line by difficult line, as a blind man. This work is *Paradise Lost*, about Adam and Eve being cast out of the Garden of Eden. It is considered one of the greatest epics ever written.

ANTHOLOGY

William Shakespeare (1564–1616)

That time of year thou mayst in me behold (Sonnet 73)

That time of year thou mayst in me behold
When yellow leaves, or none, or few, do hang
Upon those boughs which shake against the cold,
Bare ruined choirs, where late the sweet birds sang.
5   In me thou see'st the twilight of such day
As after sunset fadeth in the west;
Which by and by black night doth take away,
Death's second self, that seals all up in rest.
In me thou see'st the glowing of such fire,
10   That on the ashes of his youth doth lie,
As the deathbed whereon it must expire,
Consumed with that which it was nourished by.
    This thou perceiv'st, which makes thy love more strong,
    To love that well which thou must leave ere long.

1. Because you know this was written by Shakespeare, identify the type of sonnet used.

2. What is the statement the poet is making?

3. What is the response to this fear, loss, or regret?

4. How does he achieve the tone of sweet sadness?

5. Have you experienced this truth in love, that often we love something or someone more as our time draws to a close?

6. Trace the images that Shakespeare uses to talk about the approach of death. How do they work? What images would you use?

7. What does autumn make you think of?

8. What is the effect of the couplet at the end? Does it convince you?

John Keats (1795–1821)

On First Looking into Chapman's Homer

Much have I travell'd in the realms of gold,
  And many goodly states and kingdoms seen;
  Round many western islands have I been
Which bards in fealty to Apollo hold.
5   Oft of one wide expanse had I been told
  That deep-brow'd Homer ruled as his demesne;
  Yet did I never breathe its pure serene
Till I heard Chapman speak out loud and bold:
Then felt I like some watcher of the skies
10 When a new planet swims into his ken;
  Or like stout Cortez when with eagle eyes
He star'd at the Pacific—and all his men
Look'd at each other with a wild surmise—
  Silent, upon a peak in Darien.

1. Have you ever had the experience of reading a book that came alive and brought the writer and the story near to you?

2. What is the dilemma or question being considered in this sonnet, and where is the turn?

3. What type of sonnet is this? Do you think it is the best type for the theme?

4. Who are the figures and places mentioned here (part of being a good reader is being willing to look things up): Homer, Apollo, Chapman, Cortez, Pacific, Darien? Try Wikipedia and *Benét's Reader's Encyclopedia*. Give your class a small report and then try reading the poem again.

5. What is an odyssey? How is reading like an odyssey?

John Donne (1572–1631)

Death Be Not Proud (Holy Sonnet 10)

Death, be not proud, though some have called thee
Mighty and dreadful, for thou are not so;
For those whom thou think'st thou dost overthrow
Die not, poor Death, nor yet canst thou kill me.
5   From rest and sleep, which but thy pictures be,
Much pleasure; then from thee much more must flow,
And soonest our best men with thee do go,
Rest of their bones, and soul's delivery.
Thou'art slave to fate, chance, kings, and desperate men,
10 And dost with poison, war, and sickness dwell,
And poppy'or charms can make us sleep as well
And better than thy stroke; why swell'st thou then?
One short sleep past, we wake eternally,
And death shall be no more; Death, thou shalt die.

John Donne

1. What is this poem about?

2. How could death die?

3. Does the speaker feel any conflict in his thoughts about death?

4. What type of sonnet is this? Where is the turn?

5. Why do you think the poet violates the sonnet rhyme scheme by ending on a word that doesn't have a rhyme? (The answer isn't that Donne is a bad poet!)

Ballad

Some (namely the writer Borges in an essay called "The Telling of the Tale") have lamented the fact that the story-song aspect of the epic has passed out of our common experience in contemporary times. The ballad is an exception. While it doesn't live up to the scope and grandeur of the epic, it does combine both story and song. It is a short narrative poem that is also songlike and typically has four-line stanzas (quatrains) that are metered and rhymed. The subject matter often deals with lost love, supernatural events, and communal stories. Often the subject involves scandal—murder, disgrace, or betrayal in love. We can hear the ballad form today in country and folk music and also in rap music. The form and function of the poem lend it to dialogue and language that is close to everyday use (also called the **vernacular**). The rhyme scheme is usually *abab* or *abcb*. The meter is the same as hymn meter (see Emily Dickinson's poems in chapter twelve, page 154) which alternates four beats and three beats every other line (iambic tetrameter and iambic trimester).

Historically the role of the balladeer was defined according to his country and era. This form partakes of the oral tradition in that many times the balladeer remained anonymous and was a witness to political events, natural disasters, in essence a recorder of history. This form began as early as (and possibly earlier than) the fourteenth and fifteenth centuries. The structure and way of speaking came from conversation as opposed to being written first. The ballad is rooted in a place and often connected to a people group. Scottish ballads came with Scottish immigrants who settled in Appalachia and have carried on the tradition. The literary ballad is now a poetic and written form that took its start from this rich oral history. The communal aspect of the ballad has changed in that the person singing the story is not often singing for the group but for herself.

ANTHOLOGY

Anonymous

The Cherry-Tree Carol

i, I

Joseph was an old man,
    And an old man was he,
When he wedded Mary
    In the land of Galilee.

II

5   Joseph and Mary walk'd
    Through an orchard good,
Where was cherries and berries
    So red as any blood.

III

Joseph and Mary walk'd
10   Through an orchard green,
Where was berries and cherries
    As thick as might be seen.

IV

O then bespoke Mary,
    So meek and so mild,
15 'Pluck me one cherry, Joseph,
    For I am with child.'

V

O then bespoke Joseph
    With words so unkind,
'Let him pluck thee a cherry
20   That brought thee with child.'

VI

O then bespoke the babe
    Within his mother's womb,
'Bow down then the tallest tree
    For my mother to have some.'

VII

25 Then bow'd down the highest tree
    Unto his mother's hand:
Then she cried, 'See, Joseph,
    I have cherries at command!'

VIII

O then bespake Joseph—
30   'I have done Mary wrong;
But cheer up, my dearest,
    And be not cast down.

IX

'O eat your cherries, Mary,
    O eat your cherries now;
35 O eat your cherries, Mary,
    That grow upon the bough.'

X

Then Mary pluck'd a cherry
    As red as the blood;
Then Mary went home
40   With her heavy load.

ii, XI

As Joseph was a-walking,
    He heard an angel sing:
'This night shall be born
    Our heavenly King.

XII

45 'He neither shall be born
    In house nor in hall,
Nor in the place* of Paradise,   palace
    But in an ox's stall.

XIII

'He neither shall be clothéd
50 In purple nor in pall*,   fine cloth
But all in fair linen,
   As were babies all.

XIV

'He neither shall be rock'd
   In silver nor in gold,
55 But in a wooden cradle
   That rocks on the mould.

XV

He neither shall be christen'd
   In white wine nor red,
But with fair spring water
60   With which we were christenéd.

iii, XVI

Then Mary took her young son
   And set him on her knee;
'I pray thee now, dear child,
   Tell how this world shall be.' –

XVII

65 'O I shall be as dead, mother,
   As the stones in the wall;
O the stones in the street, mother,
   Shall mourn for me all.

XVIII

'And upon a Wednesday
70   My vow I will make,
And upon Good Friday
   My death I will take.

XIX

'Upon Easter-day, mother,
   My uprising shall be;
75 O the sun and the moon, mother,
   Shall both rise with me!'

1. Try saying this poem aloud then try to put it to a tune and sing it. What about saying it makes you think of song? What are the elements that create that sensation?

2. What is the story? How does the retelling of a familiar story change with this telling?

3. What does the cherry tree add to the story and how does the atmosphere surrounding it affect the story?

4. What is strange or unexpected about this ballad? What other aspects of the ballad do you recognize?

Anne Askew (1521–1546)

The Ballad Which Anne Askew Made and Sang When She Was in Newgate

(Askew was arrested and examined for heresy in June 1545. She was released but arrested again in June 1546, subjected to torture and burned at the stake the next month. This ballad was included in the Protestant Bishop John Bale's two accounts of her examination and death. Newgate is a London prison.)

Like as the armed knight
Appointed to the field,
With this world will I fight
And Faith shall be my shield.

5 Faith is that weapon strong
Which will not fail at need.
My foes, therefore, among
Therewith will I proceed.

As it is had in strength
10 And force of Christ's way
It will prevail at length
Though all the devils say nay.

Faith in the fathers old
Obtained rightwisness
15 Which make me very bold
To fear no world's distress.

I now rejoice in heart
And Hope bid me do so
For Christ will take my part
20 And ease me of my woe.

Thou sayst, lord, who so knock,
To them wilt thou attend.
Undo, therefore, the lock
And thy strong power send.

25 More enemies now I have
Than hairs upon my head.
Let them not me deprave
But fight thou in my stead.

On thee my care I cast.
30 For all their cruel spite
I set not by their haste
For thou art my delight.

I am not she that list
My anchor to let fall
35 For every drizzling mist
My ship substantial.

Not oft use I to write
In prose nor yet in rime,
Yet will I show one sight
40 That I saw in my time.

I saw a royal throne
Where Justice should have sit
But in her stead was one
Of moody cruel wit.

45 Absorbed was rightwisness
As of the raging flood
Satan in his excess
Sucked up the guiltless blood.

Then thought I, Jesus lord,
50 When thou shalt judge us all
Hard is it to record
On these men what will fall.

Yet lord, I thee desire
For that they do to me
55 Let them not taste the hire
Of their iniquity.

1. What do you make of the comparison of a Christian woman martyr to an armed knight?

2. What do you notice about the function of the ballad based on the way in which this story-song is identified (made and sung when she was in Newgate prison)? What are the benefits to having a form that is flexible enough to record historic stories that can be sung?

3. Do you think the ballad might be of social and political use?

Anonymous

Scarborough Fair

Are you going to Scarborough Fair?
Parsley, sage, rosemary and thyme,
Remember me to one who lives there,
For once she was a true love of mine.

5   Have her make me a cambric shirt,
Parsley, sage, rosemary and thyme,
Without a seam or fine needle work,
And then she'll be a true love of mine.

Have her wash it in yonder dry well,
10   Parsley, sage, rosemary and thyme,
Where ne'er a drop of water e'er fell.
And then she'll be a true love of mine.

Have her find me an acre of land
Parsley, sage, rosemary and thyme,
15   Between the sea and over the sand,
And then she'll be a true love of mine.

Plow the land with the horn of a lamb
Parsley, sage, rosemary and thyme,
Then sow some seeds from north of the dam
20   And then she'll be a true love of mine.

If she tells me she can't, I'll reply
Parsley, sage, rosemary and thyme,
Let me know that at least she will try
And then she'll be a true love of mine.

25   Love imposes impossible tasks,
Parsley, sage, rosemary and thyme,
Though not more than any heart asks
And I must know she's a true love of mine.

Dear, when thou has finished thy task,
30   Parsley, sage, rosemary and thyme,
Come to me, my hand for to ask,
For then thou art a true love of mine.

This is an example of a ballad that began as a poem to be sung in the oral tradition, in which people pass songs down through the generations. It has been sung by famous contemporary musicians such as Simon and Garfunkle.

1. Circle all the rhymes.

2. What is the effect of the lines that repeat?

3. Why do you think repeated lines are so common in songs?

4. What other repetitions do you notice, in addition to the refrain?

5. What is the effect of so much repetition?

6. Sing this ballad together (preferably with guitar).

7. How much of a story gets told?

8. What is the feeling that the song/poem creates? How does it create that feeling?

9. What makes this a poem rather than a song? Is there a difference between song lyrics and poetry? Argue your position with another.

Blank Verse

This is another verse form given to us by the Italians. They call it "verse free from rhyme," which is noticeable in their language since the multitude of *a* and *o* endings in Italian words creates abundant rhyme. The inspiration for developing blank verse was the classical epic, which enjoyed a renewal during the Renaissance. There were some Italians using blank verse in the early sixteenth century. In England it was the Earl of Surrey, Henry Howard, who first utilized blank verse in English. He translated *The Aeneid* by Virgil into English and used blank verse to do it.

Blank verse is an iambic line with ten stresses and five beats. It is unrhymed, and it is considered the poetic form closest to natural speech in English. It enabled poetry to be formalized without being overpowered by the hypnotic sound of rhyme. The composition could be rhythmic yet elevated, and ideas could be developed more fully with less structural complexity. Shakespeare used blank verse for his plays, as did Christopher Marlowe. John Milton used it for his epic *Paradise Lost*.

Contemporary American poetics value direct, plain speech and shorter sentences, which don't mix well with the longer, more complex sentences of blank verse. Robert Frost was really the last American poet to use blank verse significantly. While blank verse represented freedom for the Renaissance writers using it, compared to open verse (discussed in chapter 13) it is restrictive.

ANTHOLOGY

William Shakespeare (1564–1616)

The Tempest

Act 3, scene 2, lines 144–52; Caliban speaking to Stephano

> Be not afeard; the isle is full of noises,
> Sounds and sweet airs, that give delight and hurt not.
> Sometimes a thousand twangling instruments
> Will hum about mine ears, and sometime voices
> 5 That, if I then had waked after long sleep,
> Will make me sleep again: and then, in dreaming,
> The clouds methought would open and show riches
> Ready to drop upon me that, when I waked,
> I cried to dream again.

1. Count out the syllables and the stresses; there should be ten or eleven and five respectively, except in the last line.

2. Why is it significant that the rhythmic line is talking about sounds, hums, and noises?

3. Have you ever been awakened abruptly and "cried to dream again"? What does it mean to do this? Why are dreams sometimes mesmerizing in this way?

4. What about blank verse is mesmerizing and therefore enacts the sense of that line in its sound?

William Shakespeare (1564–1616)

Julius Caesar

Act 3, scene 2, lines 70–104; Antony speaking

Friends, Romans, countrymen, lend me your ears;
I come to bury Caesar, not to praise him.
The evil that men do lives after them;
The good is oft interred with their bones;
5   So let it be with Caesar. The noble Brutus
Hath told you Caesar was ambitious:
If it were so, it was a grievous fault,
And grievously hath Caesar answer'd it.
Here, under leave of Brutus and the rest—
10   For Brutus is an honourable man;
So are they all, all honourable men—
Come I to speak in Caesar's funeral.
He was my friend, faithful and just to me:
But Brutus says he was ambitious;
15   And Brutus is an honourable man.
He hath brought many captives home to Rome
Whose ransoms did the general coffers fill:
Did this in Caesar seem ambitious?
When that the poor have cried, Caesar hath wept:
20   Ambition should be made of sterner stuff:
Yet Brutus says he was ambitious;
And Brutus is an honourable man.
You all did see that on the Lupercal
I thrice presented him a kingly crown,
25   Which he did thrice refuse: was this ambition?
Yet Brutus says he was ambitious;
And, sure, he is an honourable man.
I speak not to disprove what Brutus spoke,
But here I am to speak what I do know.
30   You all did love him once, not without cause:
What cause withholds you then, to mourn for him?
O judgment! thou art fled to brutish beasts,
And men have lost their reason. Bear with me;
My heart is in the coffin there with Caesar,
35   And I must pause till it come back to me.

Notice how well the blank verse form works for an argument, for something that is complex. Notice how the form is flexible; it doesn't have to be exact; there are exceptions to the beat.

1. Shakespeare's speaker, Mark Antony, is addressing a crowd at the funeral for the assassinated emperor Julius Caesar. Where does he use repetitive refrain?

2. Is there anything in the text of the speech or in the poetic language to suggest that the speaker is using his refrains sarcastically or ironically?

3. Can you find other poems in this book or elsewhere that use repeated statements to change the tone of the speaker or to cast suspicion upon the statement itself?

Robert Frost (1874–1963)

Birches

When I see birches bend to left and right
Across the lines of straighter darker trees,
I like to think some boy's been swinging them.
But swinging doesn't bend them down to stay
5   As ice-storms do. Often you must have seen them
Loaded with ice a sunny winter morning
After a rain. They click upon themselves
As the breeze rises, and turn many-colored
As the stir cracks and crazes their enamel.
10   Soon the sun's warmth makes them shed crystal shells
Shattering and avalanching on the snow-crust—
Such heaps of broken glass to sweep away
You'd think the inner dome of heaven had fallen.
They are dragged to the withered bracken by the load,
15   And they seem not to break; though once they are bowed
So low for long, they never right themselves:
You may see their trunks arching in the woods
Years afterwards, trailing their leaves on the ground
Like girls on hands and knees that throw their hair
20   Before them over their heads to dry in the sun.
But I was going to say when Truth broke in
With all her matter-of-fact about the ice-storm
I should prefer to have some boy bend them
As he went out and in to fetch the cows—
25   Some boy too far from town to learn baseball,
Whose only play was what he found himself,
Summer or winter, and could play alone.
One by one he subdued his father's trees
By riding them down over and over again
30   Until he took the stiffness out of them,
And not one but hung limp, not one was left
For him to conquer. He learned all there was
To learn about not launching out too soon
And so not carrying the tree away
35   Clear to the ground. He always kept his poise
To the top branches, climbing carefully
With the same pains you use to fill a cup
Up to the brim, and even above the brim.
Then he flung outward, feet first, with a swish,
40   Kicking his way down through the air to the ground.
So was I once myself a swinger of birches.
And so I dream of going back to be.
It's when I'm weary of considerations,
And life is too much like a pathless wood
45   Where your face burns and tickles with the cobwebs
Broken across it, and one eye is weeping
From a twig's having lashed across it open.
I'd like to get away from earth awhile

And then come back to it and begin over.
50   May no fate willfully misunderstand me
And half grant what I wish and snatch me away
Not to return. Earth's the right place for love:
I don't know where it's likely to go better.
I'd like to go by climbing a birch tree,
55   And climb black branches up a snow-white trunk
Toward heaven, till the tree could bear no more,
But dipped its top and set me down again.
That would be good both going and coming back.
One could do worse than be a swinger of birches.

1. This is a masterful blank verse poem written by Robert Frost. How natural does it sound?

2. Can you tell there is a regular meter? Where does the poet choose to stray from the meter?

3. What is the significance of all that is contained in swinging on birches? What does it mean to the speaker, this picture of a boy swinging on birch trees? How do you know?

4. What situation or place in life might the speaker be in now as he reflects on boyhood?

5. Find three elements of poetry at work in this poem and explain how they further the poem's message or theme.

ACTIVITIES

1. Writing in each of the forms discussed in this chapter will be a huge benefit toward understanding the skill and artistry of the poems you read. It will raise your awareness about the kinds of elements that create shape, meaning, and beauty in language and enhance your admiration for the work of the masters that you are reading. Attempt a poem in each form.

2. Write a villanelle beginning with identifying the two strong, repeated lines. To help you in the writing process, choose lines from other poems (not written by you) to ensure a strong beginning and a good practice experience. Do not choose lines from other villanelles.

3. Write a sestina about a piece of art that you do not understand. Use the poem to explore possible meanings. Or write a sestina as a letter to someone and try to say something you are afraid to say. For the six repeating words, choose one adjective or adverb, one verb, and four nouns. Don't worry about making too much sense at first; just let the words guide you to a story or a subject that is important to you. Try freewriting on these words before you begin to make lines. Make lists of all the things you think of when you hear the six repeating words you've chosen.

4. Write an English or Italian sonnet. Try keeping the rhyme scheme without the iambic pentameter (work on one skill at a time to avoid feeling overwhelmed). Remember that if you choose the Italian sonnet you will have a *volta* or turn after eight lines, so tailor your choice of form according to your subject matter. Consider what your argument or question is in the poem.

5. Try writing a song together as a class about the past year, or describing (kindly) each person in the class. Use the ballad stanza. Put it to music.

6. Writing blank verse is a great way to become familiar with the rhythms in speech and to organize those rhythms. Writing blank verse also reminds us that poetry is musical and that even speaking is musical. Take one of the examples of blank verse from this book and type it into a computer file (typing it out versus copying and pasting from the Internet will help you see and hear the iambic rhythm). Insert three to six blank lines between each line of text, then print it out. Using each line as a jumping-off point, write your own lines of iambic pentameter in the spaces of this "stretched-out" poem. Then come together as a class and try to combine or reshape ten lines or more into an original poem.

7. It helps to hear a lot of blank verse to get the music of it in your ear. Watch Kenneth Branagh's film version of Shakespeare's play *Henry V,* and/or Trevor Nunn's film version of *Twelfth Night*, then read those plays aloud as a class. Try filling up two or three or ten pages in your notebook with iambic pentameter and see what happens.

VOCABULARY

Sestina: a form with six, six-line stanzas and a concluding three-line stanza. The last words of each of the first six lines of the poem must be repeated in a specific order at the ends of the lines of the next five, six-line stanzas, and all six words must finally appear in the final three-line stanza. This form originated in medieval France.

Vernacular: the plain variety of language in everyday use by ordinary people.

Villanelle: a complex form of nineteen lines and two rhymes repeated in a fixed pattern, originating in France.

11

SHAPING FORMS

{*the formal history of poetry*}

Verse forms are not the only kind of form; there are also **shaping forms**, which are not defined by meter and rhyme but rather by subject and theme. Their origin is societal. Just as words were devised from need, so too were shaping forms: the need to mourn the dead, to console the living, to celebrate and praise significant people and events, and to speak to the land from which we come. Shaping forms are communal poems and remind us that poetry has always had a place in the communities of history, for at the center of the need to be a society is the need to mark the passage of time together in poems. All of these forms came from times when poets and poetry played a very public, central role in the life of a given culture. Today these forms are kept alive by poets of all kinds, and also by government leaders, ministers and priests, famous singers and musicians, journalists, and personal or communal websites. The formal guidelines for the three shaping forms described here—the ode, the elegy, and the pastoral—are much less precise than for verse forms.

Ode

Originally a song or lyric, the ode is solemn, heroic, and elevated, often for a significant social occasion or to honor someone who has done great deeds.

This form began during the classical period with a great deal of pomp and even flattery and exaggeration. Human nature inclines us to fall into this form, as you often see when people are speaking to each other at social gatherings or public occasions. Yet as time passed, the ode form changed, and during the Romantic period other elements besides people began to be celebrated. John Keats wrote a series of historic odes to various objects and ideas, including autumn and the Grecian urn. Other poets took up the form and moved it out of its purely ceremonial (and highly political) use. Today, poets use the ode to celebrate many things, including America, animals, the Brooklyn Bridge, and large abstract ideas about meaning and existence. A commonality found in odes written across the ages is that each usually celebrates something much larger and wider than the thing itself.

LEARNING TO READ CLOSELY

Alexander Pope (1688–1744)

Ode on Solitude

I.

How happy he, who free from care
The rage of courts, and noise of towns;
Contented breathes his native air,
In his own grounds.

II.

5   Whose herds with milk, whose fields with bread,
Whose flocks supply him with attire,
Whose trees in summer yield him shade,
In winter fire.

III.

Blest! who can unconcern'dly find
10   Hours, days, and years slide swift away,
In health of body, peace of mind,
Quiet by day,

IV.

Sound sleep by night; study and ease
Together mix'd; sweet recreation,
15   And innocence, which most does please,
With meditation.

V.

Thus let me live, unheard, unknown;
Thus unlamented let me die;
Steal from the world, and not a stone
20   Tell where I lie.

Alexander Pope

Here Alexander Pope praises the life of a man who owns a few acres of land and is content to breathe "his native air." In other words, he is happy to be alone on his own land. Pope praises the self-sufficiency of such a man who has milk from his cows, who grows his own wheat for bread, whose sheep provide the wool for his clothes, and who lives wholly off of his own good land and from his own hands' work. This blessed man is further favored if he can find hours, days, years of good physical health and of mental peace. This produces good sleep, study, and ease: "sweet recreation." Somehow this keeping apart from the social world and keeping close to the natural world leads to innocence and time for meditation. The speaker goes on to say (ironically, because we are reading his poem 300 years later) that this life that he proposes is "unheard, unknown," and utterly solitary. He would like to leave the world and not have even a headstone speak of his death and life.

This solitude or withdrawal from the social realm is intertwined with the traditional "retreat to the land" mentality of the pastoral poem. The speaker is certainly not considering the stink of the animals, the back-breaking work that leaves little time for meditation, or the risk of poverty if crops should fail or disease should kill the flocks. Perhaps the speaker is meant to be a gentleman farmer who has enough income to survive without the farm and keeps it for his pleasure and leisure? There are some beautiful moments in this poem, even quotable moments ("contented breathes his native air," "sweet recreation") that are common longings. However, the poem simply omits many of the realities of the life this speaker claims to desire—not to mention the final stanza's omission of all people entirely! In this sense, Pope's poem seems an ode to a fantasy.

On the other hand, the language of this poem suggests a speaker who may in fact be well acquainted with hard work—but work of a different kind than traditional farming. We learn in the first stanza that he seeks to escape "the rage of courts" and the "noise of towns"—indicating a hectic political and urban life. Perhaps this speaker also travels a great deal, or has migrated far from his original home; he longs for "his own grounds." The final stanza, too, suggests by its exaggerated solitude—not even the stones of his land will tell where or who he is!—how deeply the speaker yearns for respite from his current life and work.

Everything in the poem works to provide this respite—if only in fantasy. Notice the formal choices of three lines of about the same length (approximately six syllables or three feet) and one short line of four syllables or two feet. The last line of each quatrain has the effect of things coming peacefully to rest, a quietness. The rhyme scheme is *abab*, which also contributes to the sense of regularity and of closure—when each wave of the rhyme scheme is completed, our expectations come to rest, to stillness. Similarly, the punctuation, which is nearly always (except once) a period, reinforces this focus on stillness.

Do you have such fantasies—either of getting away from people and the stress of your current circumstances, or of finding the right person, group, or setting? What might be the value of using the tools of poetry to write about your dreams? What might be the pitfalls?

ANTHOLOGY

Percy Bysshe Shelley (1792–1822)

Ode to the West Wind

I.

    O wild West Wind, thou breath of Autumn's being
      Thou from whose unseen presence the leaves dead
    Are driven like ghosts from an enchanter fleeing,

      Yellow, and black, and pale, and hectic red,
5   Pestilence-stricken multitudes! O thou
      Who chariotest to their dark wintry bed

    The wingèd seeds, where they lie cold and low,
      Each like a corpse within its grave, until
    Thine azure sister of the Spring shall blow

10   Her clarion o'er the dreaming earth, and fill
    (Driving sweet buds like flocks to feed in air)
      With living hues and odours plain and hill;

    Wild Spirit, which art moving everywhere;
    Destroyer and preserver; hear, O hear!

II.

15   Thou on whose stream, 'mid the steep sky's commotion,
      Loose clouds like earth's decaying leaves are shed,
    Shook from the tangled boughs of heaven and ocean,

      Angels of rain and lightning! there are spread
    On the blue surface of thine airy surge,
20   Like the bright hair uplifted from the head

    Of some fierce Mænad, even from the dim verge
      Of the horizon to the zenith's height,
    The locks of the approaching storm. Thou dirge

      Of the dying year, to which this closing night
25   Will be the dome of a vast sepulchre,
      Vaulted with all thy congregated might

    Of vapours, from whose solid atmosphere
    Black rain, and fire, and hail, will burst: O hear!

III.

Thou who didst waken from his summer dreams
30   The blue Mediterranean, where he lay,
Lull'd by the coil of his crystàlline streams,

   Beside a pumice isle in Baiæ's bay,
And saw in sleep old palaces and towers
   Quivering within the wave's intenser day,

35   All overgrown with azure moss, and flowers
   So sweet, the sense faints picturing them! Thou
For whose path the Atlantic's level powers

   Cleave themselves into chasms, while far below
The sea-blooms and the oozy woods which wear
40   The sapless foliage of the ocean, know

Thy voice, and suddenly grow gray with fear,
And tremble and despoil themselves: O hear!

IV.

If I were a dead leaf thou mightest bear;
   If I were a swift cloud to fly with thee;
45   A wave to pant beneath thy power, and share

   The impulse of thy strength, only less free
Than thou, O uncontrollable! if even
   I were as in my boyhood, and could be

The comrade of thy wanderings over heaven,
50   As then, when to outstrip thy skiey speed
Scarce seem'd a vision—I would ne'er have striven

   As thus with thee in prayer in my sore need.
O! lift me as a wave, a leaf, a cloud!
   I fall upon the thorns of life! I bleed!

55   A heavy weight of hours has chain'd and bow'd
One too like thee—tameless, and swift, and proud.

V.

Make me thy lyre, even as the forest is:
   What if my leaves are falling like its own?
The tumult of thy mighty harmonies

60   Will take from both a deep autumnal tone,
Sweet though in sadness. Be thou, Spirit fierce,
   My spirit! Be thou me, impetuous one!

Drive my dead thoughts over the universe,
   Like wither'd leaves, to quicken a new birth;
65 And, by the incantation of this verse,

   Scatter, as from an unextinguish'd hearth
Ashes and sparks, my words among mankind!
   Be through my lips to unawaken'd earth

The trumpet of a prophecy! O Wind,
70 If Winter comes, can Spring be far behind?

This famous and beautiful ode is not easy to grasp in one quick read. Take the time to read it again, out loud, noting that "thou," "thy," and "thine" are old ways of saying "you" and "your." Throughout this poem the poet is speaking directly to the West Wind.

1. Would the poem feel different if the poet had not addressed the West Wind directly and instead described the wind from the third-person voice?

2. What do you think the poet means when he asks the West Wind to "Make me thy lyre"? (Hint: He also asks the wind to "scatter…my words among mankind!")

3. What do you think the poet's state of mind is when he ends with, "If winter comes, can Spring be far behind?"? What would he be longing for in Spring, and how does this relate to the West Wind? How also does Spring relate to his ambitions for his writing life, for his words?

4. Name the meter and rhyme scheme of this poem, and identify one additional poetic tool used.

Percy Bysshe Shelley

John Keats (1795–1821)

To Autumn

1.

Season of mists and mellow fruitfulness,
  Close bosom-friend of the maturing sun;
Conspiring with him how to load and bless
  With fruit the vines that round the thatch-eves run;
5 To bend with apples the moss'd cottage-trees,
  And fill all fruit with ripeness to the core;
    To swell the gourd, and plump the hazel shells
With a sweet kernel; to set budding more,
  And still more, later flowers for the bees,
10 Until they think warm days will never cease,
    For Summer has o'er-brimm'd their clammy cells.

2.

Who hath not seen thee oft amid thy store?
  Sometimes whoever seeks abroad may find
Thee sitting careless on a granary floor,
15 Thy hair soft-lifted by the winnowing wind;
Or on a half-reap'd furrow sound asleep,
  Drows'd with the fume of poppies, while thy hook
    Spares the next swath and all its twined flowers:
And sometimes like a gleaner thou dost keep
20 Steady thy laden head across a brook;
  Or by a cyder-press, with patient look,
    Thou watchest the last oozings hours by hours.

3.

Where are the songs of Spring? Ay, where are they?
  Think not of them, thou hast thy music too,–
25 While barred clouds bloom the soft-dying day,
  And touch the stubble plains with rosy hue;
Then in a wailful choir the small gnats mourn
  Among the river sallows, borne aloft
    Or sinking as the light wind lives or dies;
30 And full-grown lambs loud bleat from hilly bourn;
  Hedge-crickets sing; and now with treble soft
  The red-breast whistles from a garden-croft;
    And gathering swallows twitter in the skies.

1. This is another ode to something in nature, but it has a very different feel and scope than Shelley's grand sweep. Can you name three ways in which the poems are similar and three ways in which they are different?

2. The poet here is extolling the season of Autumn and all that comes with it. What images or phrases in this poem struck you as exactly accurate—made you nod your head in recognition of the essence of Autumn as you have experienced it? What images or phrases surprised you?

3. As with Shelley's, this ode directly addresses Autumn as a person. In your own words, what message does Keats want to convey to Autumn in this poem?

Henry Wadsworth Longfellow (1807–1882)

The Fire of Driftwood

Devereux Farm, near Marblehead

We sat within the farm-house old,
　　Whose windows, looking o'er the bay,
Gave to the sea-breeze damp and cold,
　　An easy entrance, night and day.

5　Not far away we saw the port,
　　The strange, old-fashioned, silent town,
The lighthouse, the dismantled fort,
　　The wooden houses, quaint and brown.

We sat and talked until the night,
10　　Descending, filled the little room;
Our faces faded from the sight,
　　Our voices only broke the gloom.

We spake of many a vanished scene,
　　Of what we once had thought and said,
15　Of what had been, and might have been,
　　And who was changed, and who was dead;

And all that fills the hearts of friends,
　　When first they feel, with secret pain,
Their lives thenceforth have separate ends,
20　　And never can be one again;

The first slight swerving of the heart,
　　That words are powerless to express,
And leave it still unsaid in part,
　　Or say it in too great excess.

25　The very tones in which we spake
　　Had something strange, I could but mark;
The leaves of memory seemed to make
　　A mournful rustling in the dark.

Oft died the words upon our lips,
30　　As suddenly, from out the fire
Built of the wreck of stranded ships,
　　The flames would leap and then expire.

And, as their splendor flashed and failed,
　　We thought of wrecks upon the main,
35　Of ships dismasted, that were hailed
　　And sent no answer back again.

The windows, rattling in their frames,
　　The ocean, roaring up the beach,
The gusty blast, the bickering flames,
40　　All mingled vaguely in our speech;

Until they made themselves a part
　　Of fancies floating through the brain,
The long-lost ventures of the heart,
　　That send no answers back again.

45　O flames that glowed! O hearts that yearned!
　　They were indeed too much akin,
The drift-wood fire without that burned,
　　The thoughts that burned and glowed within.

1. What do you think this ode is celebrating or marking?

2. What does Longfellow mean when he speaks of the realization that friends sometimes know, even while they're still together, that they will have "separate ends," or when he references the "swerving of the heart"? What happens in the poem after this admission?

3. What images support the pain that he describes?

4. What are some of the formal choices that the poet makes along with the shaping and thematic choices?

Joy Harjo (1951–)

Perhaps the World Ends Here

The world begins at a kitchen table. No matter what, we must eat to live.

The gifts of earth are brought and prepared, set on the table. So it has been since creation, and it will go on.

We chase chickens or dogs away from it. Babies teethe at the corners. They scrape their knees under it.

It is here that children are given instructions on what it means to be human. We make men at it, we make women.

5   At this table we gossip, recall enemies and the ghosts of lovers.

Our dreams drink coffee with us as they put their arms around our children. They laugh with us at our poor falling-down selves and as we put ourselves back together once again at the table.

This table has been a house in the rain, an umbrella in the sun.

Wars have begun and ended at this table. It is a place to hide in the shadow of terror. A place to celebrate the terrible victory.

We have given birth on this table, and have prepared our parents for burial here.

10   At this table we sing with joy, with sorrow. We pray of suffering and remorse. We give thanks.

Perhaps the world will end at the kitchen table, while we are laughing and crying, eating of the last sweet bite.

This is an ode to a kitchen table, which is a literal piece of furniture. The poet clearly demonstrates all that happens at the table, and therefore all that is symbolized or contained within the image of the table.

1. List some of the things that happen at the table. Is the list universal, or does it seem to belong to a particular culture?

2. Learn a little bit about the poet, Joy Harjo, by checking out a book of her poems or researching her on the Internet and then revisit the previous question. Does your answer to question 1 remain the same?

3. What happens at your own kitchen table?

4. What do you make of the form of the long lines standing singly by themselves? How would the tone of the poem be different if Harjo had written in first person ("I") rather than in the third person ("we")?

5. Would the poem work if the poet had personified the table and addressed it directly? Why or why not?

6. What effect do the title and the final stanza have on the overall tone of this poem? Is it sad, happy, or something else?

Elegy

The elegy is a lament or mourning for someone who has died. It seeks consolation and describes the circumstances and nature of the loss. Sometimes it lists the virtues of the person who has died. The collected history of poetry, especially contemporary, shows many elegies of poets mourning other poets. The struggle, in the elegy, is between public manners and strong private feeling. The accomplishment is to make a tribute to the person who died and to give meaningful shape to the sadness of loss.

LEARNING TO READ CLOSELY

Ben Jonson (1572–1637)

On my first son

    Farewell, thou child of my right hand, and joy;
    My sin was too much hope of thee, loved boy.
    Seven years thou wert lent to me, and I thee pay,
    Exacted by thy fate, on the just day.
5   Oh, could I lose all father now! For why
    Will man lament the state he should envy?
    To have so soon 'scaped world's and flesh's rage,
    And if no other misery, yet age!
    Rest in soft peace, and asked, say, Here doth lie
10 Ben Jonson his best piece of poetry.
    For whose sake henceforth all his vows be such
    As what he loves may never like too much.

The speaker in this poem directly addresses his dead son, calling him "child of my right hand," which literally means "Benjamin," the name of the poet's son who died. Being at someone's "right hand" is a position of honor and importance, but beyond that Jonson calls him the child of his "joy." He calls his many eager hopes for his child and their life together "too much." Here on the page, the grieving father is reckoning with the shattered expectation that he and his son would have many years together. Here he says the boy was lent to him and that it is God's right to take the child back. The argument pushes forward and says that the child is in a state that the speaker should envy—a perfected, happy state outside of this "world's and flesh's rage." The living still endure the pain of physical aging, the speaker notes, and therefore this child has been blessed by death. By logical deduction, the fortunate child's father should be happy for him, he argues, but beneath the flawless logic we sense his deep loss and grief. He is wrestling with himself and his feelings, but he has not yet been able to win over his heart with his intellect.

The speaker, Ben Jonson, wishes his son to "rest in soft peace," and calls the boy his "best piece of poetry"—the best thing he ever made. Aptly this poem is an inadequate expression, for even a poem is slight in light of the ultimate poem—the boy. The grief-stricken father decides to "never like too much" that which he loves. This seems strange at first: how can the speaker not like too much what he loves, for "love" contains "like," doesn't it? The suggestion seems to be that he will never set his whole heart and hopes on a beloved again. This will not preclude love but perhaps will affect his expectations—he will hold those he loves more lightly from this time forward.

This poem is set in a single stanza with couplet rhymes. Couplet rhymes, with their tight sound pattern that is soon abandoned, reminds us of the child's short life and fading sound. We sense here that the speaker is trying to argue himself into a change of heart, and because the sonnet form is so often used for argument, and this poem is similar in length (this one is twelve lines; sonnets are fourteen lines), there is the echo of the sonnet. The sonnet form cut short is also appropriate for the subject matter, which dwells on this life cut short and the loss in the wake of the beloved's absence.

We know from history that Ben Jonson did lose a son, and that he lost a daughter, too. Historically at this time (1600s) it was common to lose children; almost every family lost one, and we hear that reality in the voice of the speaker. He accepts this as just and perhaps even to be expected. Yet he was nonetheless unprepared for the tragedy and he cannot align his heart with the reality.

Poetry and other art forms are a place where people can turn to pour out grief, to make something of sadness, or to simply give words to an enormous, shapeless feeling. Here Jonson works hard at the poetic craft, the art form, but suggests that no amount of skill will ever match the beauty, art, and craft of his son, "his best piece of poetry." Robert Frost once said, "Like a piece of ice on a hot stove, the poem must ride on its own melting." Jonson's terse, heartfelt elegy is a perfect example of how poems use finite language to help us access infinite mysteries.

Ben Johnson

ANTHOLOGY

Anne Bradstreet (1612–1672)

Verses upon the Burning of our House

In silent night when rest I took,
For sorrow near I did not look,
I waken'd was with thund'ring noise
And piteous shrieks of dreadful voice.
5   That fearful sound of "fire" and "fire,"
Let no man know is my Desire.
I starting up, the light did spy,
And to my God my heart did cry
To straighten me in my Distress
10   And not to leave me succourless.
Then coming out, behold a space
The flame consume my dwelling place.
And when I could no longer look,
I blest his grace that gave and took,
15   That laid my goods now in the dust.
Yea, so it was, and so 'twas just.
It was his own; it was not mine.
Far be it that I should repine.
He might of all justly bereft
20   But yet sufficient for us left.
When by the Ruins oft I past
My sorrowing eyes aside did cast
And here and there the places spy
Where oft I sate and long did lie.
25   Here stood that Trunk, and there that chest,
There lay that store I counted best;
My pleasant things in ashes lie

And them behold no more shall I.
Under the roof no guest shall sit,
30   Nor at thy Table eat a bit.
No pleasant talk shall 'ere be told
Nor things recounted done of old.
No Candle 'ere shall shine in Thee,
Nor bridegroom's voice ere heard shall bee.
35   In silence ever shalt thou lie.
Adieu, Adieu, All's Vanity.
Then straight I 'gin my heart to chide:
And did thy wealth on earth abide,
Didst fix thy hope on mouldring dust,
40   The arm of flesh didst make thy trust?
Raise up thy thoughts above the sky
That dunghill mists away may fly.
Thou hast a house on high erect
Fram'd by that mighty Architect,
45   With glory richly furnished
Stands permanent, though this be fled.
It's purchased and paid for too
By him who hath enough to do.
A price so vast as is unknown,
50   Yet by his gift is made thine own.
There's wealth enough; I need no more.
Farewell, my pelf; farewell, my store.
The world no longer let me love;
My hope and Treasure lies above.

1. For what is this poem an elegy?

2. How does the speaker in the poem deal with the loss she describes? Does her reflection offer her consolation from the loss of all of her goods? Would it console you?

3. Is there a particular line or lines that struck you, that might be worth remembering if something this difficult were to happen to you?

4. What do you think about the formal choices, again of couplets (though without stanza breaks)?

A.E. Housman (1859–1936)

To an Athlete Dying Young

The time you won your town the race
We chaired you through the market-place;
Man and boy stood cheering by,
And home we brought you shoulder-high.

5   To-day, the road all runners come,
Shoulder-high we bring you home,
And set you at your threshold down,
Townsman of a stiller town.

Smart lad, to slip betimes away
10   From fields where glory does not stay
And early though the laurel grows
It withers quicker than the rose.

Eyes the shady night has shut
Cannot see the record cut,
15   And silence sounds no worse than cheers
After earth has stopped the ears.

Now you will not swell the rout
Of lads that wore their honours out,
Runners whom renown outran
20   And the name died before the man.

So set, before its echoes fade,
The fleet foot on the sill of shade,
And hold to the low lintel up
The still-defended challenge-cup.

25   And round that early-laurelled head
Will flock to gaze the strengthless dead,
And find unwithered on its curls
The garland briefer than a girl's.

1. What is the speaker mourning in this poem?

2. How does this speaker console himself in his grief, and how is it similar to Anne Bradstreet's consolation or to Ben Jonson's?

3. What do you think the speaker means when he calls the dead boy "Smart lad"?

4. Once again, a poem that speaks of death is using a rhyme scheme that cuts short the length of time between similar sounds. What rhyme scheme is this?

5. What is the stanza form? How effective do you find it?

6. What are some of the other sound and rhythmic effects that create the musical quality of the poem?

Pastoral

The pastoral form celebrates the virtues of rural life and examines why it is good to live on the land, in the countryside.

This tradition began with the Greeks, who celebrated Arcadia, a pastoral civilization in 400 BC. Arcadia soon became a symbol of perfection in the pastoral life. This longing for the ideal, natural place was passed on throughout cultures and from poet to poet: from Greece to Italy, to England, and to all over the Western world. At certain times in history it has become a troubled and dark form. For instance, during the Industrial Revolution, the natural world was being destroyed, so the pastoral became an outcry and an escape from the indignity and losses of that time. It was during the Romantic movement in literature (the eighteenth into the nineteenth centuries) that the form reached a crisis point in history, and the pastoral seemed to gain new strength as it battled the monster of progress. In today's poetry, the relationship to nature is somewhat dependent on the individual, but it remains part of this long tradition of the pastoral. When a writer responds to nature she is usually aware of the fact that many before her have done the same thing.

ANTHOLOGY

Christopher Marlowe (1564–1593)

The Passionate Shepherd to His Love

Come live with me and be my Love,
And we will all the pleasures prove
That hills and valleys, dale and field,
And all the craggy mountains yield.

5　There will we sit upon the rocks
And see the shepherds feed their flocks,
By shallow rivers, to whose falls
Melodious birds sing madrigals.

There will I make thee beds of roses
10　And a thousand fragrant posies,
A cap of flowers, and a kirtle
Embroider'd all with leaves of myrtle.

A gown made of the finest wool
Which from our pretty lambs we pull,
15　Fair lined slippers for the cold,
With buckles of the purest gold.

A belt of straw and ivy buds
With coral clasps and amber studs:
And if these pleasures may thee move,
20　Come live with me and be my Love.

Thy silver dishes for thy meat
As precious as the gods do eat,
Shall on an ivory table be
Prepared each day for thee and me.

25　The shepherd swains shall dance and sing
For thy delight each May-morning:
If these delights thy mind may move,
Then live with me and be my Love.

1. This speaker is using the country to make a romantic appeal or proposition. What is that appeal and to whom is he making it?

2. Circle the refrain in this poem.

3. Label the rhyme scheme, and name the meter and stanza type.

4. If you were the girl to whom this speaker was appealing, what would your response be? Does the fact that his appeal is based on a place and not on the attraction of his own person strengthen or weaken his argument?

5. To what extent do you believe the picture of the country life is being glorified or romanticized here?

6. If you've spent time in the countryside, what are some of the nice aspects of that life? What is unpleasant about it? Where will you decide to live when you have the choice?

A.E. Housman (1859–1936)

Loveliest of Trees

Loveliest of trees, the cherry now
Is hung with bloom along the bough,
And stands about the woodland ride
Wearing white for Eastertide.

5   Now, of my threescore years and ten,
Twenty will not come again,
And take from seventy springs a score,
It only leaves me fifty more.

And since to look at things in bloom
10   Fifty springs are little room,
About the woodlands I will go
To see the cherry hung with snow.

1. Here the landscape reminds the speaker of a truth about his life. Can you describe that truth in your own words? What is the speaker realizing about his life?

2. Why would the action of looking at the blooms of cherry trees trigger this thought in him?

3. What do you think he is longing for, and how does that show up in his tone of voice?

4. How do the form and language choices of the poem support these thoughts?

ACTIVITIES

1. Try writing in each of the forms discussed in this chapter. Prepare by reading poems from each of the genres. What follows are some prompts for each form.

2. Ode: Make a list of things or people that you love, admire, or find quirky or interesting. Choose one or two to develop, letting your mind wander and your tongue exaggerate their virtues. Think symbolically (as in the example of *Perhaps the World Ends Here*) and make notes about all of the ideas and important events that take place surrounding this person, place, or thing. Shape this associative list into a poem, then keep writing and shaping, always seeking to relate the words and sounds to the subject you've chosen to praise.

3. Elegy: Don't limit yourself to the death of a loved one, though such a loss is certainly something about which you should feel free to write. Think about your personal anniversaries—significant moments of loss or farewell that have marked your life. Consider even what you were doing last year at this time—something you may never do again. Choose a structure or strategy that one of the elegies in this section employs—perhaps the rhyming couplet, or an examination of how the loss might be a blessing. Let images from the natural world and its seasons, so continuously dying and being reborn, seep into your writing; let your language rue the loss in whatever way is most truthful for you.

4. Pastoral: Think about your relationship to the natural world. Are you more like the person who loves everything natural and lives in harmony with the earth, or do you tend to agree with my friend who once said, "Nature wants you dead"? Regardless of your inclinations, you can write an interesting pastoral poem. Describe a scene outside your window (real or imaginary but always with reality in it), and describe it accurately according to your feelings about nature. Try using a refrain or use a line from Dylan Thomas or e.e. cummings to get you started.

5. As a class, read aloud *The Passionate Shepherd to His Love* by Christopher Marlowe, then look up *The Nymph's Reply to the Shepherd* by Sir Walter Ralegh and read that aloud in response. Choose a boy and a girl to do this, and be sure to know what the poem is saying so you can express it according to the proposal and smart-aleck reply.

6. Talk about what in your class, school, or family life is ode-worthy, elegy-worthy, and pastoral-worthy, then make lists of these and explain why you would want to memorialize them in poems.

7. Discuss the memorializing function of poems.

VOCABULARY

Shaping forms: forms that are not defined by meter and rhyme but by society and history. Their origin is societal; just as words were devised from need, so were these shaping forms.

12

EMILY DICKINSON:
A CASE STUDY IN FORM

{*the formal history of poetry*}

Emily Dickinson is considered the grandmother of American poetry. Along with Walt Whitman, she is one of the distinctive American poets who helped define the American poetic voice, distinguishing it from the poetry being produced in England. She wrote 1,775 poems in her lifetime. Eleven were published; the rest were found in her bureau drawer after her death. Even though her poems were recognized fairly quickly as being extraordinary, they were not a departure from her daily life. Dickinson's rare personhood was ingrained into all she did, said, and wrote. Her letters reflect the same texture and strangeness found in her poems, as do anecdotes told about her by family and friends. Her life has been the subject of much interest, perhaps because she was an intensely private person, but certainly because of her artistic skill and her extraordinary view of everything upon which she cast her eye.

Although she stopped attending church, and leaving her house for any social reason, at the age of thirty, her experience of and ideas about her relationship with God and with the Church were constant preoccupations in her poems. Fascinatingly, despite her religious doubts, the structure used in all of her poems is something called hymn meter or common meter. This form comes from the New England Puritan practice of singing hymns in church, songs that were primarily passed down orally during church gatherings. They followed almost exclusively a rhyming stanza form alternating four-beat lines with three-beat lines.

Form is practiced and learned as we read, but it is also learned as we live. Just as our life is full of rhythms, it is also full of forms, whether we are conscious of them or not. Hymn meter is a pattern of sound that lends itself to songs that people can easily sing in a group, such as nursery rhymes and church hymns. Part of Emily Dickinson's brilliance is that she used this simple form to craft poems that tackled the deepest subjects and ideas.

Dickinson made poems out of what she found around her; she worked from the natural experiences and contacts in her life. For instance, her noteworthy metaphors were taken from everyday Puritan life: the hearth fire, the cemetery (which she could see from her bedroom window), early death, science, nature, household items, and domestic duties, to name just a few. Her method of writing was also related to her daily experience. She did her work in the tiny bits of free time that the routines of her domestic life allowed. Some have reported that she would jot lines and phrases on slips of paper and keep them in a basket to piece together at another time. Joyce Carol Oates sums up Dickinson's method this way: "Genius employs what is close at hand."

Dickinson's repeated contact with hymn meter emerged in her own artistic work. Common meter or hymn meter is a closed poetic quatrain; that is, a four-lined stanza whose end rhymes are *abab*, in which iambic tetrameter alternates with iambic trimeter. Do you remember the definition of meter and of the iamb (see the lesson on rhythm in chapter 6)? In the following example, note that the emphasized syllables aren't exactly regular. The irregularities are part of Dickinson's strangeness and genius.

If I SHOULDn't BE aLIVE	*(seven syllables)*
When the ROBins COME,	*(five syllables)*
GIVE the ONE in RED CraVAT,	*(seven syllables)*
A MeMOrial CRUMB.	*(six syllables)*

If I COULDn't THANK you,

BEing FAST aSLEEP,

YOU will KNOW I'm TRYing

WITH my GRANite LIP!

Whenever someone is a great artist, she is able to use the past and reinvent it for her present task. Dickinson is no exception. She changes the hymn form in several ways. First, she doesn't adhere to it completely. When she needs to, she abandons the meter. Also, while hymns have a noticeable pause at the end of each line so the singer can breathe, Dickinson lets the lines spill into each other. This use of enjambment was an innovation in the time period in which Dickinson lived.

In the poem, the speaker looks toward the next spring and addresses an undefined person, saying that if she isn't still living then, please give the robin (with the "red cravat" or neck scarf) a crumb of bread for her. This is a memorial crumb—one that is in memory of something— perhaps in memory of the birds, as well as the speaker who will have died. Dickinson loved animals and felt that they were better friends than people. She also loved exploring the idea of extreme humility or smallness—"I'm nobody, who are you?" is one of her famous lines. Hence she prefers a mere "crumb" over a tombstone or other memorial.

With black humor, the speaker says that since she will be dead, or "fast asleep," when this memorial crumb gets tossed, you will have to trust that she is thanking you with her lips turned to stone, or granite. There is something grotesque about this—the image of a mouth turned to stone calls up rigor mortis, the way the body goes stiff soon after death, and the word "granite" recalls a common tombstone material. What horrifies and yet is humorous is the thought of someone being conscious or alive, even under the earth, and trying to say "thank you." Even as we laugh, however, we may catch the poignant wonder and fear that's present in these lines—none can be sure we'll be alive a year from now, and all of us face the finality and mystery of death.

With Dickinson poems, the possibilities of meaning and intent are wide—she makes statements that have multiple interpretations. This complexity stretches our interpretive skills as well as our understanding of what interpretation is. Understand that when you interpret a poem, you make a case for your opinion of what that poem means, even though there are often more ways to understand the poem.

There are some things that you will want to know about Emily Dickinson, because she is a force in the literary history of our country, but also because she is a fascinating person in her own right. She lived from 1830–1886, almost wholly in Amherst, Massachusetts. She had a strong and close family and she chose to live with them her entire life. However, she did not share all the values of her parents and siblings. She did not join the church; she did not marry (though she had friendships with men); and after the age of thirty she did not leave the house. She wrote many intense letters, sometimes to the same person every day. She helped with the housework, which in her era included everything from scrubbing floors to baking bread. Despite her close relations with her family, there were many things she kept to herself and other things that they knew about her but could not understand.

Reading was an important part of her life. She said about it: "If I read a book and it makes my whole body so cold no fire can ever warm me, I know that is poetry. If I feel physically as if the top of my head were taken off, I know that is poetry." Have you ever felt this way about reading? Do you know what she means? Sometimes the muscle of words and thoughts is so powerful to us that we are physically affected. Our hearts beat, we sweat, our heads spin or ache, or we laugh out loud. Dickinson's reading list, in addition to Shakespeare and the Bible, included Keats, Emily and Charlotte Brontë, Robert and Elizabeth Browning, Alfred Tennyson, George Eliot, Ralph Waldo Emerson, and Nathaniel Hawthorn. She never read her contemporary Walt Whitman, saying, "I never read his book, but was told that it was disgraceful." Much of her education came from books, though she did have a formal education as well (including one year of women's seminary).

She chose to live an inward life, spending most of her time in her home, though she was a passionate lover of the natural world. Her imagination was unbounded, and she lived there, too—she simplified her life to an extreme so that she could "dwell in Possibility" within her mind. This combination of serious commitment to the life of her mind and her lack of fame gives her poetry a remarkably unusual quality that other writers in her time did not share. As you study her poems, notice how much she says in such little space, how musically she says it, the strangeness and number of her metaphors, and her awareness of the qualities of our emotional lives. These are some of the reasons we continue to read Emily Dickinson today.

Here is the first letter she wrote to an editor with whom she corresponded for twenty-three years:

Mr. Higginson,

Your kindness claimed earlier gratitude, but I was ill, and write to-day from my pillow.

Thank you for the surgery; it was not so painful as I supposed. I bring you others, as you ask, though they might not differ. While my thought is undressed, I can make the distinction; but when I put them in the gown, they look alike and numb.

You asked how old I was? I made no verse, but one or two, until this winter, sir.

I had a terror since September, I could tell to none; and so I sing, as the boy does of the burying ground, because I am afraid.

You inquire my books. For poets, I have Keats, and Mr. and Mrs. Browning. For prose, Mr. Ruskin, Sir Thomas Browne, and the Revelations. I went to school, but in your manner of the phrase had no education. When a little girl, I had a friend who taught me Immortality; but venturing too near, himself, he never returned. Soon after my tutor died, and for several years my lexicon was my only companion. Then I found one more, but he was not contented I be his scholar, so he left the land.

You ask my companions, Hills, sir, and the sundown, and a dog large as myself that my father bought me. They are better than beings because they know but do not tell; and the noise in the pool at noon excels my piano.

I have a brother and sister; my mother does not care for thought, and father, too busy with his briefs to notice what we do. He buys me many books, but begs me not to read them, because he fears they joggle the mind. They are religious, except me, and address an eclipse, every morning, whom they call their "Father."

But I fear my story fatigues you. I would like to learn. Could you tell me how to grow, or is it unconveyed, like melody or witchcraft?

You speak of Mr. Whitman, I never read his book, but was told that it was disgraceful.

I read Miss Prescott's Circumstance, but it followed me in the dark, so I avoided her.

Two editors of journals came to my father's house this winter, and asked me for my mind, and when I asked them "why" they said I was penurious, and they would use it for the world.

I could not weigh myself, myself. My size felt small to me. I read your chapters in the "Atlantic," and experienced honor for you. I was sure you would not reject a confiding question.

Is this, sir, what you asked me to tell you?

Your friend,

E. Dickinson

And here is Thomas Higginson's description of meeting Emily Dickinson in person:

> I found myself face to face with my hitherto unseen correspondent. It was at her father's house, one of those large, square, brick mansions so familiar in our older New England towns, surrounded by trees and blossoming shrubs without, and within exquisitely neat, cool, spacious, and fragrant with flowers. After a little delay, I heard an extremely faint and pattering footstep like that of a child, in the hall, and in glided, almost noiselessly, a plain, shy little person, the face without a single good feature, but with eyes, as she herself said, "like the sherry the guest leaves in the glass," and with smooth bands of reddish chestnut hair. She had a quaint and nun-like look, as if she might be a German canoness of some religious order, whose prescribed garb was white piqué, with a blue net worsted shawl. She came toward me with two day-lilies, which she put in a childlike way into my hand, saying softly, under her breath, "These are my introduction," and adding, also, under her breath, in childlike fashion, "Forgive me if I am frightened; I never see strangers, and hardly know what I say." But soon she began to talk, and thenceforward continued almost constantly....[1]

1. Thomas Wentworth Higginson, "Emily Dickinson's Letters," published in *Atlantic Monthly*, October 1891. Available at: <http://capress.link/1201>.

Emily Dickinson

LEARNING TO READ CLOSELY

I dwell in Possibility

> I dwell in Possibility–
> A fairer House than Prose–
> More numerous of Windows–
> Superior–for Doors–
>
> 5   Of Chambers as the Cedars–
> Impregnable of Eye–
> And for an Everlasting Roof
> The Gambrels of the Sky–
>
> Of Visitors–the fairest–
> 10 For Occupation–This–
> The spreading wide my narrow Hands
> To gather Paradise–

The only way to begin our close reading here is to define the only word that's not a metaphor or an abstract idea: "Prose." Prose is ordinary language, any writing or speaking that's unrhymed or unmetered; in other words, prose is distant from poetry. The speaker in this poem tells us that she "dwells" or lives in a "fairer House than Prose," so that must mean that she lives in the house of poetry, though she doesn't use that word to name her house. Instead, she names it "Possibility," and the rest of the poem is a metaphorical exploration of the ways in which poetry opens us to possibility—imagination, play, mystery, and, ultimately, she claims, "Paradise."

In the first stanza, the speaker invites us into her metaphorical house by asking us to try to tease out the ways in which the description of this house might apply to poetry. She gives a tour: the house of poetry has more windows than the house of prose, which let the light in, allow you to look outside, and can be opened to fresh breezes. Another reason for the superiority of this house is its doors. Doors mark entryways, openings, barriers that, unlike walls, you can get past. Doors also suggest surprise and further possibilities—we see a closed door and we wonder what is behind it. Unlike the straightforward, literal nature of prose, poetry's sound and image tools represent multiple entryways into new perspectives, new ways of seeing life. Notice how each line extends the possibility mentioned in the first. The stanza as a whole doesn't close down at the end but, with its dashes and lack of an end mark, pushes us onward to the next.

In the second stanza we are taken deeper inside the house, into its chambers, or rooms, which are "as the Cedars." Cedars are tall trees with a distinctively fresh fragrance and with foliage so thick their tops are difficult to see. When you walk among a forest of cedars you might feel hidden and held, but you might also sense that things might be hidden from *you*. Thus cedars are "impregnable of eye," which is to say that the eye cannot penetrate or conquer the privacy of the rooms. These rooms are deeply shielded from exposure. Poetry, too, has a hidden, impregnable quality—it is hard to understand; it tells its story and subject through word pictures; and it is sometimes so dense and layered that we might never exhaust its meaning. In this very poem, for example, Dickinson has asked her readers to think of poetry as a house, but then to think of the house as a forest of trees!

The gambrel roof on this house is the sky—in other words, poetry doesn't have a roof, a containing lid. It has a structure—walls and rooms—but no limitations. Note the rhyme scheme that threads throughout the poem: every second and fourth line is rhymed (*abcb*). Note also that the sounds are like the wind of the imagination playing in the trees of language and idea. The "s" sound whistles through the lines at the beginning, middle, and end of words in this stanza: chamber*s*, cedar*s*, everla*s*ting, gambrel*s*, *s*ky.

In the third stanza we move from the physical structure of the house to the actions and habits of its occupants. Visitors, or readers of poems, who come to this house are the most beautiful ("fairest"). The work of the house's owner is to spread "wide my narrow Hands / To gather Paradise." Paradise could refer to the Garden of Eden—that first garden in the Christian story—commonly equated with perfection, which humankind lost through its arrogance. This would suggest that the poet is the gatherer of what we have lost. Paradise also commonly means heaven—a place that is eternal and delightful and in the presence of God. Hence the poet's job is large, for with her small handspan she must attempt to collect that which we are all seeking, that which is dearest and deepest and most mysterious to all mankind. In the last stanza, the words "This," and "Paradise" rhyme with each other, reinforcing the idea that this task, the work of writing itself, *is* paradise—both in its purpose and its pleasure.

The regularity of the hymn meter or common measure is particularly noticeable in this poem (look again at the poem and read it out loud to hear the beats). It sticks more closely to the meter (iambic tetrameter alternating with iambic trimester) than some of Dickinson's other poems. The movement of the poem suggests both inwardness, or movement toward some deep impenetrable center chamber, and outwardness, or movement toward the sky, the heavens, and some clearly perceived but unreachable paradise. Notice that the poem doesn't formally come to a close, for there are no punctuation marks besides dashes. (No critic has ever entirely understood this common feature of Dickinson's writing.) Dashes move us both inward and outward—inward because the words that come after a dash further describe the subject of the dash, outward because the dash as Dickinson has used it in this poem keeps us moving forward. The reader moves on to the next subject and the next stanza—on to the occupation of gathering a paradise that can't be contained or ended.

ANTHOLOGY

None of Emily Dickinson's poems have titles. For that reason, people sometimes use the poem's first line as the title. Dickinson is hard to read, so if you feel challenged or blind as you approach these poems, know that you're in good company. Try reading all of these poems aloud before you talk about any of them so that you can get a feel for the patterns of her work and of her mind. Approach the poems first as examples of intricate craftsmanship and notice the way they are made, then move on to trying to understand their general meaning. Finally, begin to piece together the meanings line by line and metaphor by metaphor. Use a dictionary as you read.

I felt a funeral in my brain

I felt a funeral in my brain,
    And mourners, to and fro,
Kept treading, treading, till it seemed
    That sense was breaking through.

5   And when they all were seated,
    A service like a drum
Kept beating, beating, till I thought
    My mind was going numb.

And then I heard them lift a box,
10   And creak across my soul
With those same boots of lead,
    Then space began to toll

As all the heavens were a bell,
    And Being but an ear,
15   And I and silence some strange race,
    Wrecked, solitary, here.

And then a plank in reason, broke,
    And I dropped down and down—
And hit a world at every plunge,
20   And finished knowing—then—

1. Count out the syllables and the stressed and unstressed beats for each line, marking them as you go along.

2. Circle the rhymes and write out the pattern of rhymes (*abab* or *abcb* or other).

3. See if you can explain how each stanza (called quatrains because there are four lines in each) is a compartment of its own.

4. Think about the way children like to write crazy stories that end with the line "and then I woke up!" Looking at the first line of Dickinson's poem and then the rest of it, is the detailed scene of a funeral a literal event she's describing, or a symbol or series of metaphors for something she is experiencing psychologically? Can you find evidence for both interpretations?

A narrow fellow in the grass

A narrow fellow in the grass
Occasionally rides;
You may have met him,—did you not,
His notice sudden is.

5   The grass divides as with a comb
A spotted shaft is seen;
And then it closes at your feet
And opens further on.

He likes a boggy acre,
10   A floor too cool for corn.
Yet when a child, and barefoot,
I more than once, at morn,

Have passed, I thought, a whip-lash
Unbraiding in the sun,—
15   When, stooping to secure it,
It wrinkled, and was gone.

Several of nature's people
I know, and they know me;
I feel for them a transport
20   Of cordiality;

But never met this fellow,
Attended or alone,
Without a tighter breathing,
And zero at the bone.

1. Many of Dickinson's poems are like riddles. What is the animal that this poem describes?

2. Make a list of the things that the poet tells us snakes do.

3. What do you notice about the verbs that describe the motion and effect of the snake: "wrinkle," "divides," "rides"?

4. Name and describe the metaphors that she makes about the snake. (Hint: The first four stanzas have them, and sometimes the metaphor is created with the verb, such as "rides.")

5. Circle all the verbs. Underline the metaphors. Circle the end rhymes. Put a star next to the end rhymes that are slant or half rhymes.

6. What does she mean when she says that the person who sees a snake feels "zero at the bone"? Have you experienced this? Describe what you think she means.

7. If you take the poem as a whole, what is the speaker's tone toward snakes? Are there different tones in the poem? Name them, and then cite language or devices in the poem that create those tones.

Because I could not stop for Death

Because I could not stop for Death,
He kindly stopped for me;
The carriage held but just ourselves
And Immortality.

5   We slowly drove, he knew no haste,
And I had put away
My labor, and my leisure too,
For his civility.

We passed the school, where children strove
10 At recess, in the ring;
We passed the fields of gazing grain,
We passed the setting sun.

Or rather, he passed us;
The dews grew quivering and chill,
15 For only gossamer my gown,
My tippet only tulle.

We paused before {a} house that seemed
A swelling of the ground;
The roof was scarcely visible,
20 The cornice but a mound.

Since then 'tis centuries, and yet each
Feels shorter than the day
I first surmised the horses' heads
Were toward eternity.

1. Count out the syllables and stresses for each line in this poem. Beat it out on the table while saying the words.

2. Circle the rhymes. Talk about what kind of rhymes they are (see chapter 5, on sound, to refresh your memory). Which are half (or slant) and which are full?

3. How is death personified in this poem, and does it seem believable to you? Describe Dickinson's characterization of death in your own words.

4. Early in the poem, Death "kindly" stops for the speaker and the two of them "slowly" drive toward eternity. Name three ways in which language and sound in the poem give the sense of either kindliness or slowness.

Much madness is divinest sense

Much madness is divinest sense
To a discerning eye;
Much sense the starkest madness.
'Tis the majority
5   In this, as all, prevails.
Assent, and you are sane;
Demur,–you're straightway dangerous,
And handled with a chain.

1. Define the words "assent" and "demur."

2. What do you think it means to be "handled with a chain"?

3. Have you ever felt that you had to go along with the "majority" and if you didn't you were "handled with a chain"?

4. Why does disagreeing with the majority make you "straightway dangerous" to the crowd?

5. Can you give an example of something that you believe that other people think is the "starkest madness"? Can you think of anything that Emily Dickinson did or believed that others might have labeled "starkest madness"?

6. Name three ways in which the language and patterning of the poem fit its message.

After great pain a formal feeling comes

After great pain a formal feeling comes–
The nerves sit ceremonious like tombs;
The stiff Heart questions–was it He that bore?
And yesterday–or centuries before?

5   The feet, mechanical, go round
A wooden way
Of ground, or air, or ought,
Regardless grown,
A quartz contentment, like a stone.

10   This is the hour of lead
Remembered if outlived,
As freezing persons recollect the snow–
First chill, then stupor, then the letting go.

1. Have you ever experienced great emotional pain?

2. What do you think of Dickinson's metaphor for the feeling that comes after having experienced something difficult like what is described in the poem?

3. How do all of the metaphors in this poem contribute to the sense of numb, stiff, stung shock that one feels after something sad or difficult or awful happens? Name them.

4. What happens to those who freeze?

5. Mark the rhyme scheme of the poem. Does it conform totally to a pattern? How does that choice fit the meaning of the poem?

Tell all the Truth but tell it slant

Tell all the Truth but tell it slant—
Success in Circuit lies
Too bright for our infirm Delight
The Truth's superb surprise
5 As Lightening to the Children eased
With explanation kind
The Truth must dazzle gradually
Or every man be blind—

1. What does it mean to tell the truth slant? How does this proverb relate to Emily Dickinson's own truth telling—her poetry?

2. Why does truth "dazzle" or blind us when we experience too much of it at once—when we have no time to gradually learn it?

3. What is the rhyme scheme of this poem and how do the rhymes serve to reinforce the point of the poem?

4. Name one other sound or rhythm tool being used in this poem.

5. If you were to write an essay or poem affirming the phrase "Success in Circuit lies," what examples would you use from your own life or the lives of people you know?

ACTIVITIES

1. As Dickinson did with her own phrases, cut scraps of text from photocopied pages (your choice of what the text is, but probably not Dickinson poems; try using different kinds of text—prose and poetry). Now take these lines and use them to make your own poem (called a "found poem"). Rearrange the lines several times to get a feel for the different possible directions you could take it in.

2. Memorize some Dickinson poems and spend a whole class period reciting them. Take the last ten minutes of class to freewrite on what you learned, enjoyed, and remember of the poems. Try to trace words, images, and themes that recur in Dickinson poems.

3. Check out a book of Dickinson's letters from the library and read through them. Write your own letter after reading them. The recipient can be a real or imagined person, but if imagined be sure the imaginary friend is important to you and open to strangeness. Don't explain everything you mean. Or write a letter, patterned after the ones in this chapter, that explains yourself in metaphor to someone who does not know you.

4. Write a riddle poem in which you describe an animal or object but don't name it. Start by freewriting in prose the qualities and observations about the animal that you'd like to include in the poem.

5. Read all of Dickinson's animal poems together (you'll need to get a book of her selected poems out of the library to do this) and then write your own. Choose lines from the poems that might serve as openers to your poem.

6. Spend a class period drawing the poem *I dwell in Possibility*. According to Dickinson's words, what would the house of poetry look like if it were a sketch?

7. As you'll learn, both Walt Whitman and Emily Dickinson frequently wrote poems in which they directly addressed animals, countries, or places as if they were people. What's the benefit of this? What might be the pitfalls?

13

OPEN VERSE

{the formal history of poetry}

There is a form of poetry called "free verse" or "open verse," which is defined as unmetrical verse or poetry made with lines that do not conform to a clear pattern according to syllable, stress, or length. Although it sounds like this form of poetry is without form, this is impossible, for art cannot be made without form. The literal phrase "free verse" comes from the French words *vers libre* and, while free verse became popular during the modernist period, it can be found in books as old as the King James Bible. In modern American times it began with force in the poetry of Walt Whitman, who drew heavily on the psalm structure for his own work. Although its lines cannot be counted numerically, open verse has lines, stanzas, and rhythms that pull us in one direction or another.

The great mid-twentieth-century poet William Carlos Williams, who wrote almost exclusively in open verse, said this about rhythm and movement in a poem: "Either the movement continues or it stops." In prose, all stops or pauses in the forward movement of the language are created by punctuation, with the period being the strongest stop (or longest pause); the comma being the weakest stop (or shortest pause); and marks like semicolons, colons, and dashes falling somewhere in between. Poetry, especially the open verse form, offers more options. When you come to the end of a line in a poem, the white space after the words on the page signals a natural pause. If there is no punctuation telling you to stop, that pause is tiny, sometimes barely noticeable, for you must push your voice over the edge of that white space and onto the next line. Thus in poetry you have the option of a pause that is shorter than a comma. Alternatively, if you match the end of a line with the end of a sentence (called a full stop), you create a pause that is longer than a period. Some poets extend this use of white space even further, placing large gaps in the middle of lines, interrupting a series of very long lines with a very short line, or shaping a series of lines in such a way that the poem makes a visual image on the page.

The following are some other specific devices used in open verse. They are less precise than the classic meter and rhyme schemes, but are nonetheless powerful and flexible:

- Anaphora repeats the same word or phrase at the beginnings of lines or clauses. Without aligning to a set pattern, the repeated words can nevertheless become a skeleton or structure for the poem. Walt Whitman used anaphora memorably and often: "Ever the hard unsunk ground / Ever the eaters and drinkers, ever the upward and downward sun, ever the air and the ceaseless tides, / Ever myself and my neighbors, refreshing, wicked, real…" (from *Song of Myself*).

- **Parallelism** repeats the way a phrase or sentence is structured, substituting new objects or actions in each repetition. The following poem by William Meredith (1919–2007) illustrates it well:

A Major Work

> Poems are hard to read
> Pictures are hard to see
> Music is hard to hear
> And people are hard to love
>
> But whether from brute need
> Or divine energy
> At last mind eye and ear
> And the great sloth heart will move.

There is much parallelism here. In the first stanza, poems, pictures, music, and people are all parallel, as are reading, seeing, hearing, and loving. In the second stanza, the parallelism is echoed or reinforced with the string of body parts—mind, eye, ear, heart—that correspond exactly to the first stanza's list of actions.

- **Climax** builds up a series of phrases, images, or ideas to some high point of realization, as in the climax of a plot. In Meredith's poem above, the climax is the realization that we can and will love each other "at last," even though it is difficult and how we do it is a mystery. The climax often comes at the end of a poem and is emphasized with distinctive language of some kind. In this example, the heart's movement ends the poem; it is surrounded by memorable adjectives; and it is visually longer than any other line in the poem. These signal the fact that we've arrived at the pinnacle, the high point.

- **Cumulative** is a term used to describe the buildup of images or ideas that lead to the climax of a poem. In *A Major Work*, the elements of need, difficulty, divine energy, along with the images of the body and of human activities are all pieces of development that lead to the climax.

- **Counterpoint** uses argument, opposition, or surprise as an organizing structure for a poem. It can be established both with ideas/words and with sound. In *A Major Work* we see a series of four claims and then the word "but," which signals that the claims are about to be refuted or qualified. Counterpoint is also present in the final line of the poem, but, coming after so many short, unadorned phrases, it surprises us with its long, wordy conclusion.

Can you see how all these devices are about organizing the forward movement of the poem? They are helpful as you look at open verse poems and try to examine whether or not the poet has successfully made a structure or form for the poem. It's also helpful to know that the micro-elements of poetic sound—alliteration, assonance, consonance, etc.—are just as important and present in open verse poems as they are in traditional poetry. When you read an open verse poem, you want to ask how it made its form and whether or not it worked, just as you would if you were creating a new sort of paper airplane—the most important question is, does it fly?

Rather than seeing traditional or verse form poetry as one thing and open verse as another, remember that open verse has been written since the beginning, when literate cultures began encoding language in an alphabet and making written poems. The modernist time period (late nineteenth century through the mid-twentieth century), when writers were experimenting with old forms, could be viewed as a dialogue, argument, or discussion with those forms. At certain times in history, open verse was a form of social and artistic rebellion, at other times it was not. One of the defining benefits of open verse is the freedom that it allows for a natural-sounding voice. Often, we come to a new place in our lives and need to make changes in the form of our expression in order to register the experience. Modernist writers, such as T.S. Eliot, William Carlos Williams, and many others, were living in a time when life experience and thought were changing. They needed forms that reflected this change and so they invented them.

All of the work that we do as writers is part of a conversation with work that has come before us. Close reading of poems, marked equally by questioning and deep respect, is an essential part of that conversation. As a writer you should feel free to talk to the poems that you have loved and even those you have loathed, with those you would rewrite in your own voice with your own opinions. There is a long tradition of this dialogue with the dead.

LEARNING TO READ CLOSELY

Elizabeth Bishop (1911–1979)

The Fish

I caught a tremendous fish
and held him beside the boat
half out of water, with my hook
fast in a corner of his mouth.
5   He didn't fight.
He hadn't fought at all.
He hung a grunting weight,
battered and venerable
and homely. Here and there
10   his brown skin hung in strips
like ancient wallpaper,
and its pattern of darker brown
was like wallpaper:
shapes like full-blown roses
15   stained and lost through age.
He was speckled with barnacles,
fine rosettes of lime,
and infested
with tiny white sea-lice,
20   and underneath two or three
rags of green weed hung down.
While his gills were breathing in
the terrible oxygen
—the frightening gills,
25   fresh and crisp with blood,
that can cut so badly—
I thought of the coarse white flesh
packed in like feathers,
the big bones and the little bones,
30   the dramatic reds and blacks
of his shiny entrails,
and the pink swim-bladder
like a big peony.
I looked into his eyes
35   which were far larger than mine
but shallower, and yellowed,
the irises backed and packed
with tarnished tinfoil

40   seen through the lenses
of old scratched isinglass.
They shifted a little, but not
to return my stare.
—It was more like the tipping
of an object toward the light.
45   I admired his sullen face,
the mechanism of his jaw,
and then I saw
that from his lower lip
—if you could call it a lip
50   grim, wet, and weaponlike,
hung five old pieces of fish-line,
or four and a wire leader
with the swivel still attached,
with all their five big hooks
55   grown firmly in his mouth.
A green line, frayed at the end
where he broke it, two heavier lines,
and a fine black thread
still crimped from the strain and snap
60   when it broke and he got away.
Like medals with their ribbons
frayed and wavering,
a five-haired beard of wisdom
trailing from his aching jaw.
65   I stared and stared
and victory filled up
the little rented boat,
from the pool of bilge
where oil had spread a rainbow
70   around the rusted engine
to the bailer rusted orange,
the sun-cracked thwarts,
the oarlocks on their strings,
the gunnels—until everything
75   was rainbow, rainbow, rainbow!
And I let the fish go.

The Fish by Elizabeth Bishop is a much loved, much anthologized poem. The poem opens with the speaker declaring that she has caught a fish. It's "tremendous," which at first we take to mean physically enormous, but as the poem proceeds, we begin to see that this exclamation means more than that. The information that the speaker relays to us about the fish accumulates in short lines, slowly, almost as if the reader were pulling a loaded fishing line out of the water. The fish immediately becomes personal: "he" doesn't fight, and we get the sense that he is resigned, perhaps, to being caught. The speaker starts gazing at her catch, giving us an incredibly detailed catalog, rife with metaphor. The brown skin is like "ancient wallpaper," for example, and the barnacles are like "rosettes" on his skin. The fisherman begins to empathize with the fish whose gills "were breathing in / the terrible oxygen," showing us that she has taken on the perspective of the fish for a moment. Then, immediately, she's back in her own perspective, calling the gills "frightening." Although the fisherman is looking at the "grunting weight" of the fish, she begins imaginatively to flay him when she thinks of his insides (notice the personal pronoun). The fish is not human, his eyes do not resemble our human eyes—"shallower, and yellowed, / the irises backed and packed / with tarnished tinfoil / seen through the lenses / of old scratched isinglass." This is a remarkable bit of description and comparison—the eye behind the irises reminds her of tarnished tinfoil seen through wavy glass that is scratched—how particular and strange, how imaginative!

From line 40 the speaker moves from description to interpretation—on line 48 she sees the fish's "lower lip / —if you could call it a lip" (still she humanizes the fish, but understands she's doing so). She notices the history of the fish's past escapes from capture—there are old pieces of fishline and hooks growing from his mouth. The speaker tells us the details of these lines, and she calls them "medals," as if the fish is a decorated veteran of war. She calls this trail of old, broken lines a "beard of wisdom" come from experience and from pain (she says his jaw is "aching"). These details affect the speaker, who tells us that she "stared and stared." She is transfixed, drawn to these marks of the fish's survival. The fish is a survivor. The speaker seems to take in all of the information and to deeply consider the fish's life.

When the poem began we heard the voice of a happy fisherman, bragging about her catch, admiring it. Then she began to gaze at the shell of the fish, comparing it to what she knows—wallpaper, tinfoil, feathers. In an understated way, the speaker has begun to see the fish symbolically as an emblem of survival, of having lived through many episodes of capture and near-death. "Victory filled up / the little rented boat," she tells us, and at first we wonder if the victory is the traditional fisherman's pride at having captured such quarry. At this moment, the speaker describes the unexpected setting for victory—a rented boat, a pool of bilge (the foul water that collects at the lowest part of a boat), leaking oil, rusted engine, sun-cracked thwarts. All of this is broken down, cracked, leaking, not an auspicious site for victory. As readers we must probe the nature of this victory.

Notice, there is a rainbow made from oil, and by the end of the poem, a few short lines later, the speaker exclaims (after staring and staring) that "everything / was rainbow, rainbow, rainbow!" The rainbow traditionally symbolizes amnesty from God after the Flood in Genesis. By it God promised not to destroy humanity with a flood ever again. Here, too, there is amnesty: the fisherman lets the fish go. From the tone of the speaker, we have the sense that this grace has somehow been extended toward the speaker as well. The poem ends its intense scrutiny with an air of joyful elation. The victory is the survival of the fish, the speaker, and humanity. The latter is only indirectly stated, but the speaker tells us as much from her

exuberant tone of voice, repetition, exclamation mark, and, of course, the surprising action of letting the venerable fish go. This fish seems worth the veneration she's paid to it. What is its value? What has the speaker "caught," though she ends the poem empty-handed? Perhaps she's gained a sense of the possibility of survival, of making it in this difficult, broken-down world. From this suggestion, we gather that the fisherman has seen and perhaps experienced suffering.

The poem is written in open verse. The lines hover in length between six and eight syllables without a specific meter. Bishop built the poem with the traditional tools of open verse: a list of minute observations, each observation contained on a single line, the weight of accumulation with each piece of information, each observation, piling in a heap until we feel the "grunting weight" of this "tremendous fish"—a weight that isn't measured simply in pounds. The poem builds to a climax near line 50 when the speaker begins to observe elements of the fish that aren't purely visual or informational but empathetic, at which time she begins to see him in human terms. At line 65, the staring reaches its apex and there is the sudden, joyous sense of victory. The poem ends abruptly as she lets the fish go.

Bishop is a master of quiet sound patterns and rhythms that are unannounced and not showy, yet which partner perfectly with the subjects of her poems. What we know from the quality of her work and from looking at her papers is that she did labor. Her decisions about sound, word choice, minute description, even her decisions of where to break each line, lead us suggestively but naturally to the essence of the thing she is describing. *The Fish* as a poem could actually be read as a little instruction manual about how to look at something, to truly see it, for the language and shape of the poem brings to life the patience and waiting involved in truly looking and gleaning all that there is to see in a scene, an object, a moment. Where most of us would leap quickly to another subject or scene, Bishop stays and unpacks, pressures the fish with her insistent gaze, and, under the pressure of that gaze, new observations and mysteries unfold. The long extension of short lines helps us to feel that pressured gaze, that sense of something important being slowly drawn toward us.

As readers we come away from the encounter refreshed, alert, sharpened, and wondering what would happen to us and our sight if we looked at the world this way more often.

ANTHOLOGY

Psalm 100

A psalm. For giving thanks.

1   Shout for joy to the LORD, all the earth.
2   Worship the LORD with gladness;
            come before him with joyful songs.
3   Know that the LORD is God.
            It is he who made us, and we are his;
            we are his people, the sheep of his pasture.
4   Enter his gates with thanksgiving
            and his courts with praise;
            give thanks to him and praise his name.
5   For the LORD is good and his love endures forever;
            his faithfulness continues through all generations.

1. Where do you see the tools of open verse poetry at work in this psalm? Name at least two examples.

2. Pay attention to the pronouns the poem's speaker uses. For and to whom does he speak?

3. Notice that the language of this poem is imperative—each of the first four stanzas begins with a command: "Shout," "Worship," "Know," and "Enter." Who or what is being commanded? Does the who or what change in each stanza?

4. Can you find another example of a poem in this book in which the speaker is commanding or directly addressing an inanimate object?

5. In addition to addressing a group of people, the speaker in this psalm includes himself in the address of the poem. Can you find another example of a poem in this book in which the speaker is commanding or directly addressing himself?

6. Why would one need to speak to oneself, and why might poetry or music be a helpful way to frame such speaking?

Christopher Smart (1722–1771)
from Jubilate Agno

My Cat Jeoffry

For I will consider my Cat Jeoffry.
For he is the servant of the Living God duly and daily serving him.
For at the first glance of the glory of God in the East he worships in his way.
For this is done by wreathing his body seven times round with elegant quickness.
5   For then he leaps up to catch the musk, which is the blessing of God upon his prayer.
For he rolls upon prank to work it in.
For having done duty and received blessing he begins to consider himself.
For this he performs in ten degrees.
For first he looks upon his forepaws to see if they are clean.
10   For secondly he kicks up behind to clear away there.
For thirdly he works it upon stretch with the forepaws extended.
For fourthly he sharpens his paws by wood.
For fifthly he washes himself.
For sixthly he rolls upon wash.
15   For seventhly he fleas himself, that he may not be interrupted upon the beat.
For eighthly he rubs himself against a post.
For ninthly he looks up for his instructions.
For tenthly he goes in quest of food.
For having consider'd God and himself he will consider his neighbour.
20   For if he meets another cat he will kiss her in kindness.
For when he takes his prey he plays with it to give it a chance.
For one mouse in seven escapes by his dallying.
For when his day's work is done his business more properly begins.
For he keeps the Lord's watch in the night against the adversary.
25   For he counteracts the powers of darkness by his electrical skin and glaring eyes.
For he counteracts the Devil, who is death, by brisking about the life.
For in his morning orisons he loves the sun and the sun loves him.
For he is of the tribe of Tiger.
For the Cherub Cat is a term of the Angel Tiger.
30   For he has the subtlety and hissing of a serpent, which in goodness he suppresses.
For he will not do destruction, if he is well-fed, neither will he spit without provocation.
For he purrs in thankfulness, when God tells him he's a good Cat.
For he is an instrument for the children to learn benevolence upon.
For every house is incomplete without him and a blessing is lacking in the spirit.
35   For the Lord commanded Moses concerning the cats at the departure of the
          Children of Israel from Egypt.
For every family had one cat at least in the bag.
For the English Cats are the best in Europe.
For he is the cleanest in the use of his forepaws of any quadruped.
For the dexterity of his defence is an instance of the love of God to him exceedingly.
40   For he is the quickest to his mark of any creature.
For he is tenacious of his point.
For he is a mixture of gravity and waggery.
For he knows that God is his Saviour.
For there is nothing sweeter than his peace when at rest.
45   For there is nothing brisker than his life when in motion.

For he is of the Lord's poor and so indeed is he called by benevolence perpetually
     —Poor Jeoffry! poor Jeoffry! the rat has bit thy throat.
For I bless the name of the Lord Jesus that Jeoffry is better.
For the divine spirit comes about his body to sustain it in complete cat.
For his tongue is exceeding pure so that it has in purity what it wants in music.
50   For he is docile and can learn certain things.
For he can set up with gravity which is patience upon approbation.
For he can fetch and carry, which is patience in employment.
For he can jump over a stick which is patience upon proof positive.
For he can spraggle upon waggle at the word of command.
55   For he can jump from an eminence into his master's bosom.
For he can catch the cork and toss it again.
For he is hated by the hypocrite and miser.
For the former is afraid of detection.
For the latter refuses the charge.
60   For he camels his back to bear the first notion of business.
For he is good to think on, if a man would express himself neatly.
For he made a great figure in Egypt for his signal services.
For he killed the Ichneumon-rat very pernicious by land.
For his ears are so acute that they sting again.
65   For from this proceeds the passing quickness of his attention.
For by stroking of him I have found out electricity.
For I perceived God's light about him both wax and fire.
For the Electrical fire is the spiritual substance, which God sends from heaven to
      sustain the bodies both of man and beast.
For God has blessed him in the variety of his movements.
70   For, tho he cannot fly, he is an excellent clamberer.
For his motions upon the face of the earth are more than any other quadruped.
For he can tread to all the measures upon the music.
For he can swim for life.
For he can creep.

1. In Latin *Jubilate Agno* means "Rejoice in the Lamb," referring to Christ. Smart modeled this long poem (longer than what we have shown here) after the biblical psalms. What free verse devices does Smart rely on most heavily to organize the poem? How is this appropriate given the kind of poem it is—a praise poem or ode?

2. How does the cat lead the speaker to a deeper appreciation for the universe and for its Creator?

3. Find a collection of lines that show a progression or movement that increases in its intensity of observation and conclusion.

4. What is the tone of voice of the speaker? How does he feel about the cat and the world the cat unveils?

Walt Whitman (1819–1892)

I Hear America Singing

I hear America singing, the varied carols I hear;
Those of mechanics—each one singing his, as it should be, blithe and strong;
The carpenter singing his, as he measures his plank or beam,
The mason singing his, as he makes ready for work, or leaves off work;
5   The boatman singing what belongs to him in his boat—the deckhand singing
    on the steamboat deck;
The shoemaker singing as he sits on his bench—the hatter singing as he stands;
The wood-cutter's song—the ploughboy's, on his way in the morning, or at the
    noon intermission, or at sundown;
The delicious singing of the mother—or of the young wife at work—or of the girl
    sewing or washing—Each singing what belongs to her, and to none else;
The day what belongs to the day—At night, the party of young fellows, robust, friendly,
10 Singing, with open mouths, their strong melodious songs.

1. How has the poet organized this poem?

2. It is a list poem—how do the poem's main idea and its form relate to each other?

3. What is happening with the punctuation? Does it make sense that the poem is one sentence?

4. What songlike elements does the poem have? How is it musical?

5. What relationship does this poem have to the psalms that you read before it?

6. What is the tone of the poem? How does the speaker feel about what he hears?

Langston Hughes (1902–1967)

The Negro Speaks of Rivers

I've known rivers:
I've known rivers ancient as the world and older than the
      flow of human blood in human veins.

My soul has grown deep like the rivers.

I bathed in the Euphrates when dawns were young.
5   I built my hut near the Congo and it lulled me to sleep.
I looked upon the Nile and raised the pyramids above it.
I heard the singing of the Mississippi when Abe Lincoln
      went down to New Orleans, and I've seen its muddy
      bosom turn all golden in the sunset.

I've known rivers:
Ancient, dusky rivers.

10   My soul has grown deep like the rivers.

1. The speaker in this poem uses the word "rivers" six times in the space of the poem—why? What is the effect of that repetition?

2. What is the effect of comparing the depth of soul to the depth of the rivers and then listing all the rivers with which the speaker says he has had a relationship?

3. Why is the title *The Negro Speaks of Rivers*?

4. What is the relationship between suffering and depth?

5. What does the symbol of the river in this poem contain?

6. What do you think it takes for a soul to grow deep like a river? Or, to put it another way, how might a river be a good metaphor for one's soul?

7. Are there other bodies of water that a soul could be like—as both positive and negative symbols?

William Carlos Williams (1883-1963)

Spring and All

By the road to the contagious hospital
under the surge of the blue
mottled clouds driven from the
northeast—a cold wind. Beyond, the
5 waste of broad, muddy fields
brown with dried weeds, standing and fallen

patches of standing water
the scattering of tall trees

All along the road the reddish
10 purplish, forked, upstanding, twiggy
stuff of bushes and small trees
with dead, brown leaves under them
leafless vines—

Lifeless in appearance, sluggish
15 dazed spring approaches—

They enter the new world naked,
cold, uncertain of all
save that they enter. All about them
the cold, familiar wind—

20 Now the grass, tomorrow
the stiff curl of wildcarrot leaf

One by one objects are defined—
It quickens: clarity, outline of leaf

But now the stark dignity of
25 entrance—Still, the profound change
has come upon them: rooted they
grip down and begin to awaken

1. Mark the few words or phrases of this poem that are about human life, rather than purely the natural life. If the poem is primarily about spring and nature, why include these human elements?

2. Circle the plural pronouns in the fifth stanza and the singular pronoun in the seventh stanza. To what are these pronouns referring?

3. Try to make some sense of the way in which the lines and stanzas are broken. What does the poet achieve by doing this?

4. What do you make of the punctuation? What might the writer be trying to do with it?

5. If you had to come up with a fresh (not clichéd) picture of spring, what would it be?

Ezra Pound (1885–1972)

Salutation

O generation of the thoroughly smug and thoroughly uncomfortable,
I have seen fishermen picnicking in the sun,
I have seen them with untidy families,
I have seen their smiles full of teeth and heard ungainly laughter.
5   And I am happier than you are,
And they were happier than I am;
And the fish swim in the lake and do not even own clothing.

1. What are some of the open verse structures (listed on pp. 168-169) that this poem uses?

2. How do these structures function to create a shape for the poem without rhyme or meter?

3. Where does the poem arrive by the end?

4. Is the ending a full circle from the opening of the poem?

5. What is the tone of voice?

6. Is there an echo of another text in the last line?

D.H. Lawrence (1885–1930)

Snake

A snake came to my water-trough
On a hot, hot day, and I in pyjamas for the heat,
To drink there.

In the deep, strange-scented shade of the great dark carob-tree
5   I came down the steps with my pitcher
And must wait, must stand and wait, for there he was at the trough before me.

He reached down from a fissure in the earth-wall in the gloom
And trailed his yellow-brown slackness soft-bellied down, over the edge of
10   the stone trough
And rested his throat upon the stone bottom,
And where the water had dripped from the tap, in a small clearness,
He sipped with his straight mouth,
Softly drank through his straight gums, into his slack long body,
15   Silently.

Someone was before me at my water-trough,
And I, like a second comer, waiting.

He lifted his head from his drinking, as cattle do,
And looked at me vaguely, as drinking cattle do,
20   And flickered his two-forked tongue from his lips, and mused a moment,
And stooped and drank a little more,
Being earth-brown, earth-golden from the burning bowels of the earth
On the day of Sicilian July, with Etna smoking.
The voice of my education said to me
25   He must be killed,
For in Sicily the black, black snakes are innocent, the gold are venomous.

And voices in me said, If you were a man
You would take a stick and break him now, and finish him off.

But must I confess how I liked him,
30   How glad I was he had come like a guest in quiet, to drink at my water-trough
And depart peaceful, pacified, and thankless,
Into the burning bowels of this earth?

Was it cowardice, that I dared not kill him?
Was it perversity, that I longed to talk to him?
35   Was it humility, to feel so honoured?
I felt so honoured.

And yet those voices:
If you were not afraid, you would kill him!

And truly I was afraid, I was most afraid, But even so, honoured still more
40   That he should seek my hospitality
From out the dark door of the secret earth.

He drank enough
And lifted his head, dreamily, as one who has drunken,
And flickered his tongue like a forked night on the air, so black,
45   Seeming to lick his lips,
And looked around like a god, unseeing, into the air,
And slowly turned his head,
And slowly, very slowly, as if thrice adream,
Proceeded to draw his slow length curving round
50   And climb again the broken bank of my wall-face.

And as he put his head into that dreadful hole,
And as he slowly drew up, snake-easing his shoulders, and entered farther,
A sort of horror, a sort of protest against his withdrawing into that horrid black hole,
Deliberately going into the blackness, and slowly drawing himself after,
55   Overcame me now his back was turned.

I looked round, I put down my pitcher,
I picked up a clumsy log
And threw it at the water-trough with a clatter.

I think it did not hit him,
60   But suddenly that part of him that was left behind convulsed in undignified haste.
Writhed like lightning, and was gone
Into the black hole, the earth-lipped fissure in the wall-front,
At which, in the intense still noon, I stared with fascination.

And immediately I regretted it.
65   I thought how paltry, how vulgar, what a mean act!
I despised myself and the voices of my accursed human education.

And I thought of the albatross
And I wished he would come back, my snake.

For he seemed to me again like a king,
70   Like a king in exile, uncrowned in the underworld,
Now due to be crowned again.

And so, I missed my chance with one of the lords
Of life.
And I have something to expiate:
75   A pettiness.

1. This poem describes a simple encounter with an animal, one that we're all likely to have experienced.
What do you notice about the level of the diction—is it elevated or down-to-earth?

2. What are some of the words that turn this story from an ordinary, backyard, childhood encounter
with an animal to something important, mysterious, and even otherworldly?

3. What are some moments in the poem in which the writer has chosen words whose sounds are
especially noticeable, either alone or in combination with other words?

4. Why does the speaker feel the way he does in the beginning, middle, and end of the poem? How do
his feelings change throughout the poem, and why might they change?

5. What about a snake might cause a negative reaction? Is there any relevant history between snakes and
humankind that might shed light on this encounter?

ACTIVITIES

1. Write a list poem.

2. Notice that several of the poems in this chapter refer to song or were written to be sung (the psalm, Smart's *Jubilate Agno*, Whitman's *I Hear America Singing*). Working individually or as a group, try putting one or all of these poems to music. Once you have done so, sing them out loud. What do you learn about the poems as a result of making them into songs?

3. Choose an object of interest, even something common, and gaze at it for a long time without doing anything else (no phone, Internet, iPod allowed here). Try to do this for twenty minutes. Then freewrite your thoughts about the object, letting your mind associate—that is, move from one thought to the next—and write the associations down. Write a poem modeled after *The Fish* in which you write in excruciating detail your observation of an object, then see what happens to your thoughts and to the significance of the object after such a detailed look.

4. Write a poem in which you take on the voice of a character from another story. Tell his story but with detail not available in the original account (as in the case of the Magi of the Bible). Find a voice— tone and personality—that matches the character.

5. Choose one of the following lines and use it somewhere in a poem of your own making:
...I always felt like crying. It wasn't fair...
...grip down and begin to awaken...
...but now the stark dignity of...
...old age is...
...I'll be at the table...

6. You'll notice that many open verse poems spend most of the poem establishing a mood or a scene and then reverse direction in the last few lines. This structure is in dialogue with the sonnet, in particular the English sonnet with its final couplet. Write a poem that has such a buildup and concluding reversal.

7. Write a poem that features an encounter with an animal (as four or five of the poems in this chapter do). Describe the animal in detail, using figures of speech to compare it to something it is not. Perhaps your animal will reveal something to you about yourself, the world, or bring you a message.

VOCABULARY

Climax: the building up of an idea to some high point, as in the climax of a plot.

Counterpoint: a statement that seems to argue with a previous statement.

Cumulative: the points that lead up to the climax, as in plot development.

Parallelism: the repetition of similar structures within phrases or sentences in the course of a poem. There is also parallelism of idea.

14

WALT WHITMAN:
A CASE STUDY IN OPEN VERSE

{the formal history of poetry}

Walt Whitman is the patriarch of American poetry. He lived from 1819–1892, during the same era as America's poetic matriarch, Emily Dickinson. His formative experiences are equally distinctive and interesting. He did not finish high school but learned the printing trade, and he held down an enormous range of jobs before he became established as a poet. He taught school in a one-room schoolhouse at the age of seventeen; he took writing jobs as a journalist; he took odd jobs as a carpenter and contractor; and he nursed soldiers during the Civil War. Unlike Dickinson, whose work did not become known until after her death, Whitman's poetry and reputation were widely known while he was alive. For the last part of his life he lived in Camden, New Jersey, entertaining writers and artists from around the world.

Whitman immersed himself in the works of Shakespeare, Homer, and Dante, as well as in the Bible. He wrote free verse that was very similar to the psalms of the Bible, employing strong rhythms that varied widely but not randomly. They sounded much closer to natural speech than the strict, elevated metric forms that other poets of the time were using. You can see in his work the tendency to ramble and talk and to be expansive, making wide claims. He celebrated things American and democratic and challenged traditional ideas. His lines are very long, wandering, and often list-like, and he makes catalogs of people, places, and things, using many adjectives. Several devices of free verse and of the psalms that are strongly present in his poems are parallelism and anaphora (see p. 167). Parallelism is the repetition of similar or identical structures within phrases or sentences, making it like anaphora, but it includes more than repetition of a single word. Anaphora is a rhetorical device in which several successive lines, phrases, clauses, or sentences begin with the same word or phrase (as in the repetition of the word "ever" in the poem below). Climax and accumulation also function in Whitman's work. The following is an example of both, from *Song of Myself*, part 42:

> Ever the hard unsunk ground
> Ever the eaters and drinkers, ever the upward and downward sun, ever the air and the
>   Ceaseless tides,
> Ever myself and my neighbors, refreshing, wicked, real,
> Ever the old inexplicable query, ever that thorn'd thumb,
>   That breath of itches and thirsts...

Notice how these sample verses repeatedly employ the same grammatical arrangement and create a frame for the poem—a series of place markers, a structure. This repetition somehow doesn't seem monotonous or robotic; rather, we feel it building up to a climax, accumulating to a high point. Notice this same pattern in Psalm 148:1-3:

> Praise the LORD.
>   Praise the LORD from the heavens,
>   Praise him in the heights above.
> Praise him, all his angels,
>   Praise him, all his heavenly hosts.
> Praise him, sun and moon,
>   Praise him, all you shining stars.

It is clear that, like Dickinson, Whitman instinctively incorporated his experience with biblical verse and with the rhythms of the human voice to create what, in retrospect, was a revolutionary form of poetry. His influence on later poets is unparalleled, for many, if not most poets were influenced by his style, which was groundbreaking. Research some of the other poets who wrote during the Victorian period of literature, many of whom are included in this book—Hopkins, Tennyson, Elizabeth Browning, Robert Browning, Matthew Arnold, Christina Rossetti, Dante Rossetti—and you will see that they were writing in contained stanzas with rhyme and meter. Many poets of later generations departed radically from strict forms and took up Whitman's style in their own particular ways. Prominent examples include, but are not limited to, Hart Crane, William Carlos Williams, Allen Ginsberg, Jack Kerouac, and Gerald Stern. The critic Harold Bloom says that when he is gloomy he reads Whitman aloud until he feels better because of Whitman's spirit and the rhythms of his line.

Whitman wrote the long, rambling, epic-length poem *Leaves of Grass* throughout his life, revising and adding to it continuously until he died. He wrote some memorable short lyrics, as well as poems that commemorated large national events, including his most famous elegy about Lincoln's death, *When Lilacs Last in the Door-yard Bloom'd.*

LEARNING TO READ CLOSELY

Song of Myself

(part 6)

A child said What is the grass? fetching it to me with full hands;
How could I answer the child? I do not know what it is any more than he.

I guess it must be the flag of my disposition, out of hopeful green stuff woven.

Or I guess it is the handkerchief of the Lord,
5   A scented gift and remembrancer designedly dropt,
Bearing the owner's name someway in the corners, that we may see and remark,
            and say Whose?

Or I guess the grass is itself a child, the produced babe of the vegetation.

Or I guess it is a uniform hieroglyphic,
And it means, Sprouting alike in broad zones and narrow zones,
10   Growing among black folks as among white,
Kanuck, Tuckahoe, Congressman, Cuff, I give them the same, I receive them the same.

And now it seems to me the beautiful uncut hair of graves.

Tenderly will I use you curling grass,
It may be you transpire from the breasts of young men,
15   It may be if I had known them I would have loved them,
It may be you are from old people, or from offspring taken soon out of their mothers' laps,
And here you are the mothers' laps.

This grass is very dark to be from the white heads of old mothers,
Darker than the colorless beards of old men,
20   Dark to come from under the faint red roofs of mouths.

O I perceive after all so many uttering tongues,
And I perceive they do not come from the roofs of mouths for nothing.

I wish I could translate the hints about the dead young men and women,
And the hints about old men and mothers, and the offspring taken soon out of their laps.

25   What do you think has become of the young and old men?
And what do you think has become of the women and children?

They are alive and well somewhere,
The smallest sprout shows there is really no death,
And if ever there was it led forward life, and does not wait at the end to arrest it,
30   And ceas'd the moment life appear'd.

All goes onward and outward, nothing collapses,
And to die is different from what any one supposed, and luckier.

Whitman is the great poet of lists and catalogs. He has an incantatory rhythm, almost as if he were casting a ritual spell with repetitions and word patterns. The poem begins so simply. Haven't you heard a child ask (or, yourself a child, asked) an enormous, unanswerable, or strange question about something you took for granted and never questioned? Here the poem opens with a child gathering a handful of grass and asking a question: "What is the grass?" The speaker in the poem, probably an adult, wonders, "How could I answer the child?" The grass and all the elements of the universe are as mysterious as they are common. Almost immediately, however, the speaker decides to take on the challenge and try to answer the question.

He begins with a one-line stanza as an answer, almost as if he is getting warmed up. The grass is like a flag of the disposition, temperament, or personality of the speaker, which he says is hopeful and green. The color green suggests newness and growth, as does hope. Clearly the speaker is playful in his response, taking it personally, starting wherever he can.

His next suggestion, comparison, or metaphor is that grass is the handkerchief of the Lord with His initials in the corner, dropped on the earth so that we humans might pick it up and wonder whose it is and ask questions about God's existence. Notice the words Whitman chooses to talk about this metaphor—a "remembrancer designedly dropt." He changes the syntax of the words to say all this quickly, in a compressed way. This stanza is longer than the previous one. It is three lines that get progressively longer.

The speaker's playfulness continues in another single-lined stanza in which he suggests that "the grass is itself a child," the baby "of the vegetation." Grass is literally the most basic and lowly vegetation in the floral kingdom, but we see the speaker moving by association as well. The child was the one who brought the grass to his attention, thus his mind is thinking about children; the grass, in its smallness, commonness, and hopeful growth is also a kind of child.

Now the grass is a hieroglyphic, which is the picture script of the ancient Egyptians or, more broadly, something that needs to be deciphered. The whole poem is a kind of deciphering of the grass and, more largely, of the universe. This is perhaps the most serious suggestion our speaker has put forth, and immediately he has more to say about it—his imagination is stirred by his own suggestion. The grass grows everywhere, among all kinds of people—black folk, white, Native Americans. "I give them the same, I receive them the same," claims the speaker, as if the presence of the same grass among all these people is reason enough for them all to be treated equally. Whitman lived during the time when Lincoln was working to abolish slavery, hence this is not a light statement. How did we get from talking about the grass to the equality of all humankind? This is called a lyric leap and it is especially delightful as we follow Whitman's mind across (or down) the poem.

Yet if you thought equality of humankind was where this speaker was going to land, you'd be wrong, because he goes on. The next stanza, another single-lined one, brings him finally to his biggest subject: death. The grass, this speaker suggests, is like hair on top of graves. In the next stanza, before we have time to register our surprise about where this poem is taking us, we are ushered into the poet's thoughts as he takes stock of his subject. He says he will use the subject of grass and death "tenderly," almost as if he is addressing the subject of his poem as an animate being. He begins to speak of how the grass grows from those dead—"the breasts of young men," for instance. Whitman lived through the Civil War and was conscious of the death surrounding him. He cared for young soldiers in their dying hours after battle. He doesn't intend for us to think only of those battle dead, but of all who die—old people, babies, mothers.

From the grass as "hair of graves" and the graves themselves, we move to an imaginative space within the poem where the speaker can hear the dead, like "so many uttering tongues." He wants to tell us what they are saying, to "translate the hints," and to explain what has become of them. He wants, finally, to speak of life after this life. His vision of this is that "there is really no death," that all these dead are alive and well; that all in the universe goes onward; and there is really no such thing as entropy. This poet believes in regeneration, in life coming from death literally—the dead body enriches the earth from which grass grows—and figuratively—dying produces life, all things are caught up in the circle of life. "Nothing collapses" he says, "And to die is different from what any one supposed," presuming that most of us think of it as an end, a sadness, and separation. He rebuts this claim and says that to die is "luckier" than we supposed.

Whether you agree with the speaker or not, look at the astonishing range of thought that we have covered and the surprising words and patterns of words that have taken us there. Did you ever in your whole life hear someone refer to death as lucky? Did you ever think of the dead as speaking from the grave with "so many uttering tongues"? Whitman is the master of surprising lyric leaps of logic and image. What about this proposition—"The smallest sprout shows there is really no death." In other words, because life comes from the earth, which is made up of dead things—plants, animals, people—therefore nothing entirely dies but simply changes form.

Look also at the astonishing formal choices that this consummate writer of free verse has used. Mostly anaphora and parallelism, where certain repeated phrases and word constructions ("Or," "Or," "Or," "It may," "It may," "It may," "Darker," "Dark," "I perceive," "I perceive," "And," "And," "And"…), comprise the scaffold of the poem. This small pool of repeated words gives a shape and a satisfaction to the poem. These long-breathed lines that don't even fit the page of your book in some cases are also reminiscent of Psalms, one of Whitman's favorite books of the Bible. Look how simple the divisions are between stanzas. When he has a new subject, he starts a new stanza. Feel the energy of these sweeping phrases—long and muscular language that carries us a great distance both in our bodies as we read out loud and in our hearts and minds as we leap where Whitman leaps.

Whether you agree with Whitman on this subject or not, the poem is a remarkable achievement. He took us from a child's question to the meaning of death and life in this universe and beyond. He gave us a simple but satisfying form and surprised us with comparisons and words that we ourselves would likely never have considered on this subject. He created a surprising but logical relationship between his metaphors. Look at the power language has to lift us to another place!

ANTHOLOGY

A Noiseless Patient Spider

> A noiseless, patient spider,
> I mark'd, where, on a little promontory, it stood, isolated;
> Mark'd how, to explore the vacant, vast surrounding,
> It launch'd forth filament, filament, filament, out of itself;
> 5 Ever unreeling them—ever tirelessly speeding them.
>
> And you, O my Soul, where you stand,
> Surrounded, detached, in measureless oceans of space,
> Ceaselessly musing, venturing, throwing,—seeking the spheres, to connect them;
> Till the bridge you will need, be form'd—till the ductile anchor hold;
> 10 Till the gossamer thread you fling, catch somewhere, O my Soul.

1. Begin by looking up the definitions of any unfamiliar words—"promontory" and "filament" are especially important to know.

2. What is being compared to the soul? What do you make of the comparison?

3. What do you know about spiders, their webs, and their movement?

4. How do you think the speaker feels about the sense of being small and finite in the face of such infinitude—exultant, overwhelmed, agitated, delighted?

5. What do you know of Walt Whitman's perspective on life (from other poems and his biography) that would help you to read the tone of this poem?

6. In these two small stanzas, Whitman employs the tools of metaphor, symbol, parallelism, repetition, alliteration, assonance, consonance, and more. Choose three tools from this list to identify in the text and explain how and why they contribute to the message or theme.

7. What are the boundaries of interpretation in poetry? How can we argue that poems can't simply mean anything you want them to, but also don't necessarily have a single true interpretation?

O Captain! My Captain!

O Captain! my Captain! our fearful trip is done,
The ship has weather'd every rack, the prize we sought is won,
The port is near, the bells I hear, the people all exulting,
While follow eyes the steady keel, the vessel grim and daring;
5   But O heart! heart! heart!
            O the bleeding drops of red!
               Where on the deck my Captain lies,
                  Fallen cold and dead.

O Captain! my Captain! rise up and hear the bells;
10   Rise up—for you the flag is flung—for you the bugle trills,
For you bouquets and ribbon'd wreaths—for you the shores crowding,
For you they call, the swaying mass, their eager faces turning;
            Here, Captain! dear father!
               This arm beneath your head!
15   It is some dream that on the deck
                  You've fallen cold and dead.

My Captain does not answer, his lips are pale and still,
My father does not feel my arm, he has no pulse nor will;
The ship is anchor'd safe and sound, its voyage closed and done,
20   From fearful trip the victor ship comes in with object won;
            Exult, O shores! and ring, O bells!
               But I, with mournful tread,
                  Walk the deck my Captain lies,
                     Fallen cold and dead.

1. This is an elegy for Abraham Lincoln—what are the clues in the language that identify it as 1) an elegy, and 2) a specific tribute to Lincoln?

2. What is the poem's emotional tone?

3. How does the poem's structure and language help you feel the metaphor of the ship and of the ship's captain having fallen?

4. What is the effect of repeating and then ending with the words "cold and dead"—how does the sound of this phrase contribute to its sense or meaning?

5. Circle or bracket all instances of parallelism in the grammar or in the ideas of the poem.

6. Have you experienced the death of a loved one? Have you ever felt this strongly about the death of someone you didn't personally know?

7. Do you think this poem adequately captures some of the qualities of grief?

I Saw in Louisiana a Live-Oak Growing

I saw in Louisiana a live-oak growing,
All alone stood it, and the moss hung down from the branches;
Without any companion it grew there, uttering joyous leaves of dark green,
And its look, rude, unbending, lusty, made me think of myself;
5   But I wonder'd how it could utter joyous leaves, standing alone there,
       without its friend, its lover near—for I knew I could not;
And I broke off a twig with a certain number of leaves upon it, and twined
       around it a little moss,
And brought it away—and I have placed it in sight in my room;
It is not needed to remind me as of my own dear friends,
(For I believe lately I think of little else than of them;)
10   Yet it remains to me a curious token—it makes me think of manly love;
For all that, and though the live-oak glistens there in Louisiana, solitary,
       in a wide flat space,
Uttering joyous leaves all its life, without a friend, a lover, near,
I know very well I could not.

1. Notice how the poet's thoughts travel—he sees an oak tree growing alone, separated from other trees, and immediately his thoughts turn to friendship. How do you explain this leap? Does your mind do this at times, leaping associatively from one thought to another, even though they might seem unconnected?

2. What do you make of the phrase "utter joyous leaves"? What's surprising about it?

3. How is the twig twined with moss a symbol? What might be its range of meanings?

4. Based on your reading of this poem, how does Whitman feel about his friends?

5. Do you think this poem captures something essential about friendship, something that you yourself feel about your friends, or is it peculiar only to Whitman?

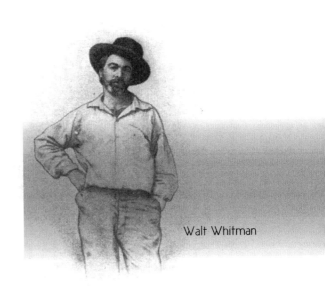

Walt Whitman

When Lilacs Last in the Door-yard Bloom'd

1

When lilacs last in the door-yard bloom'd,
And the great star early droop'd in the western sky in the night,
I mourn'd—and yet shall mourn with ever-returning spring.

O ever-returning spring! trinity sure to me you bring;
5   Lilac blooming perennial, and drooping star in the west,
And thought of him I love.

2

O powerful, western, fallen star!
O shades of night! O moody, tearful night!
O great star disappear'd! O the black murk that hides the star!
10   O cruel hands that hold me powerless! O helpless soul of me!
O harsh surrounding cloud, that will not free my soul!

3

In the door-yard fronting an old farm-house, near the white-wash'd palings,
Stands the lilac bush, tall-growing, with heart-shaped leaves of rich green,
With many a pointed blossom, rising, delicate, with the perfume strong I love,
15   With every leaf a miracle......and from this bush in the door-yard,
With delicate-color'd blossoms, and heart-shaped leaves of rich green,
A sprig, with its flower, I break.

4

In the swamp, in secluded recesses,
A shy and hidden bird is warbling a song.

20   Solitary, the thrush,
The hermit, withdrawn to himself, avoiding the settlements,
Sings by himself a song.

Song of the bleeding throat!
Death's outlet song of life—(for well, dear brother, I know
25   If thou wast not gifted to sing, thou would'st surely die.)

5

Over the breast of the spring, the land, amid cities,
Amid lanes, and through old woods, (where lately the violets peep'd from the
        ground, spotting the gray debris;)
Amid the grass in the fields each side of the lanes—passing the endless grass;
Passing the yellow-spear'd wheat, every grain from its shroud in the dark-brown
        fields uprising;
30   Passing the apple-tree blows of white and pink in the orchards;
Carrying a corpse to where it shall rest in the grave,
Night and day journeys a coffin.

6

Coffin that passes through lanes and streets,
Through day and night, with the great cloud darkening the land,
35   With the pomp of the inloop'd flags, with the cities draped in black,
With the show of the States themselves, as of crape-veil'd women, standing,
With processions long and winding, and the flambeaus of the night,
With the countless torches lit—with the silent sea of faces, and the unbared heads,
With the waiting depot, the arriving coffin, and the sombre faces,
40   With dirges through the night, with the thousand voices rising strong and solemn;
With all the mournful voices of the dirges, pour'd around the coffin,
The dim-lit churches and the shuddering organs—Where amid these you journey,
With the tolling, tolling bells' perpetual clang;
Here! coffin that slowly passes,
45   I give you my sprig of lilac.

7

(Nor for you, for one, alone;
Blossoms and branches green to coffins all I bring:
For fresh as the morning—thus would I carol a song for you, O sane and sacred death.

All over bouquets of roses,
50   O death! I cover you over with roses and early lilies;
But mostly and now the lilac that blooms the first,
Copious, I break, I break the sprigs from the bushes;
With loaded arms I come, pouring for you,
For you, and the coffins all of you, O death.)

8

55   O western orb, sailing the heaven!
Now I know what you must have meant, as a month since we walk'd,
As we walk'd up and down in the dark blue so mystic,
As we walk'd in silence the transparent shadowy night,
As I saw you had something to tell, as you bent to me night after night,
60   As you droop'd from the sky low down, as if to my side, (while the other
      stars all look'd on;)
As we wander'd together the solemn night, (for something, I know not what,
      kept me from sleep;)
As the night advanced, and I saw on the rim of the west, ere you went, how
      full you were of woe;
As I stood on the rising ground in the breeze, in the cold transparent night,
As I watch'd where you pass'd and was lost in the netherward black of the night,
65   As my soul, in its trouble, dissatisfied, sank, as where you, sad orb,
Concluded, dropt in the night, and was gone.

9

Sing on, there in the swamp!
O singer bashful and tender! I hear your notes—I hear your call;
I hear—I come presently—I understand you;
70   But a moment I linger—for the lustrous star has detain'd me;
The star, my departing comrade, holds and detains me.

10

O how shall I warble myself for the dead one there I loved?
And how shall I deck my song for the large sweet soul that has gone?
And what shall my perfume be, for the grave of him I love?

75 Sea-winds, blown from east and west,
Blown from the eastern sea, and blown from the western sea, till there on
    the prairies meeting:
These, and with these, and the breath of my chant,
I perfume the grave of him I love.

11

O what shall I hang on the chamber walls?
80 And what shall the pictures be that I hang on the walls,
To adorn the burial-house of him I love?

Pictures of growing spring, and farms, and homes,
With the Fourth-month eve at sundown, and the gray smoke lucid and bright,
With floods of the yellow gold of the gorgeous, indolent, sinking sun, burning,
    expanding the air;
85 With the fresh sweet herbage under foot, and the pale green leaves of the trees prolific;
In the distance the flowing glaze, the breast of the river, with a wind-dapple here
    and there;
With ranging hills on the banks, with many a line against the sky, and shadows;
And the city at hand, with dwellings so dense, and stacks of chimneys,
And all the scenes of life, and the workshops, and the workmen homeward returning.

12

90 Lo! body and soul! this land!
Mighty Manhattan, with spires, and the sparkling and hurrying tides, and the ships;
The varied and ample land—the South and the North in the light—Ohio's shores, and
    flashing Missouri,
And ever the far-spreading prairies, cover'd with grass and corn.

Lo! the most excellent sun, so calm and haughty;
95 The violet and purple morn, with just-felt breezes;
The gentle, soft-born, measureless light;
The miracle, spreading, bathing all—the fulfill'd noon;
The coming eve, delicious—the welcome night, and the stars,
Over my cities shining all, enveloping man and land.

13

100 Sing on! sing on, you gray-brown bird!
Sing from the swamps, the recesses—pour your chant from the bushes;
Limitless out of the dusk, out of the cedars and pines.

Sing on, dearest brother—warble your reedy song;
Loud human song, with voice of uttermost woe.

105   O liquid, and free, and tender!
      O wild and loose to my soul! O wondrous singer!
      You only I hear......yet the star holds me, (but will soon depart;)
      Yet the lilac, with mastering odor, holds me.

14

      Now while I sat in the day, and look'd forth,
110 In the close of the day, with its light, and the fields of spring, and the farmer
          preparing his crops,
      In the large unconscious scenery of my land, with its lakes and forests,
      In the heavenly aerial beauty, (after the perturb'd winds, and the storms;)
      Under the arching heavens of the afternoon swift passing, and the voices of
          children and women,
      The many-moving sea-tides,—and I saw the ships how they sail'd,
115 And the summer approaching with richness, and the fields all busy with labor,
      And the infinite separate houses, how they all went on, each with its meals and
          minutia of daily usages;
      And the streets, how their throbbings throbb'd, and the cities pent—lo! then and there,
      Falling upon them all, and among them all, enveloping me with the rest,
      Appear'd the cloud, appear'd the long black trail;
120 And I knew Death, its thought, and the sacred knowledge of death.

15

      Then with the knowledge of death as walking one side of me,
      And the thought of death close-walking the other side of me,
      And I in the middle, as with companions, and as holding the hands of companions,
      I fled forth to the hiding receiving night, that talks not,
125 Down to the shores of the water, the path by the swamp in the dimness,
      To the solemn shadowy cedars, and ghostly pines so still.

      And the singer so shy to the rest receiv'd me;
      The gray-brown bird I know, receiv'd us comrades three;
      And he sang what seem'd the carol of death, and a verse for him I love.

130 From deep secluded recesses,
      From the fragrant cedars, and the ghostly pines so still,
      Came the carol of the bird.

      And the charm of the carol rapt me,
      As I held, as if by their hands, my comrades in the night;
135 And the voice of my spirit tallied the song of the bird.

     Death Carol.

16

     Come, lovely and soothing Death,
     Undulate round the world, serenely arriving, arriving,
     In the day, in the night, to all, to each,
     Sooner or later, delicate Death.

140   *Prais'd be the fathomless universe,*
     For life and joy, and for objects and knowledge curious;
     And for love, sweet love–But praise! praise! praise!
     For the sure-enwinding arms of cool-enfolding Death.

     Dark Mother, always gliding near, with soft feet,
145   *Have none chanted for thee a chant of fullest welcome?*

     Then I chant it for thee–I glorify thee above all;
     I bring thee a song that when thou must indeed come, come unfalteringly.

     Approach, strong Deliveress!
     When it is so–when thou hast taken them, I joyously sing the dead,
150   *Lost in the loving, floating ocean of thee,*
     Laved in the flood of thy bliss, O Death.

     From me to thee glad serenades,
     Dances for thee I propose, saluting thee–adornments and feastings for thee;
     And the sights of the open landscape, and the high-spread sky, are fitting,
155   *And life and the fields, and the huge and thoughtful night.*

     The night, in silence, under many a star;
     The ocean shore, and the husky whispering wave, whose voice I know;
     And the soul turning to thee, O vast and well-veil'd Death,
     And the body gratefully nestling close to thee.

160   *Over the tree-tops I float thee a song!*
     Over the rising and sinking waves–over the myriad fields, and the prairies wide;
     Over the dense-pack'd cities all, and the teeming wharves and ways,
     I float this carol with joy, with joy to thee, O Death!

17

     To the tally of my soul,
165   Loud and strong kept up the gray-brown bird,
     With pure, deliberate notes, spreading, filling the night.

     Loud in the pines and cedars dim,
     Clear in the freshness moist, and the swamp-perfume;
     And I with my comrades there in the night.

170   While my sight that was bound in my eyes unclosed,
     As to long panoramas of visions.

18

     I saw askant the armies;
     And I saw, as in noiseless dreams, hundreds of battle-flags;
     Borne through the smoke of the battles, and pierc'd with missiles, I saw them,
175   And carried hither and yon through the smoke, and torn and bloody;
     And at last but a few shreds left on the staffs, (and all in silence,)
     And the staffs all splinter'd and broken.

I saw battle-corpses, myriads of them,
And the white skeletons of young men—I saw them;
180   I saw the debris and debris of all the dead soldiers of the war;
But I saw they were not as was thought;
They themselves were fully at rest—they suffer'd not;
The living remain'd and suffer'd—the mother suffer'd,
And the wife and the child, and the musing comrade suffer'd,
185   And the armies that remain'd suffer'd.

19

Passing the visions, passing the night;
Passing, unloosing the hold of my comrades' hands;
Passing the song of the hermit bird, and the tallying song of my soul,
(Victorious song, death's outlet song, yet varying, ever-altering song,
190   As low and wailing, yet clear the notes, rising and falling, flooding the night,
Sadly sinking and fainting, as warning and warning, and yet again bursting with joy,
Covering the earth, and filling the spread of the heaven,
As that powerful psalm in the night I heard from recesses,)
Passing, I leave thee, lilac with heart-shaped leaves;
195   I leave thee there in the door-yard, blooming, returning with spring,
I cease from my song for thee;
From my gaze on thee in the west, fronting the west, communing with thee,
O comrade lustrous, with silver face in the night.

20

Yet each I keep, and all, retrievements out of the night;
200   The song, the wondrous chant of the gray-brown bird,
And the tallying chant, the echo arous'd in my soul,
With the lustrous and drooping star, with the countenance full of woe,
With the lilac tall, and its blossoms of mastering odor;
With the holders holding my hand, nearing the call of the bird,
205   Comrades mine, and I in the midst, and their memory ever I keep—for the dead
        I loved so well;
For the sweetest, wisest soul of all my days and lands...and this for his dear sake;
Lilac and star and bird, twined with the chant of my soul,
There in the fragrant pines, and the cedars dusk and dim.

This is considered the greatest American elegy ever written. Don't try to understand every word of it. Simply read it aloud as a class, taking turns with each section. It is generally understood that Whitman wrote this after President Lincoln was assassinated, and the poem represents to Whitman his "sprig of lilac" placed on the grave of the fallen leader, so to speak.

1. Notice how he extends the lyric poem well beyond the length we usually expect—does he keep your interest? How?

2. What are the things he does in terms of repetition of ideas as well as structure and language?

3. What lines in this poem do you love because they capture something you've felt, wondered, or grieved about? What lines in this poem do you admire simply for their sound?

4. What do you think about Whitman's carol of praise to Death?

ACTIVITIES

1. Find an online recording of Walt Whitman reading his poems. Find a picture of Walt Whitman.

2. Try writing a Whitmanian poem. As a class, make a list of the elements that are characteristic of his style and decide on a minimum number that must be included in your poem. If you are daring enough as a class, after you have each written a poem, hand them out randomly to each other and have each student double the length of another student's poem, still writing in Whitman's style. Read the poems aloud to the class anonymously.

3. Try writing a poem in answer to a child's question. Take the subject far afield from the original question. "Are we there yet?" is a favorite question that could be answered in many ways.

4. Try writing some lines of poetry in which unexpected objects "utter" something—the way Whitman's live-oak "utters" its leaves. Feel free to use other verbs in a similarly surprising way.

5. Contrast the poetry of Dickinson and Whitman. Make two lists on the board that describe the differences between them, such as the different styles and interests they have as poets. Look at some of the other poems in this book that were written by Americans who lived after 1900 and try to discern toward which style the later poets lean. Have half the class dress up and/or perform a skit in which Emily Dickinson and Walt Whitman end up in the same room and have a conversation about life and poetry.

6. Make a list of adjectives to describe Whitman and Dickinson as poets or as people. What do they have in common? Think about other great writers or figures in history. Do they also share these qualities?

7. As a class memorize *A Noiseless Patient Spider* with hand motions. Write an imitation of this poem, using the following example (see below) to guide you. Find a metaphor for the soul and use the structure of Whitman's poem, borrowing what you need from his phrasing to create your own picture of the soul's work in the world.

Jessica Budd

A Heavy Wordy Book

> A heavy wordy book
> I noted where on my bed it laid still
> Impressed upon the pages, stories of distant lands
> It launches forth, words, words, words into the mind
> Ever releasing them, ever tirelessly engaging them
>
> And you O my soul where you are,
> Insightful, yet hidden, between the covers laid upon it
> Endlessly pondering, exploring, deciphering, seeking the threads to connect them
> Till the knot you will need be tied, till the wondering thoughts settle
> Till the words from the pages you cast attach somewhere, O my soul.

8. Read *When Lilacs Last in the Door-yard Bloom'd* aloud. First take time to hear its rhythms and sounds without thinking too much about meaning (except to know that it is an elegy for Abraham Lincoln). Then read it again for understanding. It is a time investment but it will be worth it. What do you observe?

9. Break up into small groups to talk about Whitman's view of death in part 6 of *Leaves of Grass*. Do you agree or disagree with his view? Why? Can you write a poem describing your view? Be sure to do it with images as he did by using the grass to explore his subject versus stating the idea first.

10. Make a list of the books and other cultural forms, such as music, that have influenced you and share it with the class. Think about how you might use this influence to create your own formal structures as a writer.

11. Many activities and professions besides poetry depend on the ability to make imaginative leaps and associations. Talk about this as a class, making a list of examples in the sciences, arts, business, politics, sports, etc., in which individuals or groups made surprising decisions or actions that resulted in dramatic change. Debate the merits of following the rules in an activity or profession versus the benefits of breaking them.

15

NARRATIVE POEMS:

AN ANTHOLOGY

{the formal history of poetry}

You have been taught to ask certain questions of poems. The first questions you ask relate to *who is speaking* and *the situation of the person speaking*. Whenever we have a character, we have a story. Narrative poems, like lyric poems, are rhythmic and finely tuned to sound. They use the line and stanza, and employ all of the elements of the poem. Their difference is one of emphasis; they tend to focus more intently on the story and have characters and plot. You have already seen that ballads and epics belong to the category of narrative poem (refer to chapter 9 to refresh your memory). Narratives entertain, inform, warn, and delight. To look at a culture's stories is to understand its deepest values, what it means to be a part of that group of people in time and place. Any of the poems in this section could have been written in prose, but their writers wanted the tension, elegance, immediacy, stark imagery, and music of the poem.

LEARNING TO READ CLOSELY

Langston Hughes (1902–1967)

Theme for English B

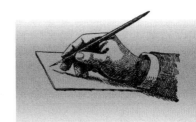

The instructor said,
    Go home and write
    a page tonight.
    And let that page come out of you—
5   *Then, it will be true.*

  I wonder if it's that simple?
I am twenty-two, colored, born in Winston-Salem.
I went to school there, then Durham, then here
to this college on the hill above Harlem.
10 I am the only colored student in my class.
The steps from the hill lead down into Harlem
through a park, then I cross St. Nicholas,
Eighth Avenue, Seventh, and I come to the Y,
the Harlem Branch Y, where I take the elevator
15 up to my room, sit down, and write this page:

  It's not easy to know what is true for you or me
at twenty-two, my age. But I guess I'm what
I feel and see and hear, Harlem, I hear you:
hear you, hear me—we two—you, me, talk on this page.
20 (I hear New York too.) Me—who?
Well, I like to eat, sleep, drink, and be in love.
I like to work, read, learn, and understand life.
I like a pipe for a Christmas present,
or records—Bessie, bop, or Bach.
25 I guess being colored doesn't make me *not* like
the same things other folks like who are other races.
So will my page be colored that I write?

  Being me, it will not be white.
But it will be
30 a part of you, instructor.
You are white—
yet a part of me, as I am a part of you.
That's American.
Sometimes perhaps you don't want to be a part of me.
35 Nor do I often want to be a part of you.
But we are, that's true!
As I learn from you,
I guess you learn from me—
although you're older—and white—
40 and somewhat more free.
This is my page for English B.

This poem tells a story that is particular to the speaker, but it is also a narrative of which many people felt the force in their own lives. The setting is New York City in the 1920s during the Harlem Renaissance. There are two characters in the story—the speaker and the "instructor"; the speaker is taking a college class in which he is the "only colored student." The narrative opens with the italicized words of the instructor giving an assignment to the class. The teacher tells his students that if they write a page that comes "out of you— / Then, it will be true." The rest of the poem is the student/speaker's response to this assignment. He queries what it means to be "you," and what it means to be true. He addresses some of the assumptions in the instructor's statement and the issue of race that runs beneath the conversation and the time period during which the poem was born.

The instructor's "assignment" is written in a rhymed and rhythmic quatrain. The speech is tighter and more artificial and formulaic in comparison with the speaker's answer, which is more conversational, less singsong. The speaker's first response also points to the possibility that the teacher is reducing the complexity of the issue—"I wonder if it's that simple?" What follows is a list of descriptive information about the speaker that locates him in time, place, and culture and brings "the elephant in the room" out of the closet. He says he's "colored" in line 7 and later in line 10, he says, "I am the only colored student in my class." He then gives us directions to his home. But this place isn't just physical; he is sketching for us his reality, or reality as he sees it, which isn't as simple as the assignment suggests. "It's not easy to know what is true for you or me," he says, and then he proceeds to have a sort of dialogue with himself. The style of this is jazzy: it echoes, is highly rhythmic, and is reminiscent of two instruments in conversation with each other. It ends by echoing the same original question: "Me—who?" as if to say what does the "me" to which you and I so easily refer mean and contain. He lists his likes and dislikes, and quickly these cascade toward the same opening subject, "I guess being colored doesn't make me *not* like / the same things other folks like who are other races."

We understand that this meditation is on race, a conversation that was raging off the page at the time the poem was composed. Slavery was long abolished at this point, but inequality and segregation remained a fact of life. The speaker, whose life details are the same as the poet's, goes on to speak of America as a place where white and black are a part of each other, whether they prefer it or not. He suggests an even ground where both races have second thoughts about being a part of each other, yet they nonetheless are, and insists that they can learn from each other. He ends with an eloquent statement about the political reality of their times—"you're older—and white— / and somewhat more free." He argues gently that the instructor, despite his age, freedom, skin color, and position as the teacher, can learn from the student—the speaker—as well.

This poem is striking for its musical, playful, jazzy, conversational style and for the ground-breaking statement it made at the time of its writing. Interestingly, it is tonally matter-of-fact. It states racial equality as a reality, but it also acknowledges the social and political actuality of inequality. It speaks for the individuals, the characters involved, but it also speaks more widely of the two racial groups. Breaking down barriers beyond race, he insists that teachers can learn from students (another potential power relationship). He uses the list format, common to Whitman and other free verse writers, and creates sequences of words in each line that rhythmically ricochet off each other (lines like "Bessie, bop, or Bach" and "hear you, hear me—we two—you, me, talk on this page"). Hughes maps out the poem in four simple stanzas that function almost like chapters in the argument: instructor says, student says, student elaborates, student closes with a single-line stanza. The language is down-to-earth, colloquial, and it seems to be simply functional in many places as opposed to beautiful or elegant. Unlike the opening quatrain, which is tight and follows clear rules, his rhyming is occasional and unpatterned. This contributes to his basic claim that "you" and "true" are not simple, easy, or apolitical categories.

It wouldn't be hard to argue that this is not a narrative poem but a lyric poem. Its theme is the equality of man and the notion of the self. The poem seems to ask what it means to be a self, an individual, and to what extent we are a part of larger forces. The word "true," as used in the opening assignment, is also somewhat ironic in the context of the untruth that the social and political forces of the time perpetuated. This speaker, so wise and yet temperate, communicates this with his mild but earnest tone of voice.

ANTHOLOGY

Henry Wadsworth Longfellow (1807–1882)

Paul Revere's Ride

Listen, my children, and you shall hear
Of the midnight ride of Paul Revere,
On the eighteenth of April, in Seventy-five;
Hardly a man is now alive
5 Who remembers that famous day and year.
He said to his friend, 'If the British march
By land or sea from the town to-night,
Hang a lantern aloft in the belfry arch
Of the North Church tower as a signal light,–
10 One, if by land, and two, if by sea;
And I on the opposite shore will be,
Ready to ride and spread the alarm
Through every Middlesex village and farm,
For the country folk to be up and to arm.'

15 Then he said, 'Good-night!' and with muffled oar
Silently rowed to the Charlestown shore,
Just as the moon rose over the bay,
Where swinging wide at her moorings lay
The Somerset, British man-of-war;
20 A phantom ship, with each mast and spar
Across the moon like a prison bar,
And a huge black hulk, that was magnified
By its own reflection in the tide.

Meanwhile, his friend, through alley and street,
25 Wanders and watches with eager ears,
Till in the silence around him he hears
The muster of men at the barrack door,
The sound of arms, and the tramp of feet,
And the measured tread of the grenadiers,
30 Marching down to their boats on the shore.

Then he climbed the tower of the
      Old North Church,
By the wooden stairs, with stealthy tread,
To the belfry-chamber overhead,
And startled the pigeons from their perch
35 On the sombre rafters, that round him made
Masses and moving shapes of shade,–
By the trembling ladder, steep and tall,
To the highest window in the wall,
Where he paused to listen and look down
40 A moment on the roofs of the town,
And the moonlight flowing over all.

Beneath, in the churchyard, lay the dead,
In their night-encampment on the hill,
Wrapped in silence so deep and still
45 That he could hear, like a sentinel's tread,
The watchful night-wind, as it went
Creeping along from tent to tent,
And seeming to whisper, 'All is well!'
A moment only he feels the spell
50 Of the place and the hour, and the secret dread
Of the lonely belfry and the dead;
For suddenly all his thoughts are bent
On a shadowy something far away,
Where the river widens to meet the bay,–
55 A line of black that bends and floats
On the rising tide, like a bridge of boats.

Meanwhile, impatient to mount and ride,
Booted and spurred, with a heavy stride
On the opposite shore walked Paul Revere.
60 Now he patted his horse's side,
Now gazed at the landscape far and near,
Then, impetuous, stamped the earth,
And turned and tightened his saddle-girth;
But mostly he watched with eager search
65 The belfry-tower of the Old North Church,
As it rose above the graves on the hill,
Lonely and spectral and sombre and still.
And lo! as he looks, on the belfry's height
A glimmer, and then a gleam of light!
70 He springs to the saddle, the bridle he turns,
But lingers and gazes, till full on his sight
A second lamp in the belfry burns!

A hurry of hoofs in a village street,
A shape in the moonlight, a bulk in the dark,
75 And beneath, from the pebbles, in passing,
      a spark
Struck out by a steed flying fearless and fleet;
That was all! And yet, through the gloom and
      the light,
The fate of a nation was riding that night;
And the spark struck out by that steed, in
      his flight,
80 Kindled the land into flame with its heat.

He has left the village and mounted the steep,
And beneath him, tranquil and broad and deep,
Is the Mystic, meeting the ocean tides;
And under the alders that skirt its edge,
85 Now soft on the sand, now loud on the ledge,
Is heard the tramp of his steed as he rides.

It was twelve by the village clock,
When he crossed the bridge into Medford town.
He heard the crowing of the cock,
90 And the barking of the farmer's dog,
And felt the damp of the river fog,
That rises after the sun goes down.

It was one by the village clock,
When he galloped into Lexington.
95 He saw the gilded weathercock
Swim in the moonlight as he passed,
And the meeting-house windows, blank
  and bare,
Gaze at him with a spectral glare,
As if they already stood aghast
100 At the bloody work they would look upon.

It was two by the village clock,
When he came to the bridge in Concord town.
He heard the bleating of the flock,
And the twitter of birds among the trees,
105 And felt the breath of the morning breeze
Blowing over the meadows brown.
And one was safe and asleep in his bed,
Who at the bridge would be first to fall,
Who that day would be lying dead,
110 Pierced by a British musket-ball.

You know the rest. In the books you have read,
How the British Regulars fired and fled,—
How the farmers gave them ball for ball,
From behind each fence and farm-yard wall,
115 Chasing the red-coats down the lane,
Then crossing the fields to emerge again
Under the trees at the turn of the road,
And only pausing to fire and load.

So through the night rode Paul Revere;
120 And so through the night went his cry of alarm
To every Middlesex village and farm,—
A cry of defiance and not of fear,
A voice in the darkness, a knock at the door
And a word that shall echo forevermore!
125 For, borne on the night-wind of the Past,
Through all our history, to the last,
In the hour of darkness and peril and need,
The people will waken and listen to hear
The hurrying hoof-beats of that steed,
130 And the midnight message of Paul Revere.

First talk as a class or in pairs about what you know about Paul Revere's ride. For younger grades consider using a picture book to compare and contrast what a narrative poem does versus a prose narrative. Then read the poem (preferably aloud with each class member taking different pieces).

1. What is the effect of poetry that is also story?

2. What are some of the elements of poetry found in this poem?

3. What are some of the typical elements of story? How do they work together?

4. What is the overall effect of all of the elements of poetry and story coming together in this poem?

Edgar Allen Poe (1809-1849)

The Raven

Once upon a midnight dreary, while I pondered weak and weary,
Over many a quaint and curious volume of forgotten lore,
While I nodded, nearly napping, suddenly there came a tapping,
As of some one gently rapping, rapping at my chamber door.
5   "Tis some visitor,' I muttered, 'tapping at my chamber door—
  Only this, and nothing more.'

Ah, distinctly I remember it was in the bleak December,
And each separate dying ember wrought its ghost upon the floor.
Eagerly I wished the morrow;—vainly I had sought to borrow
10   From my books surcease of sorrow—sorrow for the lost Lenore—
For the rare and radiant maiden whom the angels named Lenore—
  Nameless here for evermore.

And the silken sad uncertain rustling of each purple curtain
Thrilled me—filled me with fantastic terrors never felt before;
15   So that now, to still the beating of my heart, I stood repeating
  "Tis some visitor entreating entrance at my chamber door—
Some late visitor entreating entrance at my chamber door;—
  This it is, and nothing more.'

Presently my soul grew stronger; hesitating then no longer,
20   'Sir,' said I, 'or Madam, truly your forgiveness I implore;
But the fact is I was napping, and so gently you came rapping,
And so faintly you came tapping, tapping at my chamber door,
That I scarce was sure I heard you'—here I opened wide the door;—
  Darkness there, and nothing more.

25   Deep into that darkness peering, long I stood there wondering, fearing,
Doubting, dreaming dreams no mortal ever dared to dream before
But the silence was unbroken, and the darkness gave no token,
And the only word there spoken was the whispered word, 'Lenore!'
This I whispered, and an echo murmured back the word, 'Lenore!'
30   Merely this and nothing more.

Back into the chamber turning, all my soul within me burning,
Soon again I heard a tapping somewhat louder than before.
'Surely,' said I, 'surely that is something at my window lattice;
Let me see then, what thereat is, and this mystery explore—
35   Let my heart be still a moment and this mystery explore;—
  'Tis the wind and nothing more!'

Open here I flung the shutter, when, with many a flirt and flutter,
In there stepped a stately raven of the saintly days of yore.
Not the least obeisance made he; not a minute stopped or stayed he;
40   But, with mien of lord or lady, perched above my chamber door—
Perched upon a bust of Pallas just above my chamber door—
  Perched, and sat, and nothing more.

Then this ebony bird beguiling my sad fancy into smiling,
By the grave and stern decorum of the countenance it wore,
45   `Though thy crest be shorn and shaven, thou,' I said, `art sure no craven.
Ghastly grim and ancient raven wandering from the nightly shore—
Tell me what thy lordly name is on the Night's Plutonian shore!'
Quoth the raven, `Nevermore.'

Much I marvelled this ungainly fowl to hear discourse so plainly,
50   Though its answer little meaning—little relevancy bore;
For we cannot help agreeing that no living human being
Ever yet was blessed with seeing bird above his chamber door—
Bird or beast above the sculptured bust above his chamber door,
With such name as `Nevermore.'

55   But the raven, sitting lonely on the placid bust, spoke only,
That one word, as if his soul in that one word he did outpour.
Nothing further then he uttered—not a feather then he fluttered—
Till I scarcely more than muttered `Other friends have flown before—
On the morrow he will leave me, as my hopes have flown before.'
60   Then the bird said, `Nevermore.'

Startled at the stillness broken by reply so aptly spoken,
`Doubtless,' said I, `what it utters is its only stock and store,
Caught from some unhappy master whom unmerciful disaster
Followed fast and followed faster till his songs one burden bore—
65   Till the dirges of his hope that melancholy burden bore
Of `Never-nevermore."'

But the raven still beguiling all my sad soul into smiling,
Straight I wheeled a cushioned seat in front of bird and bust and door;
Then, upon the velvet sinking, I betook myself to linking
70   Fancy unto fancy, thinking what this ominous bird of yore—
What this grim, ungainly, ghastly, gaunt, and ominous bird of yore
Meant in croaking `Nevermore.'

This I sat engaged in guessing, but no syllable expressing
To the fowl whose fiery eyes now burned into my bosom's core;
75   This and more I sat divining, with my head at ease reclining
On the cushion's velvet lining that the lamp-light gloated o'er,
But whose velvet violet lining with the lamp-light gloating o'er,
She shall press, ah, nevermore!

Then, methought, the air grew denser, perfumed from an unseen censer
80   Swung by Seraphim whose foot-falls tinkled on the tufted floor.
`Wretch,' I cried, `thy God hath lent thee—by these angels he has sent thee
Respite—respite and nepenthe from thy memories of Lenore!
Quaff, oh quaff this kind nepenthe, and forget this lost Lenore!'
Quoth the raven, `Nevermore.'

85 `Prophet!' said I, `thing of evil!–prophet still, if bird or devil!–
Whether tempter sent, or whether tempest tossed thee here ashore,
Desolate yet all undaunted, on this desert land enchanted–
On this home by horror haunted–tell me truly, I implore–
Is there–*is* there balm in Gilead?–tell me–tell me, I implore!'
90 Quoth the raven, `Nevermore.'

`Prophet!' said I, `thing of evil!–prophet still, if bird or devil!
By that Heaven that bends above us–by that God we both adore–
Tell this soul with sorrow laden if, within the distant Aidenn,
It shall clasp a sainted maiden whom the angels named Lenore–
95 Clasp a rare and radiant maiden, whom the angels named Lenore?'
Quoth the raven, `Nevermore.'

`Be that word our sign of parting, bird or fiend!' I shrieked upstarting–
`Get thee back into the tempest and the Night's Plutonian shore!
Leave no black plume as a token of that lie thy soul hath spoken!
100 Leave my loneliness unbroken!–quit the bust above my door!
Take thy beak from out my heart, and take thy form from off my door!'
Quoth the raven, `Nevermore.'

And the raven, never flitting, still is sitting, still is sitting
On the pallid bust of Pallas just above my chamber door;
105 And his eyes have all the seeming of a demon's that is dreaming,
And the lamp-light o'er him streaming throws his shadow on the floor;
And my soul from out that shadow that lies floating on the floor
Shall be lifted–nevermore!

1. What is the basic story of this poem?

2. What is mysterious about the story?

3. What role does the raven play in the poem?

4. What is the state of mind of the speaker?

5. How does the poet use repetition to reinforce the speaker's mindset?

6. What are the different kinds of repetition?

7. What is the tone and emotional effect of the poem?

8. Have you ever had an experience that helps you to understand what is happening in the poem?

Alfred Tennyson (1809–1892)

The Lady of Shalott

On either side the river lie
Long fields of barley and of rye,
That clothe the wold and meet the sky;
And through the field the road run by
5   To many-tower'd Camelot;
And up and down the people go,
Gazing where the lilies blow
Round an island there below,
The island of Shalott.

10   Willows whiten, aspens quiver,
Little breezes dusk and shiver
Through the wave that runs for ever
By the island in the river
Flowing down to Camelot.
15   Four grey walls, and four grey towers,
Overlook a space of flowers,
And the silent isle imbowers
The Lady of Shalott.

By the margin, willow veil'd,
20   Slide the heavy barges trail'd
By slow horses; and unhail'd
The shallop flitteth silken-sail'd
Skimming down to Camelot:
But who hath seen her wave her hand?
25   Or at the casement seen her stand?
Or is she known in all the land,
The Lady of Shalott?

Only reapers, reaping early,
In among the bearded barley
30   Hear a song that echoes cheerly
From the river winding clearly;
Down to tower'd Camelot:
And by the moon the reaper weary,
Piling sheaves in uplands airy,
35   Listening, whispers, " 'Tis the fairy
The Lady of Shalott."

There she weaves by night and day
A magic web with colours gay.
She has heard a whisper say,
40   A curse is on her if she stay
To look down to Camelot.
She knows not what the curse may be,
And so she weaveth steadily,
And little other care hath she,
45   The Lady of Shalott.

And moving through a mirror clear
That hangs before her all the year,
Shadows of the world appear.
There she sees the highway near
50   Winding down to Camelot;
There the river eddy whirls,
And there the surly village churls,
And the red cloaks of market girls
Pass onward from Shalott.

55   Sometimes a troop of damsels glad,
An abbot on an ambling pad,
Sometimes a curly shepherd lad,
Or long-hair'd page in crimson clad
Goes by to tower'd Camelot;
60   And sometimes through the mirror blue
The knights come riding two and two.
She hath no loyal Knight and true,
The Lady of Shalott.

But in her web she still delights
65   To weave the mirror's magic sights,
For often through the silent nights
A funeral, with plumes and lights
And music, went to Camelot;
Or when the Moon was overhead,
70   Came two young lovers lately wed.
"I am half sick of shadows," said
The Lady of Shalott.

A bow-shot from her bower-eaves,
He rode between the barley sheaves,
75 The sun came dazzling thro' the leaves,
And flamed upon the brazen greaves
Of bold Sir Lancelot.
A red-cross knight for ever kneel'd
To a lady in his shield,
80 That sparkled on the yellow field,
Beside remote Shalott.

The gemmy bridle glitter'd free,
Like to some branch of stars we see
Hung in the golden Galaxy.
85 The bridle bells rang merrily
As he rode down to Camelot:
And from his blazon'd baldric slung
A mighty silver bugle hung,
And as he rode his armor rung
90 Beside remote Shalott.

All in the blue unclouded weather
Thick-jewell'd shone the saddle-leather,
The helmet and the helmet-feather
Burn'd like one burning flame together,
95 As he rode down to Camelot.
As often thro' the purple night,
Below the starry clusters bright,
Some bearded meteor, burning bright,
Moves over still Shalott.

100 His broad clear brow in sunlight glow'd;
On burnish'd hooves his war-horse trode;
From underneath his helmet flow'd
His coal-black curls as on he rode,
As he rode down to Camelot.
105 From the bank and from the river
He flashed into the crystal mirror,
"Tirra lirra," by the river
Sang Sir Lancelot.

She left the web, she left the loom,
110 She made three paces through the room,
She saw the water-lily bloom,
She saw the helmet and the plume,
She look'd down to Camelot.
Out flew the web and floated wide;
115 The mirror crack'd from side to side;
"The curse is come upon me," cried
The Lady of Shalott.

In the stormy east-wind straining,
The pale yellow woods were waning,
120 The broad stream in his banks complaining.
Heavily the low sky raining
Over tower'd Camelot;
Down she came and found a boat
Beneath a willow left afloat,
125 And around about the prow she wrote
The Lady of Shalott.

And down the river's dim expanse
Like some bold seer in a trance,
Seeing all his own mischance—
130 With a glassy countenance
Did she look to Camelot.
And at the closing of the day
She loosed the chain, and down she lay;
The broad stream bore her far away,
135 The Lady of Shalott.

Lying, robed in snowy white
That loosely flew to left and right—
The leaves upon her falling light—
Thro' the noises of the night,
140 She floated down to Camelot:
And as the boat-head wound along
The willowy hills and fields among,
They heard her singing her last song,
The Lady of Shalott.

145 Heard a carol, mournful, holy,
Chanted loudly, chanted lowly,
Till her blood was frozen slowly,
And her eyes were darkened wholly,
Turn'd to tower'd Camelot.
150 For ere she reach'd upon the tide
The first house by the water-side,
Singing in her song she died,
The Lady of Shalott.

Under tower and balcony,
155 By garden-wall and gallery,
A gleaming shape she floated by,
Dead-pale between the houses high,
Silent into Camelot.
Out upon the wharfs they came,
160 Knight and Burgher, Lord and Dame,
And around the prow they read her name,
The Lady of Shalott.

Who is this? And what is here?
And in the lighted palace near
165 Died the sound of royal cheer;
And they crossed themselves for fear,
All the Knights at Camelot;
But Lancelot mused a little space
He said, "She has a lovely face;
170 God in his mercy lend her grace,
The Lady of Shalott."

1. What happens in this story?

2. Read the poem then listen to Lorena McKennit's song of this poem on YouTube. Compare and contrast the poem and the song. Why is this poem fairly easy to put to music?

3. Is there a way in which the emotion of the song would come out if the music were not aiding you (if you were just reading it aloud)?

4. How does the power of the music add to the story? How does the music take away from the story (if at all)?

5. In what beloved family film does this poem appear?

Robert Frost (1874–1963)

Home Burial

He saw her from the bottom of the stairs
Before she saw him. She was starting down,
Looking back over her shoulder at some fear.
She took a doubtful step and then undid it
5   To raise herself and look again. He spoke
Advancing toward her: "What is it you see
From up there always—for I want to know."
She turned and sank upon her skirts at that,
And her face changed from terrified to dull.
10   He said to gain time: "What is it you see,"
Mounting until she cowered under him.
"I will find out now—you must tell me, dear."
She, in her place, refused him any help
With the least stiffening of her neck
                and silence.
15   She let him look, sure that he wouldn't see,
Blind creature; and a while he didn't see.
But at last he murmured, "Oh," and
                again, "Oh."

"What is it—what?" she said.

"Just that I see."

20   "You don't," she challenged. "Tell me
                what it is."

"The wonder is I didn't see at once.
I never noticed it from here before.
I must be wonted to it—that's the reason.
The little graveyard where my people are!
25   So small the window frames the whole of it.
Not so much larger than a bedroom, is it?
There are three stones of slate and one
                of marble,
Broad-shouldered little slabs there in
                the sunlight
On the sidehill. We haven't to mind *those*.
30   But I understand: it is not the stones,
But the child's mound—"

"Don't, don't, don't, don't," she cried.

She withdrew shrinking from beneath his arm
That rested on the banister, and slid downstairs;
35   And turned on him with such a daunting look,
He said twice over before he knew himself:
"Can't a man speak of his own child he's lost?"
"Not you! Oh, where's my hat? Oh, I don't
                need it!
I must get out of here. I must get air.
40   I don't know rightly whether any man can."

"Amy! Don't go to someone else this time.
Listen to me. I won't come down the stairs."
He sat and fixed his chin between his fists.
"There's something I should like to ask
                you, dear."

45   "You don't know how to ask it."

"Help me, then."
Her fingers moved the latch for all reply.

"My words are nearly always an offence.
I don't know how to speak of anything
50   So as to please you. But I might be taught
I should suppose. I can't say I see how.
A man must partly give up being a man
With women-folk. We could have
                some arrangement
By which I'd bind myself to keep hands off
55   Anything special you're a-mind to name.
Though I don't like such things 'twixt
                those that love.
Two that don't love can't live together
                without them.
But two that do can't live together with them."
She moved the latch a little. "Don't—don't go.
60   Don't carry it to someone else this time.
Tell me about it if it's something human.
Let me into your grief. I'm not so much
Unlike other folks as your standing there
Apart would make me out. Give me my chance.
65   I do think, though, you overdo it a little.
What was it brought you up to think it the thing
To take your mother-loss of a first child
So inconsolably—in the face of love.
You'd think his memory might be satisfied—"

70   'There you go sneering now!'

'I'm not, I'm not!
You make me angry. I'll come down to you.
God, what a woman! And it's come to this,
A man can't speak of his own child that's dead.'

75   'You can't because you don't know how.
If you had any feelings, you that dug
With your own hand–how could you?–
          his little grave;
I saw you from that very window there,
Making the gravel leap and leap in air,

80   Leap up, like that, like that, and land so lightly
And roll back down the mound beside the hole.
I thought, Who is that man? I didn't know you.
And I crept down the stairs and up the stairs
To look again, and still your spade kept lifting.

85   Then you came in. I heard your rumbling voice
Out in the kitchen, and I don't know why,
But I went near to see with my own eyes.
You could sit there with the stains on your shoes
Of the fresh earth from your own baby's grave

90   And talk about your everyday concerns.
You had stood the spade up against the wall
Outside there in the entry, for I saw it.'

'I shall laugh the worst laugh I ever laughed.
I'm cursed. God, if I don't believe I'm cursed.'

95   'I can repeat the very words you were saying.
"Three foggy mornings and one rainy day
Will rot the best birch fence a man can build."
Think of it, talk like that at such a time!
What had how long it takes a birch to rot

100   To do with what was in the darkened parlour.
You *couldn't* care! The nearest friends can go
With anyone to death, comes so far short
They might as well not try to go at all.
No, from the time when one is sick to death,

105   One is alone, and he dies more alone.
Friends make pretence of following to the grave,
But before one is in it, their minds are turned
And making the best of their way back to life
And living people, and things they understand.

110   But the world's evil. I won't have grief so
If I can change it. Oh, I won't, I won't!'

'There, you have said it all and you feel better.
You won't go now. You're crying. Close the door.
The heart's gone out of it: why keep it up.

115   Amy! There's someone coming down the road!'

'*You*–oh, you think the talk is all. I must go–
Somewhere out of this house. How can I make you–'

'If–you–do!' She was opening the door wider.
'Where do you mean to go? First tell me that.

120   I'll follow and bring you back by force. I *will!*–'

1. This is a poem made up of dialogue or conversation, between two people. Who are the two people?

2. What are they arguing about?

3. Have you ever experienced an argument like this?

4. What is the emotional state of the couple?

5. Does the argument resolve? Do Amy and her husband come to a better understanding of each other?

6. How does hearing their words powerfully communicate the story of these characters to us?

7. If you could speak to them, what would you say to each of these people to help them?

8. Do you find yourself caring about the characters?

9. Do you find yourself siding with one or the other of the characters?

10. Try to write a dialogue with a different outcome than the one in this poem and perform it in your classroom.

EPIC AS A SUBSET OF NARRATIVE POETRY

The epic poem is considered a narrative poem with distinctive characteristics. There are different meanings of the term "epic." Its specific meaning in poetry refers to the ancient epics that were written accounts of stories and information in poem form (with a meter). These grand poems were often accounts of the battles and heroic adventures of a culture and were written and collected over many, many years. The most well-known of these epics are *The Illiad* and *The Odyssey* by Homer, a Greek poet. Both epics tell about the Trojan War and its hero, Odysseus, and were composed late in the eighth century BC. These are called traditional or primary epics.

Another form of epic is the literary or secondary epic. This form is written in imitation of the primary epic but has some differences. *Paradise Lost*, written by John Milton in the eighteenth century, is the chief example of this. Milton wrote about the fall of man in the Garden of Eden and Adam and Eve's subsequent expulsion from the Garden. He used many techniques of the earlier epics but embellished and developed the biblical story from Genesis.

In modern times, poets, such as T.S. Eliot, wrote poems that are described as epic in their scale. This means something different than it did in either of the two previous examples. Eliot, in *The Waste Land*, endeavored to write about the spiritual and psychological aftermath of World War I. He uses many languages and fragments, and creates a kind of quest that is different than that of primary epics. It is dense and difficult and even long, though not as long as the preceding epics.

There are other examples, such as Walt Whitman's *Song of Myself*, Ezra Pound's *Cantos*, and Derek Walcott's (a living poet) *Omeros*. Some of the interesting questions that surround the epic tradition are: What constitutes an epic? and What kind of culture is capable of producing an epic (even written by an individual)? This anthology will not sample epics, but Padrick Collum's *The Children's Homer* is recommended on CD as well as *The Illiad* and *The Odyssey*, both available at modest prices and fairly easy to follow by ear. If your teacher does not take time in class to play these ancient story poems for you, consider listening to them on summer vacation. You won't regret it!

ACTIVITIES

(See the individual poem questions for further activity suggestions.)

1. Try acting out one or more of the poems in this chapter. Do a dramatic reading of any or all of them. Read them first quietly to yourself then read them dramatically aloud as a class with different people playing different voices or characters. Add actions. Perform this mini-play for another class. Before you perform it, have the audience read it to themselves. Afterward, discuss the difference between the two experiences of the poem.

2. Freewrite as if you were another person. Take what you wrote and create a sort of speech in the voice in which you've just written. Now craft the speech into lines. Be aware of word choices and their sounds, and try to pay attention to where you are breaking the lines and why. Consider adding another person who speaks in the poem as well, creating perhaps a conversation or an argument (as in *Home Burial*).

3. Read several lyric poems (most of the poems in this book are lyric poems) and try to imagine the suppressed or buried story in the poem. Usually lyric poems revolve around an emotional, spiritual, or intellectual insight that has been informed by a story. Tell the story behind the poem to each other, tell it alone by freewriting, then try telling it together aloud as a group. Notice the tone of voice as an indicator for how to tell the story; it will help you be faithful to the original intent submerged in the poem.

4. Draw a picture or make a collage of the story represented in the narrative poem that you are studying. Show it to the class and ask the class to tell you the story they see, then tell them the story you intended.

5. Invent a character, writing as much as you can about this person (looks, likes, dislikes, age, family, experiences, etc.). Then write a poem in the voice of this character.

16
GROWING YOUR INTEREST

{application}

STARTING A POETRY GROUP,
WORKSHOP, OR SCHOOL ELECTIVE GROUP

One way in which many writers work is as part of a writers' workshop. A writers' workshop consists of a group of writers who meet on a regular basis to critique each other's work. Ideally, each week, each individual writes a poem, and then at the meetings a "worksheet" (packet with all of the poems photocopied) is passed out. Each member sets aside a period of time to spend on each poem or story that will be involved in the discussion, and then on each of the poems in the worksheet, the members prepare comments for the following week. There can be a group moderator or a moderator or introducer for each poem. Once you have set up your own poetry group, writers' workshop, or school elective group (all of which serve the same basic function), you will find that your work improves and strengthens as you hear how others respond to and interpret what you have written.

When we write, so much of what we produce comes from the depths of our own experience and mind; the workshop is a way to help objectify your poetry, to see how much of your intent comes through, and also to see the ways in which your poetry has transcended your experience. That is the goal of all art. Poet John Hollander said, "I want my poems to be wiser than I am, to know more about themselves than I do." In the workshop, one becomes more perceptive about how the poems are functioning—what works, what doesn't, and the location of the areas of strength and weakness.

In this group you ought to spend time reading poems from your favorite poem notebook (see description on p. 219) aloud. Each week should start with such a reading. Better yet, have everyone memorize a poem and recite it for each other. Become a word-cherishing group and see what happens to your own poems. There is a dynamic relationship between the work that you internalize through this kind of study and the work that you produce in your own writing.

Since, most likely, you won't be able to do a poem per person every week (depending on the size of your group), a rotating schedule is a good idea. Try to write comments on each other's papers and pass them back even if you don't have time to "workshop" each person each week. Slowly you will begin to learn what to listen for when making your revisions. If all the critics are saying the same thing, they're most likely onto something. When someone seems to understand the poem's meaning but finds difficulty with certain parts, this is also a clear sign that she might have some constructive help for you. You can't implement every suggestion offered, but you will benefit from hearing it. You will learn to serve each other's work in the spirit of discerning helpfulness.

The sooner you build trust among your group and make it clear that you are invested in each other's progress as artists, the better. Always work toward a balance of affirming strengths and exploring weaknesses or opportunities for determining the next step for the piece. Try to read with an open and alert heart and mind, an eye for strengths, and an appetite for the unfamiliar. Avoid discussing poems on the basis of theme only or on your own biographical relationship to the subject matter. Avoid claims that are vague (*This poem is a masterpiece!*) or that are based on your own like or dislike of something (*I am not religious.*) in the poem. Try not to make an argument that is based on truth-value (*This poem is good because it is so true.*). Such claims as these are generic and dismissive of language and originality as well as of the elements you've learned in the course of this text. Focus on craft and the imagination, and look back at the chapter titles and vocabulary words in this book to find that can lead your discussion.

There will be times when you do not take the advice you are given. Elizabeth Bishop and Marianne Moore were long-time poetry friends. Moore was one of the reasons Bishop began taking poetry writing seriously. For years, Bishop sent Moore (who was the experienced writer) her poems for critique and would implement whatever Moore suggested. At a certain, more mature, point in her career, Bishop responded to Moore's close edits by saying, "Elizabeth knows best." She kept her own counsel for that particular poem. There will be times when you, like Elizabeth Bishop, will decide to overrule the given advice—but learning to recieve and implement advice will most likely be the more difficult skill to acquire.

Revision is the lion's share of the work for a writer. Your first writing is important and good, but it isn't the end of your piece. All writers everywhere, for their entire lives, revise their first try, often hundreds of times. Elizabeth Bishop spent twenty years revising her poem *The Moose*. Schedule a poetry reading for friends and parents once every six to twelve months as something that you can work toward, polishing your poems for a public presentation. Bring food and drink and send out invitations.

WRITER'S JOURNAL

Your writer's journal is your sourcebook for poems; it is your hide-and-seek game with the muse (a mythical figure of inspiration). Each day or week—however often you can—begin writing down phrases, words, and passages from books you are reading, or that you hear in conversation, that please or startle you. Collect images intently and try to notice what is around you and then find words for it. (For an expanded focus on this activity, read Annie Dillard's essay from *Pilgrim at Tinker Creek* titled "Seeing.") Stop at the end of the day and jot down the sensory impressions that you remember from the day. (For more on image collecting, read Robert Hass's essay on "Images" from his book *Twentieth Century Pleasures*.) Look up words in the dictionary and write down various definitions, or the origins of the words (other languages, for instance).

Write down the lyrics of songs that stick with you. Write down plot suggestions that run through your mind when you're at basketball practice. Most poets must begin by reading each time they sit down to write. This is a kind of tinder for the fire of the imagination and for language. Write down experiences or dialogues that you've had with friends or you've overheard. William James used to stop people in the middle of their good stories so that he could end the story the way he wanted. Argue with yourself, seek out your opinions on difficult and complicated subjects. Record the landscape through which you travel as you drive. Keep a list of activities, or of the weather, or of the birds you've seen. Poems usually don't occur spontaneously; they come from mulling, from collecting, from wondering. Many of the activities in this book could be recorded in a journal and will give you ideas for poem writing.

Some further exercises that will help you use your journal and turn your entries into poems include the following texts: *The Poet's Companion* by Addonizio/Laux and *A Poetry Handbook* by Mary Oliver. Read the journals that other writers have kept.

FAVORITE POEM NOTEBOOK

This exercise is simple—every time you find a favorite poem, copy it down (or photocopy it) and put it in a notebook. This is a wonderful source for you and a high mark for which you are aiming as a writer. You will begin to notice patterns and habits, gestures and images to which you are repeatedly drawn. You will find yourself returning to certain writers. It would be a good idea to seek out whole books written by the writers whom you most likely discovered by reading an anthology of poems. Read through one of their slim volumes in one sitting and write down your impressions in your journal. Copy all of your favorites for your notebook. Make notes on why you like them, introducing them as if you were going to show them to someone else or publish them in the newspaper as a recommendation. For an example, see Edward Hirsch's book *The Poet's Choice*, which does this nicely.

Some journals I'd recommend:

Literary journals are the place where writers publish their work before the poems go into books. There are usually articles about craft, sometimes an interview, along with a collection of newly published poems. There are countless journals. What follows is a brief list that will get you started. I'd recommend these for students in upper high school: *Poetry; Image: A Journal of the Arts & Religion; The Gettysburg Review; The Kenyon Review; Poets and Writers; The Threepenny Review; Blackbird* (online journal).

Books on poetry to begin collecting:

The Poetry Dictionary by John Drury

The Wadsworth Anthology of Poetry

The Norton Introduction to Poetry

The Norton Anthology of Poetry

How to Read a Poem and Fall in Love With Poetry by Edward Hirsch.
This book is especially good as a guide to your reading because it has lists of recommended books at the back.

Poet's Choice by Edward Hirsch

A Book of Luminous Things: An International Anthology, ed. by Czeslaw Milosz.

Check (online or in a library catalog) to see if any of the poets whose poems you have enjoyed have written prose books on the subject of poetry.

Reading by author

These are suggestions listed by author and are more or less in chronological order. All of the following writers can be found in nearly any poetry anthology. Let your interest and response guide you alongside the list. Start at the bottom, middle, or beginning or with a familiar name. There are also many wonderful foreign-language poets; a good place to begin looking for recommendations is *World Poetry: An Anthology of Verse from Antiquity to Our Time*, edited by Clifton Fadiman, and *How to Read a Poem* by Edward Hirsch, which has an extensive list of recommended authors and titles at the back. There are many excellent contemporary writers whom you will discover through the journals and websites recommended here. This is also a fine place to begin your reading plan. The important thing is to begin reading—wherever you begin you will work your way back or forward to other writers. Writing is the highest form of reading, it is the great conversation, hence you enter into the dialogue at whatever point you start.

The Illiad and *The Odyssey*, Homer (not originally English language)

The Bible (poetic and prophetic books; not originally English language)

Cædmon's Hymn

Thomas Wyatt

Sir Walter Ralegh

Edmund Spenser

Sir Philip Sidney

Mary Sidney

William Shakespeare (sonnets and plays)

John Donne (*The Holy Sonnets* in particular)

Ben Jonson

Robert Herrick

George Herbert (From *The Temple: Sacred Poems and Private Ejaculations*)

John Milton (short lyrics and *Paradise Lost*, preferably on CD)

Anne Bradstreet

Andrew Marvell

Henry Vaughan

Thomas Traherne

Alexander Pope

Charles Wesley (hymns)

Christopher Smart

William Cowper

Charlotte Smith

William Blake

Robert Burns

William Wordsworth

Mary Tighe

Lord Byron

Percy Bysshe Shelley

John Clare

John Keats

Elizabeth Barrett Browning

Robert Browning

Edgar Allen Poe

Alfred Tennyson

Henry Wadsworth Longfellow

Edward Lear

Emily Brontë

Spirituals (anonymous)

Herman Melville

Walt Whitman

Dante and Christina Rosetti

Emily Dickinson

Lewis Carroll

Thomas Hardy

Gerard Manley Hopkins

A.E. Housman

Charlotte Mew

Paul Laurence Dunbar

Robert Frost

Gertrude Stein

Carl Sandburg

Wallace Stevens

William Carlos Williams

D.H. Lawrence

Ezra Pound

Marianne Moore

H.D. (Hilda Doolittle)

T.S. Eliot

Wilfred Owen

e.e. cummings

Edna St. Vincent Millay

Jean Toomer

Hart Crane

Langston Hughes

Ogden Nash

Stanley Kunitz

Theodore Roethke

Elizabeth Bishop

Robert Hayden

John Berryman

Dylan Thomas

Gwendolyn Brooks

Allan Ginsberg

Richard Wilbur

Denise Levertov

Robert Bly

Frank O'Hara

Galway Kinnell

James Wright

Geoffrey Hill

Sylvia Plath

Seamus Heany

Eavan Boland

Louise Gluck

Dana Gioia

Scott Cairns

Gjertrud Schnackenberg

Stanley Plumly

Michael Collier

Ellen Voigt

Brigit Peegan Kelly

G.C. Waldrep

Online

There are many websites dedicated to poetry. Do some poking around to find the ones you like. You can type the words "poetry website" into a search engine and see what comes up.

The following are four excellent sites that will sustain you for years:

Poets.org: www.poets.org

This website has a wealth of resources, including essays and biographical information on poets, interviews, and poems. This site may also eventually guide you to places where you would like to send your poems to share with others.

LiterActive: http://capress.link/1601

This CD contains a remarkable cataloging of poetic elements, cultural contexts, and critical approaches to texts.

Poetry daily: www.poetrydaily.org

Contains a daily poem and an excellent selection of contemporary poems.

Poetry **magazine**: www.poetryfoundation.org

A leading journal of poetry with an online component.

George Herbert

POETRY SLAM OR PUBLIC RECITATION

A poetry slam is a public performance of a poem during which people compete and are judged according to specified criteria. A public recitation involves less performance and focuses on straight memorization and reciting of a poem. Have a competition (preferably with a prize) in which students across grades (perhaps grades 5–7, 7–9, or 10–12) memorize and practice reciting in front of an audience. Choose a panel of judges and have the contestants evaluated in five categories, worth five points each, for a total of twenty-five points:

Understanding of content: 1–5 points

Can you understand the poem's meaning because of the way in which the performer emphasizes and expresses it; does the performer know when to pause, when to have a question or a declaration in her voice; is the emotion appropriate to the meaning of the poem?

Body language: 1–5 points

Does the performer's body help to communicate, through gesture, movement, and facial expression, what is happening in the poem?

Clarity of speech/enunciation: 1–5 points

Can you understand the words clearly? What is the quality of the performer's voice?

Level of difficulty: 1–5 points

How difficult is the poem? Is it a twelve-line poem with simple language or is it longer or full of dense, complex expression?

Overall presentation: 1–5 points

What is your general, gut response to this performance, regardless of each separate category?

Just by listening, you should understand the poem as well as if you had spent time writing about it. The student performing should understand and externalize that understanding in all of his gestures, pauses, and emphases.

Teachers, consider inviting an audience of parents and other students. Consider offering a final grade boost for first through third places. Find a sponsor to offer a cash prize for winners. Be sure to have outside judges, such as other teachers, qualified students, qualified parents, or members of the community (not the teacher of the class).

To pursue this activity on a larger scale, consider **Poetry Out Loud**, which is a contest that starts at the local level and proceeds to the national with fantastic prizes and exposure. Ask your local or national arts council for information. There is also information online at the National Endowment for the Arts and at the state arts council websites. For more information, visit: <www.poetryoutloud.org/poems/browsepoems.html>.

HOSTING A READING SERIES
OR COFFEEHOUSE

Invite poets and fiction writers to read their work to an audience. Find a nice room and invite people from your school, church, neighborhood, and family. Have the writer read for a half-hour to an hour from her own work. Leave a few minutes at the end for questions. Check local colleges for writers who might be willing to read their work to middle and high school students, or ask around to find local writers. Check the schedule at local bookstores and colleges to see if there will be any readings in your area. Alternately, bring members of your school or homeschooling group together to have an evening of scheduled reading to each other. Invite others, print a schedule, and host it in an atmosphere similar to that of a coffeehouse, with small tables set around the central performance area. Offer a podium at the front and have volunteers bring finger food and hot drinks.

HOSTING A SUMMER CAMP
OR ATTENDING A SUMMER CAMP

Invite a group of students interested in any of the activities mentioned in this chapter to a summer poetry group. For a couple of hours a day, have a teacher or parent with expertise guide the group. Canvass your school community to see what expertise exists within it. Charge admission and have the group continue throughout the year on their own as a writing workshop. Obviously, there are a number of logistics to which someone familiar with event planning would have to attend.

Many colleges and universities offer such camps in the summer. BreadLoaf Writer's Conference has a version for high school students. The State Arts Council often supports such programs. In Pennsylvania, there is a Summer Arts Institute for middle school students and Governor's School for the Arts for high school students.

FINDING DEAD AND LIVE MENTORS

We all need to be apprenticed. Find a poet whose work makes you sing, who speaks to you in your inner being, and get to know all of his or her work. Read everything this poet has ever written. Take notes on what you read. Copy poems into your notebook and use them as templates to imitate. Write letters to this poet, though he may be dead. Consider spending a long stretch of time, such as a summer, reading this writer's work. This will help you to grow immensely as a writer.

Find a living mentor who may only be a step ahead of you—another student or a parent—and ask her to share what she has learned over the years. Perhaps she'd be willing to look at your poems and give you some feedback or meet on a regular basis.

ACKNOWLEDGMENTS

I have read many books and essays on poetry over the years and taught from a number of textbooks. Many of these have influenced my work in this book. A short list includes the following:

The Wadsworth Anthology of Poetry, edited by Jay Parini

The Norton Introduction to Poetry, Ninth Edition

Poetry, An Introduction by Jeffrey Hoeper and James Pickering

Discovering Poetry by Hans Guth and Gabriele Rico

The Princeton Encyclopedia of Poetry and Poetics

The Poetry Dictionary by John Drury

How to Read a Poem and Fall in Love with Poetry by Edward Hirsch

Poet's Choice by Edward Hirsch

The Electric Life by Sven Birkerts

I would like to thank Lenora Riley, who is an excellent designer, Rebecca Jekel and Danielle Sahm Surra, whose editorial work was essential to this project. This book would not exist in its current form without Judith Kuntz's outstanding efforts as content editor. My life in poetry would not be what it is if it weren't for the following friends and teachers: Douglas Basford, Annie Kantar Ben-Hillel, Michael Collier, James Hoch, Stanley Plumly, and G.C. Waldrep. Finally, thanks to Chris, the unmeasured whole.

SHORT BIOGRAPHIES OF POETS IN THIS BOOK

{appendix a}

Alighieri, Dante (1265-1321)

Dante Alighieri is perhaps the most exalted of the Italian poets. His most well-known work is *The Divine Comedy*. He studied philosophy and Provençal poetry and was politically active in Florence until he was banished in 1302 and became a citizen of all Italy, eventually dying in Ravenna. *The Divine Comedy* was composed while he was in exile. It is the tale of the poet's journey through Hell and Purgatory, guided by Vergil, and through Heaven, guided by Beatrice, for whom the poem is a memorial. It pictures a changeless universe ordered by God. Through it Dante established Tuscan as the literary language of Italy, and because of this he is seen as the architect of the modern Italian language. Others of his works include *La vita nuova* (c. 1292), a collection of prose and lyrics, treatises on language and politics, eclogues, and epistles.[1]

---

1. Information taken from the following sources: *The Concise Columbia Encyclopedia*. Copyright © 1991 by Columbia University Press; <http://www.guardian.co.uk/books/2008/jun/09/dantealighieri>.

Askew, Anne (1521–1546)

Relatively little is known about the life of Anne Askew. Her father, William Askew of Lincolnshire, England, forced her at the age of fifteen to marry Thomas Kyme. When she later tried to divorce her husband, her petition was denied, so she simply began to use her maiden name again. A Protestant, she expressed her faith in poetry and preaching and was persecuted as a heretic by those in power who did not share her faith. When she was put on trial in 1539, she wrote of the experience in *First Examination*. After she was re-arrested in 1546, she wrote *Latter Examination*. She eventually was martyred, burned at the stake in Smithfield for refusing to recant her beliefs.[2]

Bishop, Elizabeth (1911–1979)

Elizabeth Bishop was born in Worcester, Massachusetts. Her father died when she was eight months old, and five years later her mother went insane, after which Bishop never saw her again. Bishop was raised by her maternal grandparents in Nova Scotia and by an aunt who lived in Boston. She attended boarding school in Massachusetts, then Vassar College in New York. In 1934 she graduated from Vassar and met Marianne Moore, who became her writing mentor and close friend.

From 1935 to 1938, Bishop traveled extensively, visiting Belgium, France, Brittany, England, North Africa, Spain, Ireland, and Italy. In 1943 she lived for nine months in Mexico, where she became acquainted with the poet Pablo Neruda. In 1951, Bishop traveled to Brazil and decided to stay. Her travels in Brazil, which included trips up the Amazon and into the interior of the country, provided ample material for her poetry.

Bishop won the Houghton Mifflin Poetry Award for her first collection of poetry, *North and South*, as well as awards for her later work, including the Pulitzer Prize in 1956. She is known for her natural but understated voice and remarkable facility with form.[3]

Blake, William (1757–1827)

William Blake was a poet, painter, prophet, and visionary who wrote during the Romantic period of English literature. He was born in London and, despite his dislike for the city, spent nearly his entire life there. As a child he attended an art school, followed by an apprenticeship with an engraver. Then at the age of twenty-one he studied at the Royal Academy of Arts. With this background, he was able, during his career as a poet, to blend the written word with visual art.

In 1782 Blake married Catherine Boucher, whom he taught to read and write and who assisted him throughout his life. From an early age he had experienced visions of angels and other spiritual beings, and when in 1787 his brother Robert died, Blake claimed that Robert guided him and gave him visions from beyond the grave. He said, for instance, that Robert inspired him to invent the unique etching process that he used for one of his best-known works, *Songs of Innocence and Experience*.

---

2. Information taken from the following source: Edith Snook, *Women, Reading, and the Cultural Politics of Early Modern England*.

3. Information taken from the following sources: *Encyclopedia of World Biography*, 2nd ed.; Margaret Ferguson, Mary Jo Salter, and Jon Stallworthy, eds., *The Norton Anthology of Poetry*; Robert Giroux and Lloyd Schwartz, eds. *Elizabeth Bishop: Poems, Prose, and Letters*.

Blake printed the two halves of the *Songs* separately: *Innocence* in 1789, followed by *Experience* in 1794. (The poems "The Poison Tree," "The Tiger," and "The Lamb" on pp. 34, 57, and 58 respectively come from the *Songs*.) The *Songs*, though full of complex ideas, were intended for children and are much more accessible than some of his other works, many of which contain obscure prophecies relating to Blake's own particular theology and prophetic vision. He was a supporter of the French Revolution when it began, incorporating his ideas about tyranny in works such as *The Book of Urizen* and *Europe*.

In his later years, Blake continued, in spite of financial struggles, to write and engrave. Around the year 1818 he found some admiring supporters who enabled him to work until his death in 1827.[4]

Bradstreet, Anne (1612–1672)

Born in Northampton, England, Anne Bradstreet was educated by her father, and received a more thorough education than most young women of the time. She married Simon Bradstreet in 1628, and in 1630 they moved to the New World, where he served as governor of the Massachusetts Bay Colony. In spite of experiencing poor health from early childhood, Bradstreet nonetheless had eight children and worked hard as a writer.

In 1650 her brother-in-law, unbeknownst to Bradstreet, took a collection of her poetry back to England and had it published under the title *The Tenth Muse Lately Sprung Up in America*. The volume consisted of four long poems in the style of allegory. A second volume, *Several Poems*, was published after her death. In it, Bradstreet writes of the hardships of life in the New World. Several of the poems detail the early deaths of her grandchildren, others the joys and struggles of domestic life. She also wrote moving poems to her husband, whose work frequently took him away from home, causing his wife anxiety.[5]

Burns, Robert (1759–1796)

Robert Burns

Robert Burns began his life humbly, but his humble origins and the way in which they shaped his poetry eventually turned him into a nineteenth-century celebrity. He was born in Ayrshire, Scotland, the son of a farmer. His struggling father put Robert to work in the fields at the age of twelve. In the midst of his hard work, Burns enthusiastically read authors such as Alexander Pope, William Shakespeare, and John Milton. While these authors moved him, his greatest influence was local folk songs and legends. His love for Scotland led him to write in the common Scottish dialect, which was nearly incomprehensible to Scotland's English neighbors. He unashamedly wrote on subjects that previous generations of poets would have considered beneath them, a trend that was simultaneously taking place in England in the work of William Wordsworth and other Romantic poets.

---

4. Information taken from the following sources: *Encyclopedia of World Biography*, 2nd ed.; Margaret Ferguson, Mary Jo Salter, and Jon Stallworthy, eds., *The Norton Anthology of Poetry*; Frank N. Magill and Dayton Kohler, eds., *Masterplots Cyclopedia of World Authors*; Bruce Murphy, *Benét's Reader's Encyclopedia*.

5. Information taken from the following sources: *Encyclopedia of World Biography*, 2nd ed.; Margaret Ferguson, Mary Jo Salter, and Jon Stallworthy, eds., *The Norton Anthology of Poetry*; Frank N. Magill and Dayton Kohler, eds., *Masterplots Cyclopedia of World Authors*; Bruce Murphy, *Benét's Reader's Encyclopedia*.

When Burns published his first edition of poems in 1786, he became famous almost overnight. He was paid only 20 pounds, but became so well known that he earned 400 pounds for his second edition. Toward the end of his life, Burns spent a lot of his time collecting old Scottish folktales and legends, sometimes converting the material into songs. The famous song "Auld Lang Syne" is an example of this; Burns wrote the words, but the music was already popular. He is also the author of the famous poem that begins "O my Luve's like a red, red rose." By the end of his life, Burns was considered the national poet of Scotland.[6]

Carroll, Lewis (1832–1898)

Lewis Carroll was the pen name of Charles Lutwidge Dodgson. He was born in Daresbury, Cheshire, England, and with his ten brothers and sisters spent a happy childhood. He developed

Lewis Carroll

a love for puzzles and games, which later featured heavily in his writing. He attended school at Rugby, and later Christ Church, Oxford. When he graduated in 1854, he took a teaching position at the college, lecturing on mathematics. This position required him to enter the Anglican Church and remain unmarried. Dodgson was considered shy, though he had interests in theater and photography. He created his pen name, "Lewis Carroll," by translating his first and middle names into Latin, reversing their order, and translating them back into English.

In 1856 Dodgson wrote his most famous book, *Alice's Adventures in Wonderland,* for a child acquaintance of his, Alice Liddell. She and her sisters were Dodgson's earliest supporters and readers. In 1872 he wrote a sequel to *Alice,* called *Through the Looking Glass and What Alice Found There.* The poem "Jabberwocky" (see p. 72) comes from *Through the Looking Glass.*

Dodgson's works are often held up as an early example of contemporary children's literature, because, unlike most children's literature, *Alice* was meant chiefly to entertain and not to instruct. He wrote other nonsense works for children, as well as works for adults on the subject of mathematics.[7]

Collier, Michael (1953–)

Michael Collier has written poetry and edited anthologies, including the anthology *The Wesleyan Tradition: Four Decades of American Poetry.* He was born in Phoenix, Arizona, and was educated at Connecticut College and the University of Arizona. He married Katherine A. Branch, a librarian, in 1981, and they have two children. His first collection of poetry, *The Clasp and Other Poems,* appeared in 1986, followed by other volumes including *The Neighbor, Ledge,* and *Wide Dark Realm.* His poetic voice is both natural and musical. It speaks to neighbors and poets alike out a deep love for the world and a knowledge of its beauty and degradation. Associated with the Bread Loaf Writers' Conference beginning in 1992, he later became its

---

6. Information taken from the following sources: William Rose Benét, ed., *The Reader's Encyclopedia*; Margaret Ferguson, Mary Jo Salter, and Jon Stallworthy, eds., *The Norton Anthology of Poetry*; Frank N. Magill and Dayton Kohler, eds., *Masterplots Cyclopedia of World Authors*; Bruce Murphy, *Benét's Reader's Encyclopedia.*

7. Information taken from the following sources: William Rose Benét, ed., *The Reader's Encyclopedia*; *Encyclopedia of World Biography,* 2nd ed.; Margaret Ferguson, Mary Jo Salter, and Jon Stallworthy, eds., *The Norton Anthology of Poetry*; Frank N. Magill and Dayton Kohler, eds., *Masterplots Cyclopedia of World Authors.*

director. From 2001 to 2004 he served as the Poet Laureate of Maryland. Collier is a generous and beloved teacher currently sharing his knowledge and insights at the University of Maryland.[8]

cummings, e e (1894–1962)

e e cummings, whose real name is Edward Estlin Cummings, wrote poetry with typography and punctuation as odd as his choice of name presentation. He was born in Cambridge, Massachusetts. After receiving bachelor's and master's degrees at Harvard, he served during World War I with the Norton Harjes Ambulance Corps in France. Due to a military censor's error, he was imprisoned in a detention camp for three months, an experience he recorded in his book *The Enormous Room* (1922).

The way in which he used his odd style to make familiar objects and topics seem unfamiliar is a mark of modernist influence on his work. Because of his unusual style, cummings sometimes struggled to find a publisher, resulting in his publishing more than one volume at his own expense. In his book *No Thanks* (1935), he humorously listed the fourteen publishers who had rejected the manuscript, and then he thanked his mother. After World War II, cummings finally began to receive the recognition he deserved, including a fellowship from the Academy of American Poets in 1950. His last volume of poetry, *73 Poems* (1963), was praised by critics.[9]

Dickinson, Emily (1830–1886)

Although she published only a few poems during her lifetime, Emily Dickinson wrote more than 1,700 poems, and her revolutionary style continues to exert a profound influence on poets. She was born in Amherst, Massachusetts, and lived there until her death. She attended Amherst Academy, then at sixteen enrolled at Mount Holyoke Female Seminary. She did not return after her first year and, apart from a month-long visit to Washington in 1855 and time spent traveling in 1864 and 1865 for treatment of an eye disease, she never left home again.

By all appearances, Dickinson began writing poetry around 1858, gradually composing eighty packets, or "volumes," of poetry that were not discovered until after her death. She sent four of her poems to the editor of the *Atlantic Monthly*, asking for advice, and when he wrote back that her poetry seemed uncontrolled, she never sought publication again. Any poems of hers that were published were submitted anonymously by friends who wished to see her work in print.

Although she had a few good friends, was close to her family, and wrote many letters, Dickinson had very little face-to-face interaction with other people, finding it difficult and emotionally exhausting. She died of nephritis at the age of fifty-five, shortly after the death of several close friends. (For more on Emily Dickinson, see chapter 12.)[10]

---

8. Information taken from the following source: *Contemporary Authors Online.*
9. Information taken from the following sources: *Encyclopedia of World Biography*, 2nd ed.; Margaret Ferguson, Mary Jo Salter, and Jon Stallworthy, eds., *The Norton Anthology of Poetry*; Bruce Murphy, *Benét's Reader's Encyclopedia*.
10. Information taken from the following sources: William Rose Benét, ed., *The Reader's Encyclopedia*; Margaret Ferguson, Mary Jo Salter, and Jon Stallworthy, eds., *The Norton Anthology of Poetry*; Frank N. Magill and Dayton Kohler, eds., *Masterplots Cyclopedia of World Authors.*

Donne, John (1572–1631)

Born in London, England, John Donne was raised in a Roman Catholic home. His family suffered for their faith, and Donne was forced to leave Oxford early because of it. (He eventually converted to Anglicanism.) After traveling in 1596 and 1597, Donne became the secretary of Sir Thomas Egerton, but lost his post when he secretly married Anne More, Lady Egerton's niece. This left him and his growing family to live in relative poverty, alleviated only when they finally received his wife's dowry. Even then they struggled, but Donne continued to write, producing several tracts and essays on various topics. He wrote his *Holy Sonnets* mostly between the years 1607 and 1615. One of the most famous is *Death Be Not Proud* (see p. 124).

Donne was ordained as an Anglican priest in 1615 at the age of forty-three, after which he wrote fewer poems, concentrating instead on his sermons. He became very ill toward the end of his life and wrote *Devotions upon Emergent Occasions* in response.

After his death, Donne's reputation dramatically declined. A few Romantic authors appreciated him, but it wasn't until the nineteenth century that his work was resurrected by T.S. Eliot. Ernest Hemmingway quoted one of Donne's poems (*Devotions upon Emergent Occasions, no 17*) as the title of his famous book *For Whom the Bell Tolls*. Today Donne is considered one of the greatest of the metaphysical poets. His works are marked by long "conceits" (exaggerated metaphors), complex religious imagery, and unusual syntax.[11]

Doolittle, Hilda (1886–1961)

Hilda Doolittle, usually referred to as H.D., was born in Bethlehem, Pennsylvania, grew up near Philadelphia, and went to college at Bryn Mawr. At a young age she met Ezra Pound, who took an interest in her poetry and encouraged her in her writing. In 1911 she traveled to London to visit Pound and ended up living there for the rest of her life. She, Pound, and her husband, Richard Aldington (whom she married in 1913), were involved in the movement called Imagism. Imagism focused on the presentation of a central image, minimal use of words, and musical (vs. metrical) rhythm. This movement was strongly influenced by haiku poetry. In 1916 her husband left to fight in World War I, and she published *Sea Garden*, her first volume of poetry. H.D. continued to write poetry, the influences and style of which widened over the years, as well as novels and plays, until her death in 1961. Other volumes of her poetry include: *Hymen, Heliodora and Other Poems, Collected Poems, Hippolytus Temporizes, Red Roses for Bronze, Collected Poems, The Walls Do Not Fall, Tribute to Angels,* and *Flowering of the Rod*.[12]

Eliot, T.S. (1888–1965)

Thomas Stearns Eliot was one of the chief representatives of High Modernism, a movement that began in the early twentieth century and continued well into the middle of the century. Eliot was born in St. Louis, Missouri, and was educated at Harvard, the Sorbonne, and Oxford. His several occupations included teaching, working in Lloyds Bank, editing *The Criterion*, and

11. Information taken from the following sources: William Rose Benét, ed., *The Reader's Encyclopedia*; Margaret Ferguson, Mary Jo Salter, and Jon Stallworthy, eds., *The Norton Anthology of Poetry*; Frank N. Magill and Dayton Kohler, eds., *Masterplots Cyclopedia of World Authors*.

12. Information taken from the following sources: *Encyclopedia of World Biography*, 2nd ed.; Margaret Ferguson, Mary Jo Salter, and Jon Stallworthy, eds., *The Norton Anthology of Poetry*; Bruce Murphy, *Benét's Reader's Encyclopedia*.

directing Faber and Faber, a publishing firm. He officially became a British subject in 1927. His first book of poems was published in 1917. It was followed by *The Waste Land* in 1922, which engendered considerable controversy. Many critics objected to *The Waste Land* because of its difficult intellectual content, but others hailed it as a paradigm for modern poetry. Difficult reading, because of language and philosophical content, became a hallmark, not only of Eliot's poetry, but of all the modernist poets who were influenced by him.

Eliot was also an important critic, resurrecting many authors of previous centuries who had fallen out of favor, such as John Donne, John Dryden, and Dante Alighieri. Although his religious concerns in poems like *Ash Wednesday* or *The Journey of the Magi* baffled or angered many of his followers, Eliot's undeniable intelligence and scholarship, and the honesty with which he grappled with his faith, gave orthodox religion a renewed in reputation during the modernist period.[13]

Frost, Robert (1875–1963)

Robert Frost was born in San Francisco, California. When he was eleven, his father died, and his mother, with her two children, traveled across the country to comply with her husband's wish to be buried in his native New England. She could not afford the return trip to California, and so the family remained in New England. Frost went to Dartmouth at his grandfather's request, but after only one semester he left and worked at odd jobs. He attended Harvard for two years before again losing patience with formal education.

Robert Frost

In 1900 Frost began farming in hopes that the fresh air would prevent him from getting tuberculosis. His surroundings provided him with rich material for poetry, but between farming and teaching secondary school, he had no time for his literary ambitions. So in 1912, hoping to make a living by writing, Frost and his family moved to England, where he quickly assembled his collections and secured contracts. While in England, he became acquainted with other famous poets of the time, including Ezra Pound.

When World War I broke out, the Frosts returned to America, and his growing reputation allowed Frost to do readings and serve in various fellowships and creative writing positions at universities. He was awarded the Pulitzer Prize in 1924, 1931, 1937, and 1943, and received many other honors, including honorary degrees from Oxford, Cambridge, and the National University of Ireland. A mountain in Vermont is named after him. His poetry became famous because it was at once accessible and complex, having much to offer audiences of all levels of understanding.[14]

---

13. Information taken from the following sources: Margaret Ferguson, Mary Jo Salter, and Jon Stallworthy, eds., *The Norton Anthology of Poetry*; Frank N. Magill and Dayton Kohler, eds., *Masterplots Cyclopedia of World Authors*.
14. Information taken from the following sources: Margaret Ferguson, Mary Jo Salter, and Jon Stallworthy, eds., *The Norton Anthology of Poetry*; Frank N. Magill and Dayton Kohler, eds., *Masterplots Cyclopedia of World Authors*.

Harjo, Joy (1951–)

Joy Harjo, of Native American and Caucasian descent, was born in Tulsa, Oklahoma. During high school, Harjo trained in dancing and toured as an actress and dancer in one of the first Native American dance troupes in America. She had her first child (a son) at the age of seventeen, then moved to New Mexico to enroll in the premed program at the University of New Mexico. After one semester she decided to focus instead on art, going on to receive her bachelor's degree from the University of New Mexico and a master's degree in fine arts from the University of Iowa.

Harjo has won several awards for her poetry, including the William Carlos Williams Award. She has an interest in music, particularly jazz, and has written several poetic tributes to influential musicians. She also deals with the concerns and culture of Native Americans in her poetry, as can be seen in her poem *Perhaps the World Ends Here* (see p. 144), which comes from her seventh collection of poems, *The Woman Who Fell From the Sky* (1994). This work mingles the two sides of her inheritance: Native American culture and the culture of contemporary America.[15]

Hayden, Robert (1913–1980)

African American poet Robert Hayden was originally named Asa Bundy Sheffey. His parents had divorced by the time he was born and he was raised in Detroit by foster parents. He attended Detroit City College from 1932 to 1936, and was a part-time student at the University of Michigan from 1936 to 1940. He published his first poem in 1931. Then in 1940 he married Erma Inez Morris, a pianist and Julliard graduate. His first book of poetry was *Heart-shape in the Dust*. He returned to the University of Michigan in 1941 to pursue graduate studies, and while there he studied under the famous poet W.H. Auden.

In 1950 he moved his family to New York so that his daughter could attend an unsegregated school. Although he obviously had reason to be concerned about issues of race, Hayden refused to limit his poetry to that subject, a decision for which he was sometimes criticized by other African Americans. Nonetheless, he served several professorships, won many awards, and gained many distinctions for his poems, including recognition from President Jimmy Carter. He died in 1980, the day after a celebration that had been held in his honor in Ann Arbor.[16]

---

15. Information taken from the following source: Carole Barrett and Harvey Markowitz, eds., *American Indian Biographies*.

16. Information taken from the following sources: *Encyclopedia of World Biography Supplement*, vol. 22; Margaret Ferguson, Mary Jo Salter, and Jon Stallworthy, eds., *The Norton Anthology of Poetry*; Fred M. Fetrow, *Robert Hayden*; John Malcolm and Bill Read, eds., *The Modern Poets*.

Herbert, George (1593–1633)

George Herbert was born at Montgomery Castle, Wales. He won a scholarship to Trinity College, Cambridge, and earned a B.A. in 1613 and M.A. in 1616. Coming from a military and political background, he considered a career in government, and he earned some fame as a public orator in the service of James I. However, upon James's death, he decided instead to become an Anglican priest and was given a parish in Bemerton. He died there three years later. Herbert's poetry was religious, as one might expect, but much of it catalogued not only his calling to serve God, but also worldly ambition and his struggle to subject himself to the will of Christ. Some of his best-known poems, including *Easter Wings* and *The Altar*, are "pattern poems," a form in which the lines are arranged to create a shape that reinforces the main idea of the poem.[17]

Hopkins, Gerard Manley (1844–1889)

Though no more than forty of Gerard Manley Hopkins's poems have survived, he is considered one of the major English poets. Educated at Balliol College, Oxford, Hopkins converted to Catholicism in 1866. Two years later, he became a Jesuit novitiate and was ordained in 1877. In 1868 he stopped writing poetry because he thought that it interfered with his commitments as a priest, even going so far as to destroy all of the poetry he had written up until that point. Fortunately, in 1875, he broke his silence in order to write *The Wreck of the Deutschland*, a poem requested by one of his superiors. After this, Hopkins realized he could dedicate his poetic ability to God, though it remained a tension throughout his life. Most of his poetry is extremely religious, but not all of it is positive; what are known as his "terrible" sonnets chronicle some of his darkest struggles with his Maker. All of Hopkins's poetry is marked by an inventiveness of meter and language that was ahead of its time. "Sprung rhythm" was the term he coined to refer to the unique rhythm of his poetry. That unique rhythm, along with his extensive use of alliteration, adds richness to Hopkins's poetry. He died of typhoid fever in 1889.[18]

Housman, A.E. (1859–1936)

Alfred Edward Housman was born in Fockbury, Worcestershire, the oldest of seven children. He began his education at Oxford but, despite initially doing well, he did not obtain his degree. Embarrassed by his failure, he moved to London to take up a job at the Patent Office, but continued his studies of classical Latin and Greek works. His first of two volumes published during his lifetime was *A Shropshire Lad*, which dealt with rural interests. It made him famous as a poet, though fairly late in life. Because of the high caliber of his essays on the classics, he was offered the chair of Latin at London University in 1892 and the chair of Latin at Cambridge in 1911. In 1922 he published his second volume of poetry, *Last Poems*. A third volume, *More Poems*, was published by his brother after the poet's death.[19]

---

17. Information taken from the following sources: Margaret Ferguson, Mary Jo Salter, and Jon Stallworthy, eds., *The Norton Anthology of Poetry*; Bruce Murphy, *Benét's Reader's Encyclopedia*.

18. Information taken from the following sources: William Rose Benét, ed., *The Reader's Encyclopedia*; *Encyclopedia of World Biography*, 2nd ed.; Margaret Ferguson, Mary Jo Salter, and Jon Stallworthy, eds., *The Norton Anthology of Poetry*; Frank N. Magill and Dayton Kohler, eds., *Masterplots Cyclopedia of World Authors*.

19. Information taken from the following sources: William Rose Benét, ed., *The Reader's Encyclopedia*; *Encyclopedia of World Biography*, 2nd ed.; Margaret Ferguson, Mary Jo Salter, and Jon Stallworthy, eds., *The Norton Anthology of Poetry*; Frank N. Magill and Dayton Kohler, eds., *Masterplots Cyclopedia of World Authors*.

Hughes, Langston (1902-1967)

Langston Hughes was a poet, columnist, playwright, and novelist whose writing was significant for its contributions to the Harlem Renaissance. Hughes was born in Joplin, Missouri, and grew up in Missouri, Kansas, Illinois, and Ohio. After graduating from high school, Hughes spent a year in Mexico and a year at Columbia University, during which time he worked as a launderer, assistant cook, and busboy, and traveled to Europe as a seaman. He published his first book of poems, *The Weary Blues*, in 1926, and his first novel, *Not Without Laughter*, in 1930. From 1928 to 1930 he lived in New York City, where he was a key figure in the Harlem Renaissance. He is known for his insightful, colorful portraits of African American life, his engagement with jazz culture, and his desire to tell the stories of his people in ways that reflected their culture.[20]

Jonson, Ben (1572-1637)

Playwright Ben Jonson was one of the most famous of William Shakespeare's contemporaries. Scholars are not certain about many of the details of his life, but most agree that he was born in Westminster. He attended school there, learning a love for classical languages and literature from William Camden, his tutor. After leaving school, Jonson worked in turn as a bricklayer, a soldier, and a traveling actor. It is thought that he was married to Anne Lewis. The death of their first son is recorded in his poem *On my first son* (see p. 145). Though Jonson's tone in this poem is tender, he was a rough person who had several brushes with the law. He even killed a fellow actor in a duel.

Jonson performed as an actor and, like Shakespeare, wrote plays for the stage and for the court. A folio, or collection, of Jonson's plays was published the year that Shakespeare died. At the time, Jonson was ridiculed for calling his plays *Works*, as plays were not considered literature. But Jonson's folio paved the way for the publication of Shakespeare's folio, and without these publications many of the best works of literature of the time would have been lost. Jonson contributed a poem to Shakespeare's folio entitled *To the Memory of my Beloved, the Author, Mr. William Shakespeare*.[21]

Kantar, Annie (1976-)

Annie Kantar

Annie Kantar's poems and translations of poetry have appeared in *The American Literary Review*, *Barrow Street Review*, *Born Magazine*, *Post Road*, *Smartish Pace*, *Tikkun*, and other publications. She is the recipient of an Academy of American Poets Prize (2000), and in 2001–2002 was a Fulbright Scholar at Tel Aviv University, where she worked on translating Israeli poetry. She has recently completed a manuscript titled *With This Night*, a translation from the Hebrew of the last collection of poetry that the Israeli poet Lea Goldberg published during her lifetime. Kantar lives in Jerusalem with her husband and two children.[22]

20. Information taken from the following sources: Margaret Ferguson, Mary Jo Salter, and Jon Stallworthy, eds., *The Norton Anthology of Poetry*; Bruce Murphy, *Benét's Reader's Encyclopedia*.

21. Information taken from the following sources: William Rose Benét, ed., *The Reader's Encyclopedia*; Margaret Ferguson, Mary Jo Salter, and Jon Stallworthy, eds., *The Norton Anthology of Poetry*; Frank N. Magill and Dayton Kohler, eds., *Masterplots Cyclopedia of World Authors*.

22. Information provided by the author.

Keats, John (1795–1821)

John Keats was an English poet who wrote during the Romantic period. He was a contemporary of William Wordsworth, Percy Shelley, and Robert Burns. As a young man he studied medicine, but he was more interested in writing poetry. A school friend showed one of his poems, *On First Looking into Chapman's Homer* (see p. 123), to a publisher, and it became the first of Keats's poems to be published. One of the most famous lines of poetry, "A thing of beauty is a joy forever," is from the pen of Keats, taken from his work *Endymion*.

Keats's mother and brother both died of tuberculosis, and toward the end of his life Keats began to show signs of the illness as well. Though he did not live long, he was very productive, seeming to well up with creativity even as his health declined. Most of his most famous poems, including *To Autumn* (see p. 142), *On a Grecian Urn*, *To a Nightingale*, and *On Melancholy*, were composed between 1818 and 1820. In 1820 he accepted an invitation from Shelley to travel to Italy, and he died in Rome in 1821.[23]

Kunst, Judith (1970–)

Judith McCune Kunst graduated from Sarah Lawrence College. Her poetry has appeared in *The Atlantic Monthly*, *Poetry*, *Southern Poetry Review*, *Lumina*, and other journals. She is the author of *The Burning Word: A Christian Encounter with Jewish Midrash* (Paraclete Press, 2006), and she lives and works at The Stony Brook School in New York with her husband and two sons.[24]

Judith Kunst

23. Information taken from the following sources: William Rose Benét, ed., *The Reader's Encyclopedia*; *Encyclopedia of World Biography*, 2nd ed.; Margaret Ferguson, Mary Jo Salter, and Jon Stallworthy, eds., *The Norton Anthology of Poetry*; Frank N. Magill and Dayton Kohler, eds., *Masterplots Cyclopedia of World Authors*.

24. Information provided by the author.

Lawrence, D.H. (1885–1930)

David Herbert Lawrence was an English novelist, short-story writer, and poet. He led a difficult life, beginning in his childhood when his alcoholic father would sometimes beat his wife and children.

After receiving his degree from Nottingham University, Lawrence held various teaching posts, until he contracted pneumonia in 1911. In 1912, having written two novels, Lawrence made the first of many controversial decisions when he eloped with Frieda Von Richthofen Weekley, a mother of three and wife of a professor at Nottingham. In 1915 he published *The Rainbow*, which many critics called obscene for its frank descriptions of sexuality and portrayal of values that conflicted with the norms of his time. Later novels suffered under recurring censorship for their obscenity, particularly *Lady Chatterley's Lover*. In nearly all of his work, Lawrence mingled art with his controversial messages about sexuality, European decadence and mannerisms, and the relationships between people.

Lawrence and his wife traveled extensively. They lived in Italy just after World War I, then traveled through New Zealand on their way to living in an artist commune in New Mexico. These travels provided him with material for some of his novels, as did his hometown, a mining town called Eastwood.[25]

Longfellow, Henry Wadsworth (1807–1882)

Henry Wadsworth Longfellow was born in Portland, Maine. He was educated at Bowdoin College, where he also eventually taught modern languages. After traveling through Europe, during which time his first wife, Mary Potter, died, he returned to accept the chair of modern

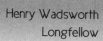

Henry Wadsworth Longfellow

languages at Harvard. In 1939 he published his first volume of poems, *Voices of the Night*, and continued to publish popular poetry that illustrated uniquely "American" themes. He married his second wife, Frances Appleton, in 1843, but she died in 1861 in a fire. Longfellow, seriously injured in the same fire, was left unable to write for some time afterward. Some of his most famous works are *Hiawatha*, *The Courtship of Miles Standish*, and *Evangeline*, which are notable for the way in which they deal with early American concerns and legends.[26]

---

25. Information taken from the following sources: William Rose Benét, ed., *The Reader's Encyclopedia*; Frank N. Magill and Dayton Kohler, eds., *Masterplots Cyclopedia of World Authors*.

26. Information taken from the following sources: William Rose Benét, ed., *The Reader's Encyclopedia*; *Encyclopedia of World Biography*, 2nd ed.; Margaret Ferguson, Mary Jo Salter, and Jon Stallworthy, eds., *The Norton Anthology of Poetry*; Frank N. Magill and Dayton Kohler, eds., *Masterplots Cyclopedia of World Authors*.

Marlowe, Christopher (1564–1593)

Christopher Marlowe, an English playwright, was born in Canterbury about two months before William Shakespeare. He received his early education at King's School in Canterbury and, on the strength of a scholarship, went to Cambridge. He graduated in 1587, but Cambridge authorities threatened to withhold his degree since they suspected that he had not fulfilled the terms of his scholarship. Queen Elizabeth intervened, however, in thanks for espionage work Marlowe had done for her, or so rumor had it. After graduating, Marlowe traveled to London, where he developed a reputation for wild behavior and was briefly imprisoned in 1589 for killing a man in a duel.

Between the time of his graduation and his death, Marlowe composed six or seven plays, the best known of which were *The Jew of Malta* and *Doctor Faustus*. *Doctor Faustus*, his most famous play and likely the last one that he wrote, is a story about a scholar who, hungry for knowledge, sells his soul to the devil and must endure the consequences. Some of Marlowe's contemporaries accused him of atheism, an imprisonable offence. But before his case could be decided, Marlowe died in a bar brawl.[27]

Meredith, William (1919–2007)

William Meredith was born in New York City and grew up in Darien, Connecticut. He graduated from Princeton University in 1940. After graduating, he worked as a reporter for the *New York Times*, then served in the U.S. Army Air Corps and the navy during World War II. His experiences in the military provided material for his first collection of poetry, published by the Yale Series of Younger Poets. When the war ended, Meredith returned to Princeton and became acquainted with the poet John Berryman. During the Korean War, Meredith served as a pilot, an experience that, he said, gave him a new start as a writer. Upon returning to the United States, he became a professor in Connecticut, then taught at the Bread Loaf School of English in Vermont, where he met Robert Frost. In 1983 he suffered a stroke, which immobilized him for two years and impeded his ability to speak and write, forcing him to stop teaching and writing. He eventually regained his ability to write after extensive therapy and went on to travel to Ireland. He died in New London, Connecticut.[28]

27. Information taken from the following sources: William Rose Benét, ed., *The Reader's Encyclopedia*; *Encyclopedia of World Biography*, 2nd ed.; Margaret Ferguson, Mary Jo Salter, and Jon Stallworthy, eds., *The Norton Anthology of Poetry*; Frank N. Magill and Dayton Kohler, eds., *Masterplots Cyclopedia of World Authors*.

28. Information taken from the following sources: Margaret Ferguson, Mary Jo Salter, and Jon Stallworthy, eds., *The Norton Anthology of Poetry*; Guy Rotella, *Three Contemporary Poets of New England: William Meredith, Philip Booth, and Peter Davison*.

Millay, Edna St. Vincent (1892–1950)

Edna St. Vincent Millay was born in Rockland, Maine. She attended Vassar, then moved to Greenwich Village, a place where the low rent and good company made it attractive to bohemian artists, writers, musicians, and radical thinkers. There Millay associated with some well-known writers of her day, including Hart Crane, Wallace Stevens, and Eugene O'Neill. She published her first volume of poetry, *Renascence*, in 1917. In 1923 she married Eugen Jan Boissevain and they lived together on a farm called Steepletop in Austerlitz, New York. Millay is well known for her formal poetry. Her collection of poems entitled *The Harp Weaver and Other Poems* (1923) won the Pulitzer Prize. She also wrote a variety of other genres, including short fiction published under the pseudonym Nancy Boyd and an opera called *The King's Henchman* (1927), which was the most successful American opera to that point. Toward the end of her life her popularity waned due to her political views, and she suffered a nervous breakdown in 1944 when the Nazis invaded Holland, causing her husband to lose his assets. She died of a heart attack a year after her husband's death.[29]

Milton, John (1608–1674)

John Milton is best known for his epic poem, *Paradise Lost*, interpreted by some as an imaginative rendering of the Genesis story and by others as a revision of it. Most consider it to be one of the greatest poems in the English language.

Milton's businessman-musician father strongly encouraged Milton to study and learn. He was first privately tutored, then attended school at St. Paul's. When he was fifteen, he went to Christ's College, intending to become a priest. He was briefly expelled for disagreeing with his tutor there, an experience that, he wrote to a friend, he found to be quite relaxing. When he returned to college, he wrote some poetry while earning his bachelor's degree. After graduation he returned to his home and was allowed by his father to read and travel for several years.

Milton felt strongly that marriage should be a union of love between two equals, not a mere contract, and expressed this idea in his pamphlets on divorce. His convictions about marriage gained strength when, in 1642, he married a woman named Mary Powell and quickly encountered difficulties. She left him temporarily, but eventually asked for his forgiveness and returned.

In addition to writing pamphlets on divorce, Milton also wrote about freedom in education and about the evils of censorship. By 1652 he became completely blind, a state which he laments in sonnets like *On His Blindness* (see p. 120).

In 1656, four years after his first wife's death, Milton married Katherine Woodcock, who died two years later in childbirth. In 1660 Charles II took the throne, putting Milton in danger for his eloquent support of the execution of Charles I, whom he considered a tyrant. Some of his books, which many considered indecent, were burned publicly, but he eventually received a pardon for supporting the overthrow of the king. In 1663 Milton married a third time, and in 1667 his great work *Paradise Lost* was published. Its sequel *Paradise Regained* followed in 1671.

---

29. Information taken from the following sources: William Rose Benét, ed., *The Reader's Encyclopedia*; *Encyclopedia of World Biography*, 2nd ed.; Margaret Ferguson, Mary Jo Salter, and Jon Stallworthy, eds., *The Norton Anthology of Poetry*.

In all of his work, Milton focused on the need for personal freedom. His religious themes often involve efforts to interpret the Bible by what it actually says, not by tradition.[30]

Moore, Marianne (1887–1972)

Marianne Moore was born in St. Louis, Missouri. She attended Bryn Mawr University and, after graduating, spent some time teaching in Carlisle, Pennsylvania. She worked at the New York Public Library for some time, a fact to which her friend and mentor Elizabeth Bishop alludes in her tribute to Moore, *Invitation to Miss Marianne Moore*. (As you found out in the "Growing Your Interest Chapter," Moore and Bishop were friends and Moore helped Bishop grow and mature as a writer.) Moore also edited the literary magazine *The Dial* from 1925 to 1929.

Moore's poetry is of the sort called "objectivist," which means that nearly all of her poems observe an object, person, information, or scene with precision and attention to detail. This quality of her poetry can be seen in *The Fish* (see p. 88). Her *Collected Poems* won the Pulitzer Prize in 1952.[31]

Poe, Edgar Allen (1809–1849)

Edgar Allen Poe is considered one of the most important American authors of the nineteenth century, a time that was very formative for American literature. He is said by many to have invented the mystery story, a claim arising from the many elements of horror, mystery, crime, and Gothicism that appear in his short stories and poetry. Poe's material may very well have come from the darker aspects of his unhappy life. After the death of his parents, Poe went to live with John Allan, a tobacco merchant. He attended the University of Virginia, accumulating many debts there. The debts were the source of arguments between him and Allan. Poverty-stricken, Poe left to join the army. After a brief stint in the army, Poe published a few poems, and then married his cousin, Virginia Clemm, in 1836. She died tragically in 1847.

Edgar Allen Poe

In 1845, Poe gained notoriety for *The Raven* (see pp. 206–208). Though he published several more well-received poems and short stories, including *Annabel Lee* and *The Fall of the House of Usher*, Poe died an alcoholic and pauper in 1849.[32]

---

30. Information taken from the following sources: William Rose Benét, ed., *The Reader's Encyclopedia*; *Encyclopedia of World Biography*, 2nd ed.; Margaret Ferguson, Mary Jo Salter, and Jon Stallworthy, eds., *The Norton Anthology of Poetry*; Frank N. Magill and Dayton Kohler, eds., *Masterplots Cyclopedia of World Authors*.

31. Information taken from the following sources: Margaret Ferguson, Mary Jo Salter, and Jon Stallworthy, eds., *The Norton Anthology of Poetry*; John Malcolm, and Bill Read, eds., *The Modern Poets*.

32. Information taken from the following sources: William Rose Benét, ed., *The Reader's Encyclopedia*; Margaret Ferguson, Mary Jo Salter, and Jon Stallworthy, eds., *The Norton Anthology of Poetry*; Frank N. Magill and Dayton Kohler, eds., *Masterplots Cyclopedia of World Authors*.

Pope, Alexander (1688–1744)

Alexander Pope, an English poet, is considered by many to be the model of a neo-classical writer. He was born in London, the son of a Roman Catholic. The Glorious Revolution, in which Protestant King William III overthrew Catholic King James II, occurred in the same year as his birth. Pope was unable to attend school for fear of anti-Catholic sentiment. Due to a serious childhood illness, Pope became crippled and never grew taller than four and a half feet.

His work entitle *Pastorals* was published in 1709 and *Essay on Criticism* in 1711, but what brought immediate fame to Pope was *The Rape of the Lock* in 1712. It was based on a breach Pope had heard about between two prominent Catholic families: A man named Lord Petre had fallen love with a woman named Arabella Fermor and, without her permission, he had cut off a lock of her hair by which he would remember. In *The Rape of the Lock*, Pope satirized the disagreement by portraying it in an epic light to show the pettiness of the ensuing disagreement.

After *The Rape*, Pope wrote several more poems, as well as translations of Chaucer and Homer. The humor he had shown in *The Rape* also revealed itself in his other works, many of which comically attacked his critics and earned him the nickname "Wicked Wasp of Twickenham." Pope wrote for the rest of his life, producing, among other works, his famous poem *An Essay on Man*.[33]

Pound, Ezra (1885–1972)

Ezra Pound was an American poet, translator, editor, and critic. He was born in Hailey, Idaho, but grew up mostly in Pennsylvania. He attended the University of Pennsylvania, and after two years transferred to Hamilton College in New York. While earning a master's degree in 1906, he taught at the University of Pennsylvania, where one of his students was William Carlos Williams. In 1908 Pound traveled in a cattle boat to London, and he lived there until 1920. In 1920 he moved to Paris and lived there for four years, becoming acquainted with other expatriates of the time, including Gertrude Stein. Then, in 1924, he moved to Italy and spent most of the rest of his life there.

During World War II he broadcasted radio talks from Rome in which he attacked American democracy and discussed the duty of an artist to society. He was accused by the American government of treason and in 1945 was sent to America to stand trial. His lawyer entered a plea of insanity and Pound was incarcerated at St. Elizabeth's Hospital in Washington, D.C. In 1958, through the influence of T.S. Eliot, William Carlos Williams, and other famous poets, Pound's indictment was dismissed and he immediately returned to Italy where he planted grapes and wrote. In 1962 he suffered a heart attack, after which he became something of a recluse. He died of intestinal blockage in Venice in 1972.

Pound's early work was influenced by Romantic writers and by the poetry of Robert Browning, but gradually over his lifetime he developed modernist theories and reflected them in his poetry. Many poets and critics admired his work, but his behavior and political stances sometimes interfered with his reputation as a poet.[34]

---

33. Information taken from the following sources: William Rose Benét, ed., *The Reader's Encyclopedia*; *Encyclopedia of World Biography*, 2nd ed.; Margaret Ferguson, Mary Jo Salter, and Jon Stallworthy, eds., *The Norton Anthology of Poetry*; Frank N. Magill and Dayton Kohler, eds., *Masterplots Cyclopedia of World Authors*.

34. Information taken from the following sources: *Encyclopedia of World Biography*, 2nd ed.; Margaret Ferguson, Mary Jo Salter, and Jon Stallworthy, eds., *The Norton Anthology of Poetry*; John Malcolm and Bill Read, eds., *The Modern Poets*.

Ralegh, Sir Walter (1552–1618)

Sir Walter Ralegh (often spelled Raleigh)—statesman, soldier, courtier, explorer, and poet—lived during the time of Queen Elizabeth. A member of a prominent family in Devonshire, Ralegh was educated at Oriel College, Oxford. In 1569 he joined the Huguenot army in the French religious war and spent five years in battle. By 1576 he was back in London and publishing poetry, which differed from the ornate poetry of his contemporaries because of his down-to-earth language and directness.

In 1578 Ralegh went with his half-brother on a voyage that began as an exploration but turned into privateering. This damaged his reputation, which suffered even more when he was involved in several personal conflicts and ended up in jail for six months for disturbing the peace.

After his release, he sailed to Ireland to join in the effort to put down the Irish rebellion. For two years he took part in battles and massacres, then was sent back to London for criticizing his superiors. However, by that point he was an expert on Ireland and he found a place at Elizabeth's court, where he became one of the queen's advisers.

A newly wealthy man, Ralegh was now authorized to explore the New World. He financed much of the early efforts to colonize America, and in June of 1584 he founded Roanoke, the "lost colony" that disappeared by 1591. He gave Virginia its name in honor of the queen and was knighted in 1585. But in 1592 when Ralegh married one of the queen's maids without permission, he lost the queen's favor for a time but continued to give himself to naval exploits and further exploration of the New World.

In 1603 Elizabeth died and was succeeded by James I, who imprisoned Ralegh in the Tower of London and took much of Ralegh's property and money from him because of his marriage. Eventually James released Ralegh to go on one last voyage in search of gold mines in Guiana. The voyage ended in failure, however, and during it Ralegh's son Walter (to whom *To His Son* on p. 59 is addressed) was killed. Upon returning to England, Ralegh was sentenced to death and beheaded in 1618 as a scapegoat to appease the Spanish for the ransacking activity of his men on the journey.[35]

Sir Walter Ralegh

---

35. Information taken from the following source: *Encyclopedia of World Biography*, 2nd ed.

Rilke, Rainer Maria (1875–1926)

Rainer Maria Rilke is generally considered Germany's greatest lyric poet. He was born in Prague and grew up in a middle-class family. He was expected to enter the military and therefore spent five years in military academy. After graduation, he spent one year studying literature at the German University of Prague before moving to the University of Munich. When he was nineteen, he published, at his own expense, his first collection of poems, *Life and Songs*. Other poetry and pieces of prose followed.

In 1930, he moved to an artist colony where he met a sculptress, Clara Westhoff, and married her. Their marriage did not last for long; in 1901, a few months after the birth of their daughter, Ruth, Rilke left his family to go to Paris. There he worked as secretary to the sculptor Auguste Rodin. His observations of Rodin's work, as well as Rodin's insistence that the artist study and observe reality rather than waiting for inspiration to descend, heavily influenced Rilke's poetry. Some of his most famous poems—among them those collected in *New Poems*—show this influence, especially his *Ding-Gedichte* or "thing-poems." These poems (an example of which, *The Panther*, can be seen on p. 4) transformed things he had observed into poetic symbols.

Restless and lonely, Rilke left Paris in 1909 in order to travel extensively, but when World War I began he was trapped in Germany. During this time he went from expressing his patriotism in *Five Songs* to opposing the German war effort by the end of the war. In 1919 he was invited to lecture in Switzerland, then spent much of the rest of his life there. Between 1921 and 1922 he composed poetry in a deserted medieval tower, producing the 1923 publication of the *Duino Elegies* he had been composing for a long time. This was followed by *Sonnets to Orpheus* and translations of various French works. He died in 1926 of leukemia in a sanatorium in Valmont.[36]

Robinson, Edwin Arlington (1869–1935)

Before gaining success and recognition for his poetic abilities, American poet Edwin Arlington Robinson suffered from depression and financial difficulties. He attended Harvard University but had to leave after only two years because he could no longer afford it. Although his first book of poems, *The Torrent and the Night Before* (1896), was well received by some critics, it was the publication of *Captain Craig* (1902) that gained him notice. Theodore Roosevelt read Robinson's poetry and was impressed by his abilities. He gave him a position in the New York City custom house, which enabled Robinson to continue writing. In 1910 he managed to make his living from writing alone, and in 1922 his *Collected Poems* won the first Pulitzer Prize to be given for poetry. He won the Pulitzer Prize again in 1925 and 1928, and enjoyed several more recognitions, prizes, and honorary degrees before his death.[37]

---

36. Information taken from the following sources: William Rose Benét, ed., *The Reader's Encyclopedia*; *Encyclopedia of World Biography*, 2nd ed.

37. Information taken from the following sources: William Rose Benét, ed., *The Reader's Encyclopedia*; Margaret Ferguson, Mary Jo Salter, and Jon Stallworthy, eds., *The Norton Anthology of Poetry*.

Rossetti, Christina (1830–1894)

Christina Rossetti wrote during the Victorian period in England, a time when studies of science and history had shaken many intellectuals' faith in Christianity. Her poems, though, still contained Christian themes and messages, and Rossetti herself held tight to her faith despite what was going on around her. She was born in London, the sister of painter Dante Gabriel Rossetti. Her brother was one of the foremost founders of a group of writers and artists called the Pre-Raphaelites, or the Pre-Raphaelite Brotherhood, which was formed in London in 1848. Christina Rossetti was a member of this group. She began writing poetry very early in life, and her first poems were printed on her grandfather's printing press. She contributed to her brother's journal, *The Athenaeum*, under a pseudonym, but it wasn't until twelve years later that her collection *Goblin Market and Other Poems* appeared in print. Though remarkably gifted, she actually published very few poems. She died single, having turned down two offers of marriage because the men who made them did not share her beliefs.[38]

Rossetti, Dante (1828–1882)

The poet, painter, and designer Dante Gabriel Rossetti, born Gabriel Charles Dante Rossetti, helped to found the Pre-Raphaelites, a group of English painters and poets who hoped to bring to their art the richness and purity of the medieval period. Rossetti was the son of the exiled Italian patriot and scholar Gabriele Rossetti and brother of the poet Christina Rossetti. He was fluent in Italian and English and showed literary talent early, winning acclaim for his poem *The Blessed Damozel* (1847) before he was twenty years old. As a student at the Royal Academy Antique School from 1845–1847, he met William Holman Hunt and John Millais, with whom he launched the Pre-Raphaelite Brotherhood in 1848. Romantic love was a major theme in both his poetry and painting. His poetry is noted for its pictorial effects and its atmosphere of lavish beauty. Although there is always passion in his verse, there is also thought. He was a master of the sonnet form, and his sonnet sequence *The House of Life* is one of his finest works.[39]

Shakespeare, William (1564–1616)

William Shakespeare

William Shakespeare, one of the best-known and most frequently praised writers of the English language, wrote both plays and poetry. Many of the details of Shakespeare's life remain in dispute. He was born in Stratford-Upon-Avon to a father who worked as a farmer and glove maker. He probably attended school at the Stratford grammar school, receiving a classical education like most of his contemporaries and possibly leaving school early in order to help his father through financial difficulties. He married Ann Hathaway when he was eighteen, and they had three children together. Shakespeare seems to have left his young family to become a traveling actor or schoolteacher, although his exact activities between 1585 and 1592 have remained a mystery.

38. Information taken from the following sources: William Rose Benét, ed., *The Reader's Encyclopedia*; Margaret Ferguson, Mary Jo Salter, and Jon Stallworthy, eds., *The Norton Anthology of Poetry*; Frank N. Magill and Dayton Kohler, eds., *Masterplots Cyclopedia of World Authors*; <http://www.poets.org/poet.php/prmPID/716>.

39. Information taken from the following sources: The Columbia Encyclopedia, Sixth Edition, "Dante Rossetti." Available at: <http://www.bartleby.com/65/ro/RossetDG.html>; <http://www.ibiblio.org/wm/paint/auth/rossetti/>.

Shakespeare's first known play, *The Comedy of Errors*, appeared around 1590. He then wrote several more comedies, histories, and tragedies, all of which have come to be known as masterpieces of the English language. From 1593 to 1594, when the theaters were closed in an effort to stem the spread of the plague, Shakespeare turned to writing poetry to support himself. His 154 sonnets may have been written during this time, though they were not published until 1609 (see *Sonnet 73* on p. 122).

In 1594 Shakespeare became the principal writer for the Lord Chamberlain's Men, a company of actors who built the Globe Theater in 1599. All theaters were required by law to be built outside the city limits because the audiences were suspected of indecent behavior, but the daytime performances were extremely popular. It was at about this time that Shakespeare composed *Julius Caesar* (see p. 131 for an excerpt).

When King James I took the throne in 1603, his enthusiasm for theater led him to give his patronage to the Lord Chamberlain's Men, who then became the King's Men. During this latter period of his life, Shakespeare produced few plays, but they are considered by many of today's critics to be some of his better plays. *The Tempest* (see p. 130 for an excerpt) was probably the last of the plays he wrote before he retired and returned to Stratford.[40]

Shelley, Percy Bysshe (1792–1822)

Though he lived a relatively short life, Percy Bysshe Shelley managed to make a significant impact on the English Romantic movement. He was one of the major English Romantic poets and is widely considered to be among the finest lyric poets in the English language. Widely anthologized pieces include: *Ozymandias*, *Ode to the West Wind*, *To a Skylark*, and *The Masque of Anarchy*. However, his major works are long visionary poems including *Alastor*, *Adonais*, *The Revolt of Islam*, *Prometheus Unbound* and the unfinished *The Triumph of Life*. From a very early age, Shelley was known as a sensitive and unusual person. For one thing, he became an atheist at an early age, later writing an essay called "On the Necessity of Atheism." He led an unconventional life and was an idealist. He married twice and had numerous affairs, and because of his irresponsible behavior lost custody of his two children in 1817. In response to this heartbreak, Shelley moved to Italy. There he became close friends with Lord Byron, another vivid personality among the English Romantics. In 1822 Shelley drowned in a storm in the Adriatic Sea.[41]

Sidney, Sir Philip (1554–1586)

Sir Philip Sidney, though poor for much of his life, was considered by many to be the model of courtly, chivalrous gentlemen during the Renaissance. Born at Penshurst in the county of Kent, he studied at Oxford and Cambridge. He traveled in Europe from 1572 to 1575, returning to the court in England where he began to build his reputation. During a long absence from the court, he wrote *Old Arcadia*, which is dedicated to his sister (see pp. 116–117 for an excerpt). Upon returning to court, he wrote *Astrophel and Stella*, the first of his famous English sonnet cycles. (A

---

40. Information taken from the following sources: William Rose Benét, ed., *The Reader's Encyclopedia*; *Encyclopedia of World Biography*, 2nd ed.; Margaret Ferguson, Mary Jo Salter, and Jon Stallworthy, eds., *The Norton Anthology of Poetry*; Frank N. Magill and Dayton Kohler, eds., *Masterplots Cyclopedia of World Authors.*
41. Information taken from the following sources: William Rose Benét, ed., *The Reader's Encyclopedia*; *Encyclopedia of World Biography*, 2nd ed.; Margaret Ferguson, Mary Jo Salter, and Jon Stallworthy, eds., *The Norton Anthology of Poetry*; Frank N. Magill and Dayton Kohler, eds., *Masterplots Cyclopedia of World Authors.*

cycle is a series of sonnets, often about an unapproachable woman and her disappointed lover.) In 1583 Sidney was knighted and married Frances, the daughter of Sir Francis Walsingham. At about this same time Sidney worked on his *Defense of Poesie* (or, as he originally titled it, *Apologie for Poetrie*), in which he defended poetry's ability to teach and entertain.

In 1585 Sidney entered into military service against Catholic forces in the Netherlands under the command of his uncle, the Earl of Leicester. After engaging in several battles, he was fatally wounded during a cavalry charge. The story is often told that as he lay wounded, he was offered a cup of water, but insisted it be given to the soldier lying next to him who, he said, had greater need than he.[42]

Smart, Christopher (1722-1771)

Christopher Smart

Christopher Smart was born in Shipbourne, England. He grew up in a natural setting, a fact reflected in his poetry, which often extols the beauty of his surroundings. His father died when he was eleven. While in his early thirties, Smart suffered from the first of the lapses into madness that would haunt him for most of his life. He attended Cambridge University, but left it in 1749 due to debt and a drinking problem in order to become a journalist in London. In 1750, 1751, 1752, 1754, and 1756 he won the Seatonian Prize, an award for the individual who could best celebrate God's divine attributes in poetry. His early poems were fairly standard fare compared with his later ones.

Between 1756 and 1763, Smart suffered from recurring bouts of mental illness and was repeatedly confined to asylums. His madness sometimes involved violence; at other times he would get down on his knees in public, sometimes naked, and ask passersby to pray with him. Despite his illness, he was still able to write and read. He was most likely in an asylum when he composed *A Song to David*. According to rumor, he scraped his *Jubilate Agno* on the walls of a madhouse room using a key. His contemporaries, knowing of his struggle with mental illness, sometimes had difficulty knowing how to respond to his poetry, and alternately attributed its uniqueness to his madness or his genius.

Smart died in debtor's prison in 1771. Based on surviving fragments of the manuscript, *Jubilate Agno* was first published in 1939, and again in 1954 in the proper order. (*My Cat Jeoffry* on pp. 174–175 comes from *Jubilate Agno*.)[43]

---

42. Information taken from the following sources: William Rose Benét, ed., *The Reader's Encyclopedia*; Margaret Ferguson, Mary Jo Salter, and Jon Stallworthy, eds., *The Norton Anthology of Poetry*; Frank N. Magill and Dayton Kohler, eds., *Masterplots Cyclopedia of World Authors*.

43. Information taken from the following sources: Margaret Ferguson, Mary Jo Salter, and Jon Stallworthy, eds., *The Norton Anthology of Poetry*; Geoffrey Grigson, *Christopher Smart*.

Stevens, Wallace (1879-1955)

Wallace Stevens was born in Reading, Pennsylvania. He attended Harvard and the New York Law School and practiced law in New York City. Later he became a businessman, serving as vice president of the Hartford Accident and Indemnity Company. Unlike many poets who seek out the company of fellow writers and join societies, Stevens remained voluntarily separated from literary society for his entire writing career. His first book of poems, *Harmonium*, was published when he was forty years old. He lived in Hartford, Connecticut, with his wife and daughter until his death. His poetry is often labeled as objectivist because of its careful examination of individual pictures through sound and imagery, appreciating the objects themselves, not what they could or could not symbolize. He won a Pulitzer Prize in 1955 for his *Collected Poems*.[44]

Stevenson, Robert Louis (1850-1894)

Robert Louis Stevenson

Robert Louis Stevenson is best known for his adventure stories, among them *The Arabian Nights* (1882), *Treasure Island* (1883), *The Strange Case of Dr. Jekyll and Mr. Hyde* (1886), and *Kidnapped* (1886). He was born in Edinburgh, Scotland, and contracted tuberculosis at a young age. Although he suffered from the disease for much of his life, Stevenson lived adventures as well as wrote them. After briefly studying to be a lawyer, he traveled to Switzerland, France, the United States, and the South Seas. He reportedly prepared for his writing career by laboriously copying the writings of famous authors like William Defoe and Nathaniel Hawthorne. His travels provided the material for his adventure stories. He also wrote some travel sketches describing the places he visited.

Stevenson married Fanny Osbourne in 1879 and they suffered hardships until he achieved fame with the publication of *Treasure Island*, which he wrote for the entertainment of his stepson. The family moved several times in hopes of finding a place where he could enjoy good health, but he died suddenly of epilepsy, leaving behind an unfinished manuscript that many say would have been his finest book. His books of poetry include: *Underwoods* (1887), *Ballads* (1891), *Songs of Travel and Other Verses* (1896), *Prayers Written At Vailima* (1904), and *New Poems* (1918) and have made him beloved of children and adults alike.[45]

Tennyson, Alfred (1809-1892)

Alfred Tennyson is considered by many, including his contemporaries, to be the greatest poet of Victorian England. He and his eleven siblings were born in Somersby to the Reverend George Clayton Tennyson and Elizabeth Fytche Tennyson. His father, though educated, struggled financially, and as he grew older, he drank and suffered from madness, which sometimes led to violence against his family.

44. Information taken from the following sources: William Rose Benét, ed., *The Reader's Encyclopedia*; Margaret Ferguson, Mary Jo Salter, and Jon Stallworthy, eds., *The Norton Anthology of Poetry*; John Malcolm, and Bill Read, eds., *The Modern Poets*.

45. Information taken from the following sources: William Rose Benét, ed., *The Reader's Encyclopedia*; Frank N. Magill and Dayton Kohler, eds., *Masterplots Cyclopedia of World Authors*.

Tennyson attended Trinity College, Cambridge, where he met his close friend Arthur Henry Hallam. In 1832, Tennyson published a volume called *Poems*, which contained, among other things, "The Lady of Shalott" (see pp. 209–211). Arthur Hallam died only a year later, and Tennyson spent the next seventeen years composing *In Memoriam*, a long poem dedicated to Hallam's memory and considered by many to be his finest work. Besides immortalizing Tennyson's love for his friend, *In Memoriam*

Alfred Tennyson

deals with themes common to Tennyson's contemporaries, such as the loss of faith in the face of scientific advancements. Tennyson went on to write plays and poetry prolifically, including: *Becket, Harold: A Drama, Queen Mary: A Drama, The Cup: A Tragedy, The Falcon, The Promise of May, Idylls of the King, The Early Poems of Alfredy Lord Tennyson, Poems,* and *Chiefly Lyrical.*

In 1836 Tennyson fell in love with Emily Sellwood, but the marriage was long postponed for financial reasons. Finally, in 1850, *In Memoriam* was published and Tennyson was appointed Poet Laureate of England. With this turn in fortune, he and Emily were married.

Over the next twenty years Tennyson wrote *The Idylls of the King*, a series of poems that dealt with the Arthurian legends. In his last years, Tennyson produced several plays and enjoyed honors and recognition for his work. The widowed Queen Victoria said that, next to the Bible, *In Memoriam* was her greatest solace. Tennyson died in 1892 and was buried in Westminster Abbey.[46]

Toomer, Jean (1894–1967)

Jean Toomer, born Nathan Eugene Pinchback Toomer, began life in the home of his maternal grandfather, who was governor of Louisiana, the first state governor of African American descent. After high school, Toomer attended several universities and studied a wide range of subjects, including agriculture, psychology, and literature. He never earned a degree, but in 1918 began his writing career, producing short stories and poems. His early work was not particularly well received, but he kept trying. When he moved to Georgia in 1921, the blatant segregation of races there forced him to deal with the racial conflicts he witnessed. In his novel *Cane* he took up those subjects. Other of his works include: *Blood Burning Moon* (1923); *Problems of Civilization*, to which Toomer contributed along with Ellsworth Huntington, Whiting Williams, and others; and *The Collected Poems of Jean Toomer*.

For a while he moved in literary and art circles freely, from Chicago to Harlem, Washington to California. In 1935, Toomer settled down with his second wife in Doylestown, Pennsylvania, and the next year founded the communal-living "Mill House," where people were invited to set aside religious and racial segregation. In 1938, the Toomers traveled to India seeking insights to apply to their failing Mill House experiment. At that point, Toomer had largely set aside his writing. In 1940, he formally joined the Society of Friends. The Harlem Renaissance revived interest in his work and he became a cultural icon.[47]

46. Information taken from the following sources: William Rose Benét, ed., *The Reader's Encyclopedia*; *Encyclopedia of World Biography*, 2nd ed.; Margaret Ferguson, Mary Jo Salter, and Jon Stallworthy, eds., *The Norton Anthology of Poetry*; Frank N. Magill and Dayton Kohler, eds., *Masterplots Cyclopedia of World Authors*.

47. Information taken from the following sources: *Encyclopedia of World Biography Supplement*, vol. 23; Margaret Ferguson, Mary Jo Salter, and Jon Stallworthy, eds., *The Norton Anthology of Poetry*.

Whitman, Walt (1819–1892)

Walt Whitman was born in West Hills, Long Island. He had a meager public school education and entered the working world at a young age, eventually becoming a teacher on Long Island. Following that, he involved himself in the print and journalism fields for some time. He started and then abandoned a newspaper, worked as a printer in New York City, edited a daily paper called *Aurora* (at the age of twenty-three), worked on the Long Island *Star*, edited the Brooklyn *Eagle* for two years, worked briefly on the New Orleans *Crescent* in 1848, and then returned to Brooklyn and edited a paper called the *Freeman*.

For five years after that he dabbled in real estate, but then returned to journalism and edited the Brooklyn *Times*. During all this time, he published a few poems and stories in newspapers and magazines. But it was not until he published (at his own expense) the first edition of *Leaves of Grass* that he became a serious poet. This volume was recognized by a few, including Ralph Waldo Emerson, but was ignored or rejected by most for its unusual free verse and frank language and images. Whitman, a somewhat compulsive revisionist, nonetheless had two more editions printed.

During the Civil War, Whitman sought work in Washington hospitals caring for injured soldiers, and his experiences formed the poems collected in *Drum Taps*. His *O Captain! My Captain!* (see p. 190) and *When Lilacs Last in the Door-yard Bloom'd* (see pp. 192–197) dealt with the tragic assassination of Lincoln, and helped popularize Whitman. His fame grew in the latter part of his life largely because of his unashamed self-promotion and the controversy surrounding some of his poetry. At the time of his death he was more popular in Europe than in his own country, but in the twentieth century, critics and poets came to realize the full extent of his influence on the development of American poetry. (For more information on Whitman, see chapter 14.)[48]

Williams, William Carlos (1883–1963)

William Carlos Williams, born in Rutherford, New Jersey, was educated at the University of Pennsylvania, earning a degree in medicine there. During his early life he met and associated with other famous poets of the time, including Ezra Pound and H.D. He then became a pediatrician in Rutherford, where he lived and worked until his death. His work as a physician influenced much of his poetry, which is distinctive for its concern with American language and commonplace urban scenery.

As a poet, Williams was a follower of the Imagist movement, and later a proponent of objectivism, both of which focused on appreciating images and objects in their own right, not as symbols. Williams's poetry was known particularly for its understanding of lower-middle-class Americans, the people whom Williams served as a doctor and a poet. In 1963 he won the Pulitzer Prize for *Pictures from Brueghel* (see *The Dance* on p. 42, which is from this collection).[49]

---

48. Information taken from the following sources: William Rose Benét, ed., *The Reader's Encyclopedia*; Margaret Ferguson, Mary Jo Salter, and Jon Stallworthy, eds., *The Norton Anthology of Poetry*; Frank N. Magill and Dayton Kohler, eds., *Masterplots Cyclopedia of World Authors*.

49. Information taken from the following sources: Margaret Ferguson, Mary Jo Salter, and Jon Stallworthy, eds., *The Norton Anthology of Poetry*; John Malcolm, and Bill Read, eds., *The Modern Poets*; Bruce Murphy, *Benét's Reader's Encyclopedia*.

Wordsworth, William (1770-1850)

William Wordsworth, along with his friend Samuel Coleridge, was a pioneer of the Romantic movement in England. Born in Cockermouth, Cumberland, he endured a hard childhood. His mother died when he was eight, and his father, who had encouraged Wordsworth's literary leanings, died when Wordsworth was thirteen.

He attended Cambridge, interrupting his studies briefly in order to travel in Switzerland, France, and Italy. Then, after finishing school, he went to France and became involved in the French Revolution. When it turned violent and excessive, he returned to England, leaving behind a lover and a daughter.

Back in England, he shared a house with his sister, Dorothy, who was also a poet. (The two were very close and remained so throughout Dorothy's life.) In 1794 he met Coleridge and they, along with Dorothy, developed a warm working friendship.

In 1789, Coleridge and Wordsworth published a joint collection of poetry, *Lyrical Ballads*, which, despite a less than enthusiastic welcome upon publication, played an important role in the development of Romantic literature. At that point, Wordsworth became known not only for *Lyrical Ballads*, but also for a love of nature, the sublime, and common men and women that was manifest in all his work.

In 1802, upon receiving a long-postponed inheritance, Wordsworth married Mary Hutchinson, and by 1810 they had five children. Wordsworth's pen continued to be prolific. In 1810, he and Coleridge had a falling out and they were estranged for some years. The death of two of Wordsworth's children in 1812 likewise affected him deeply. The tenor of his writing also began to change with the years, as he reversed his earlier revolutionary views.

Though his best writing was now behind him, Wordsworth continued to receive acclaim. In 1843 he was made Poet Laureate of England and remained in that post until his death in 1850. After his death, his widow had *The Prelude*, written in 1805, published posthumously. It is considered Wordsworth's masterpiece.[50]

---

50. Information taken from the following sources: William Rose Benét, ed., *The Reader's Encyclopedia*; Margaret Ferguson, Mary Jo Salter, and Jon Stallworthy, eds., *The Norton Anthology of Poetry*; Frank N. Magill and Dayton Kohler, eds., *Masterplots Cyclopedia of World Authors*.

Yeats, William Butler (1865–1939)

William Butler Yeats was born at Sandymount, near Dublin, Ireland. His father was a fairly well-known artist, and Yeats studied painting early in his life. But gradually he took an interest in Irish folk tales, studying them extensively in the British Museum and incorporating them, with increasing success, in his own work.

A distinctive of Yeats's poetry is mysticism and symbolism. This probably stemmed from (or perhaps fed into) his interest in spiritualism, an interest shared by his wife, who was a medium and held daily séances in which Yeats participated.

He was one of the chief instigators of the Irish Renaissance, or Revival, which took place toward the end of the nineteenth century. This movement aimed to restore Irish language and culture to importance after it had degenerated under English influence. In his own work, Yeats made explicit references to his country's concerns (for an example, see *An Irish Airman Foresees his Death* on p. 73) and expressed a longing for the beauty of Ireland (see *The Lake Isle of Innisfree* on p. 87).

William Butler Yeats

Yeats encouraged some of his contemporaries to participate in the Irish Renaissance, and he is credited with persuading Lady Gregory, George Moore, and John M. Synge—all important participants in the movement—to give Ireland primacy in their work. These same individuals worked with Yeats to found the Irish Literary Society in London and in Dublin, and the Irish Literary Theatre. The Irish Literary Theatre later became the Abbey Theatre, also known as the National Theatre of Ireland, which has produced many significant plays.[51]

---

51. Information taken from the following sources: William Rose Benét, ed., *The Reader's Encyclopedia*; Margaret Ferguson, Mary Jo Salter, and Jon Stallworthy, eds., *The Norton Anthology of Poetry*; Frank N. Magill and Dayton Kohler, eds., *Masterplots Cyclopedia of World Authors*.

CHRISTINE PERRIN
CONSULTING

{appendix b}

Christine Perrin, MFA, is the Director of Writing at Messiah College and has taught literature and creative writing at Johns Hopkins University, with Gordon College's Orvieto Program, through the Pennsylvania Arts Council to students of all ages, and at the local classical school where her children attended. She consults and speaks on the topics of poetry, literature, and Writing & Rhetoric.

For information about Christine's consulting and speaking, visit https://classicalacademicpress.com/consulting/christine-perrin/.

A SIMPLIFIED PLAN:
POETRY IN THE CLASSROOM OR AT HOME

{appendix c}

These are a few simple practices that will help to initiate you into the world of poetry. The following is a summary of the practices that this book encourages and supports.

READ ALOUD

Poetry was meant to be read with the instrument of the body. For centuries, even before written language, this is how generations were taught poetry. This is an essential pleasure of poetry; it is also a skill that aids all kinds of objectives, including the ability to speak in front of others, a growth in the appreciation of language, and a lack of self-consciousness surrounding expressive reading. The reverence for the word as that which is fundamental to our humanity and our faith is cultivated in this activity. I recommend making texts available and, at the start of each day, having each student choose a poem he or she likes to read.

MEMORIZE

Our relationship to language changes when we commit words, phrases, and sentences to memory. We suddenly become aware of how the words in a sentence fit together, or why a line break was chosen for a certain place, or how the images are in relation to each other. We also feel the language and rhythms differently in our mouths when we aren't working to read them but are pulling them from memory and long association. It requires understanding and many readings to memorize a poem. These poems will become dear to students simply for having memorized them. You can start by having them memorize the same poem with hand motions with you in class and branch out to individual memorization and recitation. Take it a step further and have a recitation contest with judges and prizes for the students who excel.

BUILD A COLLECTION
AND NETWORK THE POEMS TO YOUR
CLASSROOM EXPERIENCE

Get a recommendation of good poetry texts to purchase for the library or classroom and lend them out to students. Start reading them yourself and excitedly share a recent find with your students. Use the poems to clarify or reference a particular truth, idea, or emotion that crops up in the course of your conversation or in reference to a Bible passage or a time in history that you are studying. Don't simply select poems for their ideas or treat them as a means to an end, however. Read them for beauty's sake, or for pure pleasure. Choose all kinds of poems—high serious poems (Keats, Milton, Homer) and less important, funny poems (Ogden Nash, for instance). Read poems from all time periods, giving students a taste of different eras, including their own. Read psalms and talk about the biblical poetic tradition.

BEGIN SPEAKING
ABOUT FORM AND CONTENT

Don't be afraid of what you don't know. The students will see things that you can't see; the meaning of the poem will emerge. Even if it doesn't entirely come forth, something will have been gained. Simply reading a poem aloud and discussing it for a few minutes has inestimable worth. The talking is only a fraction of the benefit. Talk about whatever formal aspects you can identify (rhythm, rhyme, sound devices, structure, stanzas, line breaks, inherited forms) and what might be the meaning and how the two might be related to each other. Be especially attentive to the way in which ideas and images cling to each other. Metaphor is the microcosm of the poem and of all human thought. In science, for instance, metaphor has guided our understanding of many concepts that are difficult to grasp—the atom being one example. Try talking about not only what a poem means but how it means—how it makes its meaning.

BUY: A LIMITED RECOMMENDATION LIST

The Art of Poetry by Christine Perrin

For young elementary:

Talking Like the Rain, edited by X.J. and Dorothy Kennedy

For older elementary:

A Child's Anthology of Poetry, edited by Elizabeth Hauge Sword

Poetry for Young Readers Series (Whitman, Dickinson, Poe, Sandburg)

For middle and high school:

Poet's Choice, edited by Edward Hirsch

A Book of Luminous Things, edited by Czeslaw Milosz

The Wadsworth Anthology of Poetry, edited by Jay Parini

The Norton Anthology of Poetry

The Psalms

GLOSSARY OF TERMS

Abstract language: words that suggest concepts, ideas, and generalizations, such as peace and justice. *Chapter: 1*

Alliteration: repetition of consonant sounds at the beginning of words next to each other (initial consonant sounds) such as roof/ruthlessness, brain/British. *Chapter: 5*

Anaphora: several lines, phrases, clauses, or sentences that begin with the same word or phrase. *Chapters: 6, 13*

Association: a leap that the mind makes when one thing or idea makes you think of another. When this is recorded it is called stream of consciousness—the stream of thought that the mind runs along at any given time. *Chapter: 1*

Assonance: repetition of vowel sounds inside words near each other: *"tinfoil winking," grape/ shave, pine/ripe, bee/meet. Chapters: 4, 5, 7*

Ballad: a narrative poem originally meant to be sung with a regular rhyming stanza. *Chapters: 5, 9, 10*

Blank verse: unrhymed iambic pentameter (used widely by Shakespeare and Milton). *Chapters: 9, 10*

Cacophony: harsh, rough sounds: *screech. Chapter: 5*

Caesura: a pause in the middle of a line of poetry marked by punctuation. *Chapter: 1, 3, 6, 7, 10*

Cinquain stanza: a five-line stanza. *Chapter: 7*

Cliché: an expression that has lost ingenuity, originality, and impact and become commonplace by long overuse. *Chapter: 2*

Climax: the building up of an idea to some high point, as in the climax of a plot. *Chapter: 13*

Concrete language: words that describe particular things (bug, table, nose) as opposed to words that are abstract. *Chapter: 1*

Connotation: emotional associations of a word that give words different shades of expression. *Chapter: 4*

Consonance: repetition of consonant sounds at the beginning of words next to each other (alliteration) or at the ends of words: *book/rack, stood/rude. Chapters: 4, 5*

Conventional symbol: meaning recognized by a society or culture (flag, cross). *Chapter: 3*

Counterpoint: a statement that seems to argue with a previous statement. *Chapter: 13*

Couplet stanza: a two-line stanza. *Chapter: 7*

Cumulative: the points that lead up to the climax (as in plot development). *Chapter: 13*

Dead metaphor: a metaphor with which we have become so familiar we are no longer aware that it is a metaphor. *Chapter: 2*

Denotation: literal, dictionary definition of a word. *Chapter: 4*

Diction: a writing style determined by the kinds of words you choose. *Chapters: 4, 8*

Eclogue: a pastoral poem, often in dialogue form. *Chapter: 9*

Ekphrasis: a poem written in response to, or in dialogue with, a visual piece of art. *Chapter: 4*

Elegy: a lament or mourning for someone who has died. It seeks consolation and describes the circumstances and nature of the loss. *Chapters: 9, 11*

End-stop (or end-stopped line): a line that ends with a definite halt, sometimes marked by punctuation (period, comma, question mark, colon, semicolon), but always a thought or phrase that is completed. *Chapters: 3, 4*

Enjambment: in a poem, a line whose sense and rhythmic movement continues to the next line, the opposite of an end-stopped line. This technique tends to cause the reader to move on quickly at the end of a line instead of pausing. *Chapters: 3, 4, 13*

Epic: a long, narrative poem that tells the stories central to the myths and beliefs of a people group. *Chapters: 5, 9, 10, 15*

Euphony: smooth, pleasing, harmonious sounds: *lilting. Chapter: 5*

Extended metaphor: a sustained comparison in which the whole poem consists of a series of related metaphors, or a single metaphor stretched throughout the whole poem. It is also called a conceit (*Hope is the thing with feathers* does this). *Chapter 2*

Eye rhyme: words that look like they rhyme to the eye but don't to the ear: *love/move. Chapter: 5*

Family of images: a collection of images in a single poem that work together to form an intentional group of concrete details that create a larger picture of significance. *Chapter: 1*

Figurative language: language that imposes a figure on the surface or content of what is actually there (the literal). Metaphor, simile, and symbol all do this; they suggest something beyond what they say. *Chapter: 1*

Figure of speech: saying one thing and suggesting another, so that words have significance beyond the literal meaning. To compare one thing to another. Literally, to superimpose a figure upon the surface of what is truly there. *Chapters: 1, 3*

Foot: a unit of measure in a metrical line. *Chapter: 6*

Formal diction: elevated words, words with careful manners. *Chapter: 4*

Free verse: also known as open verse, it is unmetrical verse with lines that are not measured according to syllable, stress, or length. *Chapters: 4, 13*

Full rhyme: when the sounds fully resemble each other, sound alike: *brake/shake. Chapter: 5*

Hymn meter: a pattern of sound that lends itself to songs that a lot of people can easily sing, like nursery rhymes and church hymns. It is a closed poetic quatrain—a four-lined stanza whose end rhymes are *abab*, in which iambic tetrameter alternates with iambic trimeter. Also known as common meter. *Chapters: 7, 10, 12*

Iamb: word or phrase that has two syllables with the first one unstressed and the second one stressed. *Chapter: 6*

Iambic pentameter: five iambs together. *Chapter: 6*

Iambic tetrameter: four iambs together. *Chapter: 6*

Image: a concrete detail that speaks to the senses. *Chapters: 1, 2, 3*

Imagery: a concrete piece of information gathered with the senses. *Chapters: 7, 8*

Imperfect rhyme: words that nearly rhyme but not exactly: *brake/spoke. Chapter: 5*

Informal diction: casual words, everyday language, ordinary speech. *Chapter: 4*

Line (or line break): the place where the poet deliberately ends a line, a distinctive feature of poetry, as opposed to prose in which the lines are not broken by the writer but by the margins of the page. Also referred to as "verse" or "stitch." *Chapters: 1, 7*

Literal: that which actually is there, concrete. *Chapter: 1*

Literary symbol: a person, object, image, word, or event with meaning beyond itself that is defined by its context in a particular work. There are also literary symbols that are conventional, having taken on meaning because they've been repeatedly used in literature in similar ways. Winter = old age, spring = renewal, lamb = innocence. *Chapter: 3*

Lyric poetry: short musical poems spoken in the voice of an individual; one of the three main categories of poetry. *Chapter: 5*

Metaphor: a comparison between two things that are unlike; a resemblance forged in the mind of the poet between two unlike things. *Chapters: 1, 2, 3*

Meter: the rhythmic measure of a line of verse. *Chapter: 6*

Monostich stanza: a one-line stanza. *Chapter: 7*

Narrative poetry: poetry that tells a story; another of the main categories of poetry. *Chapter: 5*

Near rhyme: words that nearly rhyme but not exactly: *brake/spoke. Chapter: 5*

Octave stanza: an eight-line stanza. *Chapter: 7*

Ode: a song or lyric that is solemn, heroic, and elevated, often for an occasion. This form began by celebrating people but developed into a commemoration or study of various objects or occasions. *Chapters: 9, 11*

Off rhyme: words that nearly rhyme but not exactly: *brake/spoke. Chapter: 5*

Onomatopoeia: a word that imitates the sound of the word's meaning, as in splash, sizzle, or buzz. *Chapters: 4, 5*

Open verse: unmetrical verse with lines that are not measured according to syllable, stress, or length. *Chapter: 13*

Parallelism: is the repetition of similar structures within phrases or sentences in the course of the poem. There is also parallelism of idea. *Chapter: 13*

Pastoral: a poem that traditionally extols the virtues of rural life and describes why it is good to live in the countryside. These poems reflect changes in the relationship between man and nature that occur at different time periods in history. *Chapter 11*

Perfect rhyme or full rhyme: when the sounds fully resemble each other; sound alike: *brake/shake. Chapter: 5*

Personification: a metaphor that gives human characteristics to something that is not human. *Chapter: 2*

Polarity: an opposite (another way of speaking about counterpoint). *Chapter: 13*

Quatrain stanza: a four-line stanza; the most common stanza in English. *Chapter: 7*

Repetition: a duplication of words, sounds, order of words, or phrases for effect. *Chapters: 3, 8, 13*

Rhyme: when words repeat or echo the same sound. *Chapter: 5*

Rhyme scheme: the pattern of rhymes used in a poem; indicates which words rhyme with each other. *Chapters: 5, 7, 8, 10, 11*

Rhythm: the beat of the words together; the recurrence of movement and sound; the way sounds move; the rise and fall of words together. *Chapters: 2, 5, 6*

Scan: to identify and determine the pattern of stressed and unstressed syllables of a poem. *Chapter: 6*

Senses or sensing: our ability to perceive with our sense organs—touch, taste, hear, see, smell. *Chapter: 1*

Septet stanza: a seven-line stanza. *Chapter: 7*

Sestet stanza: a six-line stanza. *Chapter: 7*

Sestina: a form with six, six-line stanzas and a concluding three-line stanza. The last words of each of the first six lines of the poem must be repeated in a specific order at the ends of the lines of the next five, six-line stanzas, and all six words must finally appear in the final three-line stanza. This form originated in medieval France. *Chapter: 10*

Shape: the element that most closely involves the visible form of the poem on the page. Also referred to as "form." *Chapters: 1, 5, 7*

Shaping forms: forms that are not defined by meter and rhyme but by society and history. Their origin is societal; just as words were devised from need, so were these shaping forms. *Chapter: 11*

Simile: a metaphor or comparison that uses "like" or "as." *Chapter: 2*

Slant, half, near, off, imperfect rhyme: words that nearly rhyme but not exactly: *brake/spoke. Chapter: 5*

Sonnet: a poem of fourteen lines in iambic pentameter with varying rhyme schemes: Petrarchan (or Italian), which is divided into eight rhymed lines and six rhymed lines, and Shakespearean (or English), which is divided into three quatrains and a final couplet. *Chapters: 9, 10*

Stanza: the equivalent of the paragraph in prose, a group of lines gathered as a unit in a poem. It comes from an Italian word which means room: each stanza in a poem is like a room, a distinct space. *Chapters: 1, 7*

Stanza types: (Chapter: 7)

Monostich—a one-line stanza.

Couplet—a two-line stanza.

Tercet—a three-line stanza.

Quatrain—a four-line stanza, the most common stanza in English.

Cinquain—a five-line stanza.

Sestet—a six-line stanza.

Septet—a seven-line stanza.

Octave—an eight-line stanza.

Stressed syllable: a syllable where the emphasis of the voice (or intonation) falls (for example the first syllable in the word BARKing is stressed). *Chapter: 6*

Subject: the basic theme a poem is exploring. *Chapters: 3, 8*

Symbol: use of a person, object, image, word, or event to evoke a range of meaning beyond the thing itself; an important image in a poem that has multiple, unspecified meanings and suggestions in its use. *Chapters: 1, 3*

Symbolism: representing things by symbols, or investing things with a symbolic meaning or character. *Chapter: 1*

Syllable: a basic unit of speech consisting of a single cluster of sound as simple as "I" or as long as "breathe." *Chapter: 6*

Tercet stanza: a three-line stanza. *Chapters: 3, 7*

Tone: the attitude of the poem, of the poet toward the subject of the poem; the emotional atmosphere of the poem. *Chapters: 2, 8*

Unstressed syllable: a syllable in a word or phrase where the emphasis does not naturally fall. In the word "basic," the emphasis is on the first syllable not on the second, so we say that the second syllable, "ic," is unstressed. *Chapter: 6*

Verse forms: all traditional or received forms with structural rules or keys that guide the poet in decisions about line length, rhyme scheme, stanza length, and other patterns. *Chapters: 9, 10*

Villanelle: a complex form of nineteen lines and two rhymes repeated in a fixed pattern, originating in France. *Chapter: 10*

Word pictures: another name for a metaphor. *Chapter: 1*

BIBLIOGRAPHY

Anonymous. "An Autumn Greeting," [online]. April 1, 2009. Available from: <http://www.storyit.com/Classics/JustPoems/autumngreet.htm>.

Bishop, Elizabeth. *Elizabeth Bishop: Poems, Prose and Letters*. New York: Library of America, 2008.

Burns, Robert. *Burns: Complete Poems and Songs*. New York: Oxford University Press, 1969.

Carroll, Lewis. *The Complete Illustrated Lewis Carroll*. Ware, UK: Wordsworth Editions, Ltd., 2008.

Collier, Michael. *The Ledge*. New York: Houghton Mifflin, 2000.

Columbia University Press, ed. "Dante Alighieri." *The Concise Columbia Encyclopedia*. Irvington, NY: Columbia University Press, 1991.

Cummings, Edward Estlin. *E.E. Cummings: Complete Poems, 1904–1962*. New York: Liveright, 1994.

Dickinson, Emily. *The Collected Poems of Emily Dickinson*. New York: Barnes & Noble Classics, 2003.

Donne, John. *The Complete Poetry and Selected Prose of John Donne*. New York: Modern Library, 2001.

Doolittle, Hilda. *Collected Poems, 1912–1944*. New York: New Directions, 1986.

Eliot, T.S. *Collected Poems, 1909–1962.* Orlando, FL: Harcourt Brace Jovanovich, 1991.

Erdman, David V. and William Golding, eds. *The Complete Poetry and Prose of William Blake.* New York: Anchor Books, 1997.

Frost, Robert. *Robert Frost: Collected Poems, Prose and Plays.* New York: Library of America, 1995.

Harjo, Joy. *The Woman Who Fell From the Sky.* New York: W.W. Norton, 1996.

Harmon, William. *The Top 500 Poems.* New York: Columbia University Press, 1992.

Hayden, Robert. *Collected Poems.* New York: Liveright, 1997.

Hensley, Jeannine, ed. *The Works of Anne Bradstreet.* Cambridge, MA: Belkna, 2007.

Herbert, George. *The Complete English Poems.* New York: Penguin, 2005.

Hopkins, Gerard Manley. *Poems and Prose.* New York: Penguin Classics, 1953.

Housman, A.E. *The Collected Poems of A.E. Housman.* Ware, UK: Wordsworth Editions, Ltd., 1999.

Hughes, Langston. *The Collected Poems of Langston Hughes.* New York: Vintage Books USA, 1995.

Jonson, Ben. *The Complete Poems.* New York: Penguin, 2006.

Justice, Donald. *New and Selected Poems.* New York: Knopf, 1997.

Keats, John. *Complete Poems and Selected Letters of John Keats.* New York: Modern Library, 2001.

Kunst, Judith. "The Crow," first published by *Poetry* Magazine, May 2003.

Lawrence, D.H. *Complete Poems.* New York: Penguin Classics, 1994.

Longfellow, Henry Wadsworth. *Henry Wadsworth Longfellow: Poems and Other Writings.* New York: Library of America, 2000.

Marlowe, Christopher. *The Complete Poems and Translations.* New York: Penguin Classics, 2007.

Meredith, William. *Effort at Speech: New and Selected Poems.* Evanston, IL: TriQuarterly Books, 1997.

Millay, Edna St. Vincent. *The Selected Poetry of Edna St. Vincent Millay.* New York: Modern Library, 2002.

Milton, John. *The Complete Poetry and Essential Prose of John Milton.* New York: Modern Library, 2007.

Moore, Marianne. *Complete Poems.* New York: Penguin Classics, 1994.

Parini, Jay. "Scarborough Fair," by Anonymous. *The Wadsworth Anthology of Poetry.* Florence, KY: Wadsworth Publishing, 2006.

Poe, Edgar Allen. *The Complete Tales and Poems of Edgar Allen Poe.* New York: Vintage Books USA, 1975.

Pope, Alexander. *The Poems of Alexander Pope: A Reduced Version of the Twickenham Text.* New Haven, CT: Yale University Press, 1966.

Pound, Ezra. *Ezra Pound: Poems and Translations.* New York: Library of America, 2003.

Rilke, Rainer Maria. *New Poems* [1907], a bilingual edition translated by Edward Snow. Translation copyright © 1984 by Edward Snow. New York: North Point Press, 2001.

Robinson, Edwin Arlington. *Selected Poems.* New York: Penguin Classics, 1997.

Rossetti, Christina. *The Complete Poems.* New York: Penguin Classics, 2001.

Shakespeare, William. *The Complete Works of William Shakespeare.* New York: Oxford University Press, 2005.

Shelley, Percy Bysshe. *The Complete Poems of Percy Bysshe Shelley.* New York: Modern Library, 1994.

Sidney, Sir Philip. *Sir Philip Sidney: The Major Works.* New York: Oxford University Press, 2009.

Smart, Christopher. *Christopher Smart: Selected Poems.* New York: Penguin Classics, 1991.

Stevens, Wallace. *Wallace Stevens: Collected Poetry and Prose.* New York: Library of America, 1997.

Stevenson, Robert Louis. *The Collected Poems of Robert Louis Stevenson.* Edinburgh, UK: Edinburgh University Press, 2003.

Tennyson, Alfred. *The Works of Alfred Lord Tennyson.* Ware, UK: Wordsworth Editions Ltd., 1998.

Toomer, Jean. *The Collected Poems of Jean Toomer.* Chapel Hill, NC: University of North Carolina Press, 1988.

Whitman, Walt. *The Complete Poems.* New York: Penguin Classics, 2005.

Williams, William Carlos. *The Collected Poems of William Carlos Williams.* 2 vols. New York: New Directions, 1991.

Woodring, Carl and James S. Shapiro. *The Columbia Anthology of British Poetry.* New York: Columbia University Press, 1995.

Wordsworth, William. *The Collected Poems of William Wordsworth.* Ware, UK: Wordsworth Editions, Ltd., 1998.

Yeats, William Butler. *The Collected Poems of W.B. Yeats.* New York: Scribner, 1996.

Works Consulted for Poet Biographies

Barrett, Carole and Harvey Markowitz, eds. *American Indian Biographies*. Pasadena, CA: Salem Press, 2005.

Benét, William Rose, ed. *The Reader's Encyclopedia*. Binghamton, NY: Thomas Y. Crowell Company, 1963.

The Columbia Encyclopedia, Sixth Edition. "Dante Rossetti." Available at: <http://www.bartleby.com/65/ro/RossetDG.html>.

Contemporary Authors Online. Gale, 2009. Reproduced in *Biography Resource Center*. Farmington Hills, MI: Gale, 2009. Available at: <http://galenet.galegroup.com/servlet/BioRC>.

Encyclopedia of World Biography, 2nd ed. 17 vols. Gale Research, 1998. Reproduced in *Biography Resource Center*. Farmington Hills, MI: Gale, 2009. Available at: <http://galenet.galegroup.com/servlet/BioRC>.

Encyclopedia of World Biography Supplement, vol. 22. Gale, 2002. Reproduced in *Biography Resource Center*. Farmington Hills, MI: Gale, 2009. Available at: <http://galenet.galegroup.com/servlet/BioRC>.

Encyclopedia of World Biography Supplement, vol. 23. Gale, 2003. Reproduced in *Biography Resource Center*. Farmington Hills, MI: Gale, 2009. Available at: <http://galenet.galegroup.com/servlet/BioRC>.

Ferguson, Margaret, Mary Jo Salter, and Jon Stallworthy, eds. *The Norton Anthology of Poetry*. New York: W. W. Norton & Company, 1997.

Fetrow, Fred M. *Robert Hayden*. Boston, MA: Twayne Publishers, 1984.

Giroux, Robert and Lloyd Schwartz, eds. *Elizabeth Bishop: Poems, Prose, and Letters*. New York: Library of America, 2008.

Grigson, Geoffrey. *Christopher Smart*. New York: Longmans, Green & Co., 1961.

Magill, Frank N. and Dayton Kohler, eds. *Masterplots Cyclopedia of World Authors*. 2 vols. New York: Salem Press, 1958.

Malcolm, John and Bill Read, eds. *The Modern Poets*. New York: McGraw-Hill, 1970.

Markoe, Arnold, Karen Markoe, and Kenneth T. Jackson, eds. *The Scribner Encyclopedia of American Lives*. Vol. 7: 2003–2005. Detroit: Charles Scribner's Sons, 2007. Reproduced in *Biography Resource Center*. Farmington Hills, MI: Gale, 2009. Available at: <http://galenet.galegroup.com/servlet/BioRC>.

Murphy, Bruce. *Benét's Reader's Encyclopedia*. New York: Harper Collins, 1996.

Rotella, Guy. *Three Contemporary Poets of New England: William Meredith, Philip Booth, and Peter Davison*. Boston: Twayne Publishers, 1983.

Snook, Edith. *Women, Reading, and the Cultural Politics of Early Modern England*. Farnham, UK: Ashgate Publishing, 2005.

Yoder, Brian, Carol Gerten-Jackson, John F. Brenner. "Dante Rossetti." WebMuseum. Available at: <http://www.ibiblio.org/wm/paint/auth/rossetti/>.

INDEX OF
AUTHORS AND TITLES

John Keats

Logic

We use logic every day, especially to distinguish *logical* arguments from those that are unreasonable. As a fundamental part of the trivium, logic is a paradigm subject by which we evaluate, assess, and learn other subjects, growing ever closer to their mastery.

Informal Logic
(Grades 7–12)

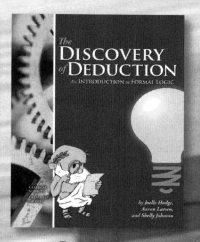

Formal Logic
(Grades 8–12)

Logic/Pre-Rhetoric
(Grades 8–12)

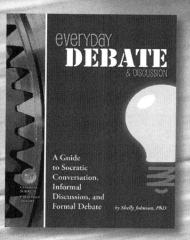

Speech & Debate
(Grades 8–12)

❝ *The Art of Argument* **is a thorough study of the fallacies, written in an organized, engaging manner. It is a great mix of instruction and application. I would highly recommend it for teaching logic. ❞**

—Kathy Gelzer, *The Old Schoolhouse Magazine*

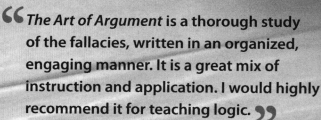